Tl CONDITION OF MADNESS

Brian Grant

University Press of America,® Inc.
Lanham • New York • Oxford

Copyright © 1999 by
University Press of America,® Inc.
4720 Boston Way
Lanham, Maryland 20706

12 Hid's Copse Rd.
Cumnor Hill, Oxford OX2 9JJ

Library of Congress Cataloging-in-Publication Data

Grant, Brian W.
The condition of madness / Brian Grant.
p.   cm.
1. Mental illness—Philosophy. 2. Psychiatry—Philosophy. I.
Title.
RC437.5.G73   1999 616.89'001—dc21   99—30115 CIP

ISBN 0-7618-1443-4 (cloth: alk. ppr.)
ISBN 0-7618-1444-2 (pbk: alk. ppr.)

♾™ The paper used in this publication meets the minimum
requirements of American National Standard for Information
Sciences—Permanence of Paper for Printed Library Materials,
ANSI Z39.48—1984

Contents

Preface

This is a book about a profession or discipline, that of psychiatry. It is also about *DSM-IV*, the American Psychiatric Association's most recent contribution to the taxonomy of mental disorders. It is also and inevitably about the mad—though not always as the profession sees them, the American branch or any other. I am—the book is written by—a philosopher. It is thus, if you like, a philosophy of madness, an inquiry into a certain area in the philosophy of mind. In the first half, the first three chapters, I concentrate, often anyway or mostly or more or less, on facts and issues, views, disagreements and definitions that have to be understood and assimilated before one can begin to think philosophically about madness. It is the second half, the final long chapter or essay, that is, more strictly speaking, a sort of philosophy of madness. I hope the book will be of interest to philosophers, psychiatrists, neurologists, psychologists, journalists, lawyers, witch-doctors of one school or another, sales managers, anthropologists, sociologists of course since they care about everything—and, insofar as this is possible, to the mad themselves. I hope it will be of interest to people of various kinds.

An acknowledgement is due—a grave bow or inclining of the head—to madness, a mental and, in itself, an abstract state or condition that can, nevertheless, be manifest in this or that individual with insupportable and undeniable immediacy.

Chapter 1

The Pioneers—From Freud to Pharmacology and California

To come to terms with psychiatry, we need to look first of all at its past. So this is the history of, not a science and not really or just an art, but a field, certainly, or a discipline, an area where training, experience and expertise have a crucial place. It is—I will confine myself to—comparatively recent history, that of the last hundred years. But this is arguably the complete history, the history of the field or the subject from its origins or, at any rate, its more or less critical and halfway promising though sometimes confused or primitive origins. We are now, roughly speaking, at the centenary of the first landmarks that are clearly recognizable from a contemporary perspective. This is a good time to take stock and to go over what has happened. It is also a difficult, even a chaotic, time—for the field is exploding. We can, however, leave that until the later parts of the chapter.

I will begin with Freud, which is to be unavoidably arbitrary; there are always the earlier thinkers, the debts and the influences. But to begin with Freud is also to begin with Kraepelin for while Kraepelin's reputation was established before Freud's, their careers overlap. So—ignoring one or two minor anachronisms—first Freud, then Kraepelin.[1]

I am going to spend a considerable—in a way, a disproportionate—amount of time discussing Freud. His views have cast a large shadow over the twentieth century and they are still very much alive, inside the profession as well as outside. But these views are complex and they are often misunderstood or misrepresented, inside the profession and out. The complexity, moreover, is primarily conceptual. So even though the present chapter is an introductory and a historical one, parts of this long section on Freud are given over to philosophical analysis. But it is also true that Freud wrote a great deal on a wide array of topics over a span of more than forty years. We have to distil it to see what Freudian theory and therapy amount to.[2]

Freud was trained—and did research for quite some time—in neurology. And in a relatively early transitional manuscript, "A Project for a Scientific Psychology"—with Freud professionally set up at this point but still feeling his way intellectually—he gives a sketch of a "psychology for neurologists." It is a remarkable document. The background assumption is that of a principle of conservation of energy, the physical "Q" or "Quantity", whose nature is not further specified. The fundamental neurological units, "neurones", are engaged in a continuous attempt to divest themselves of Q or to maintain it at as low a level as possible. There are also "contact-barriers" or synapses between the neurons and three different neuronal systems, one for perceptions, another for memories and a third, intimately tied to the perceptual system, that is supposed to account for "quality" or consciousness. Only perceptions and memories then—and it is perceptions that are, in the first instance or primarily, conscious. So pretty crude psychology. Still, Freud does recognize other mental states or occurrences—and he tries to locate them within these two or three systems. Thus, pains, emotions and wishes, dreams and various kinds of thinking, are all explained in these puzzling neurological terms.

Freud does not, in spite of this psychological/neurological pidgin, reject Interactive Dualism in favour of Materialism. "It is only a question," he says in speaking of consciousness, in particular, "of establishing a coincidence between the characteristics of consciousness…and processes in…neurones which vary in parallel with them." Neither, of course, does he believe that the mind is the brain, as many brain-scientists do, without, apparently, ever having heard of, let alone thought about, an alternative. Rather, his neurological psychology seems dualistic or it can, perhaps, be read with more licence as being compatible with either Interactionism or Identity Theory—though it is worth pointing out in this connection that Freud never wavered from the position that any psychology must, in the end, be underwritten by and somehow justified on the basis of neurology.[3]

But along with all of this sometimes ingenious neurological speculation, the *Project* contains the seeds at least of several of the better-known views in normal and abnormal psychology. So there is talk, however brief or sporadic, of the mental being "conscious" or "unconscious", of "repression" and its consequences, of "primary and secondary" processes, of dreams as "wish-fulfilments" and their similarities to neurotic symptoms. There is even an "ego", a group of neurons endowed with special supervisory powers. As will become clear, it is of some significance that much of the preliminary working out of these views was done in a largely neurological context.[4]

And then, very quickly, psychology won out; it had already been in the forefront in the still earlier investigations into hysteria. Freud, being Jewish, had been unable to obtain a permanent teaching position and he had opened his practice in Vienna. The patients trickled in, then came referrals and more patients, many of them neurotic—and about five years after finishing the *Project*, he published *The Interpretation of Dreams*, a book that is as self-indulgent as it is, at times, implausible. It is also pulled quite out of shape by its absolute unswerving conviction. It is, nevertheless, full of detailed and often riveting examples and intriguing views and ideas and it is Freud's single most important work. Almost all of the later, more central views are already firmly in place and they are presented with what is, by Freud's formidable standards, a minimum of sometimes dubious theoretical overlay.

The principal focus of attention is the eminently normal but quasipathological phenomenon of dreaming. That dreams are wish-fulfilments is, again, insisted on at the expense of claiming, among other things, that in certain seemingly recalcitrant cases the wish can only be to prove the wish-fulfilment theory mistaken—a very slippery wish indeed—as well as endorsing the Hume-like supposition that "nothing but a wish can set our mental apparatus at work"—which would make all mental processes or all movements of the mind, much less interestingly, wish-fulfilments. The wish, for Freud, is the central element of a dream's "latent content" as opposed to its "manifest content" and a substantial part of *The Interpretation of Dreams* is taken up with an account of how the latent content is transformed, by means of "condensation", "displacement", "visual representation" and "secondary revision" or the dreaming perspective or filter, into the manifest content, the content that is directly available to the dreamer. But the wish behind a dream is now assigned to the "unconscious" or the "Ucs", one of two or three major systems or agencies that make up the mind. For the neuronal systems of the *Project* have not only had others superimposed on them; the new ones—as well as the old to the extent to which they remain—are thought of, unequivocally, as mental systems or agencies. The Ucs is contrasted with the Cs, for "conscious", and the Pcs, for "preconscious". But since the distinction Freud is mostly concerned with is that between the Ucs and the rest of the mind, the Cs and Pcs are often lumped together as one—the Cs (or Pcs) or the Pcs (or Cs). Some explanations are in order.[5]

First, the simple picture. Whatever is repressed is thereby unknown and belongs to the Ucs. It is repressed, moreover, because it is enormously painful or distressing. The Pcs, on the other hand, includes all those mental phenomena that are "merely latent", as Freud often puts it, or known about without presently being objects of attention. It includes, that is, the vast majority of our memories, beliefs, desires, intentions and so on. The Cs—which is, in its functional aspect, the analogue for the internal world of the external senses—contains, at any given moment, the relatively small subset of the mental that is then impinging on the attention. It contains exactly what the stream of consciousness does.

There are difficulties here—and there are gaps. The one feature of the above picture Freud might seem to disagree with is that the Pcs is, or is often, transparent to its owner. In one passage in *The Interpretation of Dreams*, he describes a wish as "unconscious (that is to say, preconscious)". He also says that the "excitations [of the Pcs]—after observing certain rules, it is true, and perhaps only after passing a fresh censorship...—are able to reach consciousness." What rules?—and what censorship? If we are asked whether we remember this or want that, we can often reply immediately, without reflection. There is no question that we know even though, before we were asked, the memory or the desire might have been the farthest thing from our mind. This apparent disagreement is the result of a confusion on Freud's part, a confusion he never manages to resolve. It becomes perfectly clear in later writings that mental phenomena that are known about but not presently exercising the attention should indeed be included in the Pcs. But Freud's philosophy teacher, Brentano, was a good Humean. And Freud was a good student; the philosophical mistakes he learned from Brentano stayed with him. Hume, notoriously, thought of the entire mind in stream of consciousness terms—as though the Pcs did not exist. While this is not, of course, what Freud believes, he inherits enough of the confusion to be chronically uncertain as to whether what is not conscious can nevertheless be known. So we can clean Freud up on this point and save him from himself by insisting that the Pcs does include, not merely the latent or not necessarily, but the merely latent.

It is, again, made much clearer in later writings that repression is a deliberate and selective as well as a typically ongoing process. The repressing agency, the Cs (or Pcs), must, to make sense of this, have some knowledge of what is repressed—however murky or fugitive that knowledge might be. If repression is going to succeed, the Cs (or Pcs) can have very little knowledge of the contents of the Ucs. Very little—but if repression is going to be possible, the Cs (or Pcs) cannot be completely ignorant. In a similar way, there must be some wilfulness and some dishonesty. Very little again—but the Cs (or Pcs) cannot be completely absolved of responsibility and blame for repression and for what is repressed. The knowledge, murky as it is, is critical definitionally; the responsibility, minimal as it is, provides some excuse—not very much, to be sure, but some—for the view that Freudian cases involve malingering.

Repressed mental items belong to the Ucs. Does nothing else?—or is the Ucs broader than the repressed? Freud says that "Everything conscious has an unconscious preliminary stage" and he speaks of "a psychical activity which has remained unconscious" with the obvious assumption that they all start out like that. And yet it would be ludicrous to suppose that all of the mental is repressed at the very moment it comes into existence. But no more ludicrous, surely, than supposing, with Freud, that it must start out as unconscious. A belief, an emotion or an intention might well have its inception in the most limpid and unambiguous light of consciousness. A growing but perhaps disturbing conviction, the first unmistakable stirrings of embarrassment, the plan that slowly unfolds in your mind as you're walking the dog. Even more indisputably, perhaps, a vivid image or a sudden pain. One of Freud's reasons for this queer view seems to be that "memories [for example]...are in themselves unconscious." This, however, is not the expression of a genetic or temporal view; it is no more than the denial of the view that they must, by definition, be conscious. Freud also says that the wishes of infants or small children are "unrepressed". And in other writings, he occasionally suggests that the whole of an infant's mental life is unconscious. But in *The Interpretation of Dreams*, he deals faithfully with the issue: "in...children...there is as yet no division...between the Pcs and Ucs." There are no unproblematic examples here, then, of what is unconscious but not repressed. So we can safely ignore this sort of reason for maintaining, as Freud often does, that the Ucs is broader than the repressed. We can, unless persuaded otherwise, treat these notions as coextensive.

What, finally, of mental phenomena that are unknown but not because they are repressed? Are there such mental phenomena? Of course. Someone might fail to realize he is ambitious or depressed or has changed his mind on some issue because he is stupid, careless or not particularly reflective. Freud is curiously unconcerned about such cases—or not fully or clearly aware of them. If one is half-inclined to think of the Pcs as unknown, it might be extremely difficult to pick out the present group of cases at all accurately. We can, if we like, include them in the Ucs as long as we are prepared to acknowledge that this system will then contain two very different kinds of case. We can, with a similar proviso, include them in the Pcs. Or we can—there is nothing sacrosanct about the number two or the number three—invent a category for them all of their own. We can call it the "Nonsc" or the "Asc"—or whatever. It doesn't much matter which option we choose.[6]

And now for an assorted set of claims that I gather together from *The Interpretation of Dreams* with an eye to what is to come. For both neuroses and dreams, "[unconscious] wishes...are...of infantile origin." Further, "only sexual wishful impulses...are...able to furnish the motive force of psychoneurotic symptoms"—and while there are dark hints to the effect that the same thing is true of dreams, Freud decides, in the end, to leave this as an "open question". More generally, unconscious processes or thoughts "which are mutually contradictory make no attempt to do away with each other"; they are the "primary" ones and are subject to the "unpleasure principle"; they are "indestructible" and "so to say, immortal"; they are incapable of "satisfying our needs in relation to the external world"; they are not, it seems, associated with "verbal memories".[7]

And now for a couple of larger problems. While it is true that not all of the mind is conscious, how, exactly, are we to understand the Ucs and its peculiar inaccessibility to its owner? One of Freud's answers to this has to do with "mental topography"; another with "cathexis" or psychic energy, the direct descendant, in the more mature psychology, of the *Project*'s Q. The different parts of the mind and their relations to one another are described, in *The Interpretation of Dreams*, in spatial but, it is emphasized, nonanatomical terms. There are even diagrams, drawings inserted into the text, of a number of mental systems or agencies and how they are linked together. But Freud is careful to point out that this talk and these diagrams rely on mere "analogies" and "metaphors". What is not merely analogical or metaphorical, according to Freud, and what "replaces" mental topography and so gives it plain literal content is cathexis and its attachment to or detachment from individual mental phenomena or entire systems. Again there is the assumption, on a purely mental level, of a principle of conservation of energy and the mind itself along with all its states and operations— dreams and the various neuroses, of course, but also memory and perceptions, the satisfaction of wishes and the interplay of emotions— all these are explained by following out the nonspatial paths taken by quantities of cathexis, "hypercathexis" sometimes and sometimes "anticathexis". Freud never abandoned this theory. It is, quite simply, nonsense—aside from the fact that there is no discernible connection between mental topography and psychic "dynamics" or "economics", no way of moving from an aspect of the one to an aspect of the other. We do, certainly, have a limited and, so to speak, a patchwork notion of mental energy or intensity. We can all think of odd or isolated examples. What we do not have, and what Freud comes nowhere near providing us with, is a notion with the wholly general applicability and the relative precision he requires. Neither are we given any reason for thinking that if an unpleasant or disquieting memory fades or a desire becomes less insistent, the power it used to possess must turn up somewhere else. Freud's neurological background here playing him false. But if mental topography won't do and psychic energy fares little better, what on earth will or does?[8]

A second problem arises from what Freud says about the scope of his views. We all dream—or almost all of us do. And since dreams are rooted in the Ucs, almost all of us at least have a Ucs. The issue is clear to Freud: "The two psychical systems, the censorship upon the passage of one of them to the other…the relations of both of them to consciousness…all these form part of the normal structure of our mental instrument." And as for the abnormal, things are, for Freud, clearer still. Everyone has a Ucs. There is no warrant for this—any more than there is for the view that we're all selfish or hedonistic or all basically decent really. Some people are too simple-minded to have a Ucs. Some are too ingenuous. Some are not emotionally complex enough and some don't care enough—about sex or anything else. Some people grow up in circumstances so grim or so bizarre as to make a mockery of any attempt to generalize about the mind. And a lot of us don't have a Ucs that covers very much territory or results from very severe traumas—or is, by now anyway, of very great importance to us. Once we have realized this, we should reexamine our attitudes towards the abnormal, in particular. Many cases of neurosis or of symptomatic neurosis, as it were, do, I think, involve a Ucs or a substantial or more or less full-blown one—and I will have more to say about this in a while. Perhaps some cases of psychosis do; perhaps, even, some apparently normal cases do. Predictions can sometimes be made on the basis of symptoms but whether or not a case is of this sort depends, ultimately, on what the result of conscientious and painstaking analysis would be, on what is counterfactually so. We can still agree, if we think this is right, that "the interpretation of dreams is the royal road to a knowledge of the unconscious." We just have to restrict the scope of this piece of methodological advice—and be on our guard against the sense of sin and its endemic nature that permeates large stretches of this close to Victorian classic. Close to Victorian—and Viennese, of course, and middle-class and sexist too in certain ways. So there are deep and sometimes disturbing biases here, obstacles to a clear understanding. And Freud was, it should be emphasized, one of the great generalizers. But he was, by the turn of the century, in his mid-forties. He had been married since 1886, he was the father of six children, he was on the verge of becoming financially successful or at least solvent—and the foundations of psychoanalysis had now been laid. He was ready, warts and all and whatever their nature, to take on the world.[9]

Progress is made, in subsequent writings, on only the first of the above two problems—though even there, Freud's remarks need disentangling and shoring up. But we are getting ahead of ourselves. In "The Unconscious", one of a series of metapsychological papers he wrote during an extremely short but fertile period some fifteen years after *The Interpretation of Dreams*, he offers what seems to be a definition of the "Ucs": *"exemption from mutual contradiction, primary process* (motility of cathexis), *timelessness,* and *replacement of external by psychic reality*—these are the characteristics which we may expect to find in processes belonging to the system Ucs." Moreover, "the conscious idea comprises the concrete idea plus the verbal idea corresponding to it, whilst the unconscious idea is that of the thing alone. The system Ucs contains the thing-cathexes of the objects, the first and true object-cathexes...". We have come across all this before. The only difference is that, in "The Unconscious", Freud himself groups these claims together rather than making them at various points and in various contexts as he does in *The Interpretation of Dreams*. They are not, on examination, very helpful. The major axis of contradiction within the mind runs, surely, between the Ucs and the Cs (or Pcs). There might be contradictions in the Ucs but these are also contradictions—in ordinary cases of self-deception, for example—in the Cs (or Pcs). Given that primary process is explained in terms of cathexis, it is, once again, irredeemably opaque. And while Freud sometimes explains it in terms of the unpleasure principle—by now referred to, more cheerfully, as the "pleasure principle"—it is then hard to distinguish from being subject to psychic, as opposed to external, reality. The Ucs is not timeless in any strict sense if only because of the possibility of successful analysis. Still, we might allow that any changes in it must, by and large anyway, be relatively slow-paced. The final characteristic is also explained in terms of cathexis. Subtracting this, we might feel sympathy for the view that the Ucs is nonverbal. We might. But the Cs (or Pcs) sometimes is. And what is the alternative for the Ucs? What sorts of mental phenomena are nonverbal—and how, exactly? As I say, none of this helps very much in trying to come to grips with the peculiar nature of the Ucs.[10]

There is one other thing we should take note of in "The Unconscious", the explicit claim that "Everything that is repressed must remain unconscious; but...the repressed does not cover everything that is unconscious." And Freud hints at a further reason for the view: "it is not only the psychically repressed that remains alien to consciousness, but also some of the impulses that dominate our ego." This reason and the view itself are made somewhat clearer in *The Ego and the Id*, which was published in 1923.

In that shortest of books—and now the going gets tougher, the argument denser—Freud announces what he sees as the most important theoretical shift in his views after they were originally formulated in *The Interpretation of Dreams*. The structure of the mind, he tells us, has to be redescribed along the following lines. The "ego" is the Cs (or Pcs) with two additions: the unconscious resistance to certain topics that patients display in analysis and the unconscious sense of guilt that many neurotics suffer from. They are attributed to the "super-ego", a "precipitate" or "residue" in the ego responsible for "self-criticism and conscience". Correspondingly, the "id" is the Ucs with these two items omitted. The claim about resistance applies equally to repression, of course. The former, after all, is nothing but the public face of the latter. And the id or what remains of the Ucs is, to be sure, "unknown and unconscious". But we are also told that the id contains "the passions", many of which at any rate are conscious. In another passage, this is said, marginally less implausibly, to be true of only "the lower passions" and it is, presumably, no more than a gratuitous and unthinking borrowing from Hume's view of the passions. Finally, Freud says—not once but on a number of occasions—that "the ego is part of the id". This is inconsistent with his view of the relation between the Cs (or Pcs) and the Ucs as well as the one diagram of the mind that appears in *The Ego and the Id*. I will ignore these last two claims and concentrate on those having to do with resistance or repression and the sense of guilt.[11]

The most obvious question to ask is: Does the new account constitute an improvement over the old? Another, equally crucial for our purposes, is: Does it throw any light on Freud's view that the Ucs is broader than the repressed? But first I am going to say a few words about a question I have so far left to Freud, that of how we are to understand the Ucs.

One model we can make use of—and one I have mentioned before—is an ordinary, not particularly pathological, case of self-deception. Most of us have first-hand experience here with regard to our children or our talents or some other aspect of our lives. In this sort of case, there is a split in the mind between what one thinks one believes or wants or feels and what one really believes or wants or feels, a split in the Cs (or Pcs) between the "superficial" and the "deep". This division is not, except metaphorically, topographical; it is, rather, a matter of comparative recalcitrance to change. And this, in turn, is a matter of what is apparent to the deceiver on the basis of relatively casual or hasty reflection, if any, and what would be apparent on the basis of more careful, honest and perhaps prolonged reflection. So we have a continuum here of different kinds of reflecting. But essential to a case of self-deception is that the split be, to some extent and often with considerable subtlety, deliberately brought about and maintained. Typical of it is that there is, from time to time at least, some knowledge at the superficial level of what is deep. The continuum, it should be noticed, must have ordinary limits; otherwise we could never be confident that anyone really believes or feels anything. All we need do to understand the Ucs is extend the continuum to extraordinary limits to accommodate what would be apparent after years of analysis, usually with outside help. And in doing so, we will simply be turning our attention away from the division between the superficial and the deep in the Cs (or Pcs) and directing it, by analogy, towards that between the Cs (or Pcs) and the Ucs.[12]

A second model is a case of a radical change or deterioration in memory, intelligence and personality over a brief period of time, a favourite or a best sort of case for Locke of two people. So imagine a car wreck—and a man who was warm, witty and engaging suddenly thrust into a slow and sullen world, his past reduced to mere fragments. And imagine that this lasts, that things don't revert to normal. Some of us are prepared to talk of a different, a quite different, person on the slightest of pretexts—a resolution to exercise more frequently or a cooling of affections. We should, of course, beware of the extravagance. The above is not the best case of two people. That is me and you, for example. It is not the best case of one person either. That is me today, for example, and me yesterday. And surprised or repelled, perhaps, as much by the undeniable similarity as the profound difference in a case of extreme and sudden change, we might well feel the insistence that it is the same person to be blind, insensitive, bureaucratic—for the categories of truth and falsity don't come close to covering everything we meaningfully say. So not, unproblematically, two people but not unproblematically one person either. And the application to a Freudian case—to the one who possesses the Cs (or Pcs) and the one with the Ucs—should not need spelling out. Indeed, we can build into Locke's sort of case, given its plasticity and without affecting its essentially indeterminate nature, an analogue for every detail we happen to find in a Freudian case. The only ineliminable difference is that between "over time" and "at a time". We have, then, very much the same grounds for refusing to talk of one person in each of them.[13]

Several points should now be made and some conclusions drawn. The notion of the Ucs is, on either of these models, a perfectly legitimate one. Philosophical doubts about its sense are as empty as they are, typically, downright positivistic. As for whether or not abnormal cases that turn on the insidious or baleful effects of a Ucs actually exist, Freud's writings are sometimes strained or far-fetched. But their overall impact—and with regard to neurotics, in particular—is, it seems to me, decisive. The real proofs lie in the case studies—in what Freud thinks of as the results of his "practical method"—among which are the most compelling of his attempts to establish "the necessity and legitimacy" of the Ucs. All that is really needed here is for there to be one convincing case. One case in all of Freud's writings—or those of anyone else, for that matter—that is described in Freudian and convincing terms. I don't see how anyone who has read Freud could possibly deny it. The only question then is for just how many cases of madness and neurosis does this sort of account seem right. This is the question of whether we all—or all of the mad or neurotic—have a Ucs. That Freud is wrong about it should not be allowed to obscure the fact that Freudian cases do exist.

And Freud himself—remember mental topography and mental economics—suggests the second of the above models for understanding them. He does have a habit of describing any part or aspect of the mind, even an individual memory or desire, in disconcertingly personal terms. In *The Ego and the Id*, however, this chronic background way of thinking comes to the forefront and takes on the role, almost, of official doctrine. Thus, the ego is a "monarch", a "submissive slave" or "love-object", a "physician", a "politician" and a "man on horseback" with the id as subject, lover, patient, constituent, the ridden horse. Two people—or, with an emphasis on the primitive character of the id, one person and an animal—or, as I say and more soberly, not unproblematically one.[14]

But this new picture of the mind is not, as Freud believes, an improvement. The two-person model that he flirts with in *The Ego and the Id* could just as easily have been given prominence earlier. And, in his talk of resistance and the sense of guilt, Freud leaves something out. Distress, the motive for resistance or repression and so the process of resistance or repression itself, must, along with the guilt, be attributed to the same person as the moral standards that account for them. My shame can't be explained by your standards. There is, of course, no such requirement for the more neutral concept of a mental system or agency. Nevertheless, what is repressed and produces the distress and the guilt still belongs to the id. Something crucial must if a two-fold division is going to work. This might be all right for systems but it certainly isn't for people. My memories won't explain your sorrow. The stumbling block here is that resistance or repression and the sense of guilt are among the important features of Freudian cases that make them no more than problematic cases of two people. Taken in their full complexity, they point towards one. But that Freudian cases are problematic cases of two people is a brute fact. It can't be altered by carving up the landscape differently.[15]

Neither does the new theory help with Freud's view that the Ucs is broader than the repressed. Resistance or repression and the sense of guilt are unconscious. They can't, as Freud realizes, be seen for what they are when what gives rise to them is unconscious. And he says of the former that "the process of making it conscious" encounters "great difficulties", of the latter that it is "particularly difficult" to get the patient to admit to. Why doesn't it follow that they are repressed? Freud has nothing to say in response to this, nothing at all. Perhaps he is thinking that repression should be assigned to the grey area he sometimes refers to between the ego or the Cs (or Pcs), on the one hand, and the id or the Ucs on the other. But if what we have is only a grey area for repression, so too we have only a grey area for the Ucs. Or—and this, it seems to me, is much more likely—perhaps he is worried about the threat of a regress if he concedes that repression might be repressed. But that threat arises wherever one locates repression—and one can't defuse a regress by just denying that it exists.[16]

That's about all. Although Freud returns to some of these issues in later writings, there are no significant changes or refinements. Much of the time that remained to him until his death in London in 1939 was taken up with, not the intricacies of psychoanalytic theory, but the extension of its principles to broader and broader areas of experience. So what have we got? What is Freud's notion of the Ucs or of the unconscious, as he puts it, in the systematic sense?

What is unconscious, I am going to suppose—and in spite of Freud's protestations to the contrary—is repressed. It is repressed because it is distressing or painful, unbearably so. The result of repression is that it is, very largely but not entirely, unknown to its owner. It is relatively impervious to change, we might add, and obeys merely psychological laws as opposed to those of rationality—though we would do well to think harder than Freud did about his account of the former in terms of "pain" and "pleasure". And there is, again, no good reason for preferring the "id" to the "Ucs"—or the "ego" to the "Cs (or Pcs)". Indeed, many Freudians use the two sets of terminology interchangeably. It's nice to know—after having gone through Freud— that this is the sensible thing to do. And it's nice to know that your intelligent lay version of Freud, your better cocktail party version, is pretty close, at any rate, to the truth. We might have expected as much. For this concept of the unconscious is not the exclusive preserve of psychiatry. Freud gave it, not just to the profession, but to all of us.

I have, let me emphasize, said nothing about many of Freud's views, his views on society and culture, for example, or art or religion. These are large matters—but Freud's views here, whatever one makes of them, lie at a considerable distance from the definitional core of the notion of an unconscious part of the mind. Sex? Sin again and the Victorians. The fact is that a lot of people think about, discuss and engage in it in almost every conceivable situation. Most people do it in many situations. Some do it in only a few or none at all. One can't generalize here. Childhood? It is a strange time. A sort of long slowly dissipating trance that is often fantastic and sometimes very frightening. And those who develop a Ucs at that age mishandle it—perhaps because it is impossible not to. Others might develop a Ucs around puberty or from being subjected to physical or psychological torture at almost any age. We do, almost all of us, forget a great deal. Roughly speaking or with few exceptions, the less sure our grip on reality at the time and the longer ago it was, the more difficult to remember.

What follows from all this is that Freud's developmental theory with its infantile sexuality and alleged Oedipal conflicts is just that, a theory. It is not a part of what "unconscious" means for him. Is it a correct theory? For every one of us?—and whatever circumstances we grew up in? No, of course not. We've been through all that. It does, nevertheless—or so it seems to me—capture some important truths about a lot of people.

Freudian therapy? It will be that therapy appropriate to the theory. Freud, notoriously, experimented with hypnosis, then dropped it— perhaps too hastily. Hypnosis, God knows, can be dangerous but I know of nothing to show it might not be extremely valuable in trying to get at the unconscious. Freud was an indifferent hypnotist, however, and relied for most of his career on free association where the patient talks at random, though often of dreams, while Freud, behind the couch, took very little directive part, concerned, no doubt, at times during the long and frequently repetitive hours of analysis with how his doctrine of transference might be manifesting itself. Some of this should perhaps be modified. The couch, certainly, isn't necessary. And transference, together with the special bond between analyst and patient that is supposed to arise from it, can be overplayed and overrated. Besides, self-analysis is sometimes a possibility. And there are some impressive results from short-term versions of a talking therapy whose focus of attention is repression, the disturbing, the unknown. Free association? It seems to work. But the more directive the therapy, of course, the less free the association. Freudians do, after all, tend to go on about, not only dreams, but the apparently banal and the blatantly nasty. And other methods might help. Hypnosis might, as I've said— or being isolated for months or taking psychogenic drugs. The therapy will be Freudian provided that Freud's notion of the unconscious lies at its centre.[17]

Kraepelin, unlike Freud, had only the occasional private patient. A student of Wundt's and a university professor, he spent his time lecturing on clinical or forensic problems and doing experimental work on word associations, speed of response, intelligence testing, the effects of poisons, including alcohol, and various pathologies of the brain with the patients and ex-patients from the mental hospital attached to the university as his subjects. He thus saw many more psychotics and cases of obvious neurological damage than Freud did. Kraepelin was a good Prussian but an avid traveller and he did some work in compara-tive psychology. He was also something of an amateur botanist and his most significant contribution, meticulously sifted from an extensive collection of file-cards he kept on his patients, is in the taxonomy of mental disorders.

His text-book of psychiatry was first published in 1883 but it was not until the fifth and sixth editions of 1896 and 1899 that the fully elaborated taxonomy made its appearance. Dementia praecox or schizophrenia was organized into a single entity from previously recognized elements. It consisted, at first, of two types, catatonic and hebephrenic. The symptoms emphasized were hallucinations, delusions and emotional incongruities in a clear sensorium. Paranoid was then added as a type and, later on, simple—and a correspondingly more flexible symptomology was embraced. Paranoia or "paraphrenia" was distinguished from paranoid schizophrenia. And there were all sorts of other psychoses: "organic psychoses" of several kinds, among which were those having to do with the thyroid, the "exhaustion psychoses", collapse delirium, amentia and, oddly, acquired neurasthenia, and "dementia paralytica" or grand paresis. But Kraepelin also unified and refined the so-called "mood" disorders into very much their present form. There were the bipolar disorders, both severe and more mild, although involutional melancholia was set off in another chapter—and Kraepelin was as coy about the existence of unipolar mania as are most contemporary psychiatrists. The neuroses were given short shrift with one chapter devoted to the epileptic, hysterical and traumatic varieties. Obsessive-compulsive disorder, however, was included—along with congenital neurasthenia and certain "contrary sexual instincts"—as a "constitutional psychopathic state" in a later chapter. Strangely, to a modern eye, there was no place for the phobias or panic disorders and no place really for the personality disorders.

The bare bones of this taxonomy—and its picture of schizophrenia and the "mood" disorders, in particular—are still with us and are assumed without question by *DSM-IV*. Kraepelin's belief that the course of schizophrenia is invariably downwards into dementia whereas that of manic-depressive disorder is more benign has, by contrast, been abandoned. But it would be unfair to Kraepelin and a distortion of history not to mention, again, the experimental work, the research with drugs, the attention paid to the brain. Freud, again, did not reject such methods in principle; he just didn't think they would show very much in the way of results in his lifetime. Nevertheless, this division between the brain or drug merchants and the Freudians or talkers was to haunt the profession for a long time to come. As the roughest of generalizations, Europe went its Kraepelian way while America fell in love with Freud. The geographical representation has changed and the pendulum has swung towards the brain but the division too is still with us. The issue has not been resolved.

Freud, incidentally, had relatively little interest in taxonomy. If psychoanalysis is indicated in all cases, diagnosis, as others have observed, becomes less important. It all started, again, with hysteria. But by the very early years of this century, anxiety along with the

phobias, conversion hysteria, obsessive-compulsive disorder, hypochondria or neurasthenia, the amnesias and the dissociations—most of
the standard or classical neuroses—had been separated out. Freud did,
certainly, have a hand in that. But there is not much in Freud's writings
about personality disorders as opposed to neuroses. That is a later,
largely collaborative and often American development—although some
of the neuroses have obvious connections with some of our personality
disorders. And while Freud was, by the time his work matured—
somewhere, let's say again, in the very early years of this century, not
many years after the publication of the sixth edition of Kraepelin's textbook—as familiar with schizophrenia and its types, paranoia, bipolar or
"cyclic" disorders and the various kinds of depression as anyone else,
he used these notions. He did not examine them, or not with taxonomy
in mind.[18]

The stage is almost set. But first a few terminological and conceptual remarks—and a few about the Russians and the Americans. Eugen
Bleuler, a Swiss psychiatrist, and not Kraepelin, invented the word
"schizophrenia"—or, as he preferred, "the schizophrenias"—in 1911.
He meant by it a split or fragmentation in personality though not, of
course, of the kind exhibited in multiple personality disorder. The
"fundamental" symptoms were a loosening of associations, affective
indifference or inappropriateness, autism—another term coined by
Bleuler—and ambivalence. Bleuler's other, more dubious, claim to
fame is that he encouraged Jung to go to Vienna to work with Freud.
But it was Kurt Schneider, a German psychiatrist, who suggested many
years later that there are "first-rank" symptoms of the "end-state" of
schizophrenia. Schneider's symptoms are voices, thought manipulation
and certain hallucinations or delusions—very much the "psychotic"
symptoms that *DSM-IV* requires for the alleged "active phase" of the
disorder. It should be said, however, that Schneider's emphasis on an
"end-state" makes his suggestion less useful for diagnosis than for
conceptual purposes. But meanwhile in Russia, Pavlov had already
earned the Nobel prize—in 1904, in fact—for his research on dogs and
conditioned reflexes. The experiments were meant to show that no
mental processes were involved. They didn't show this—any more
than Descartes showed that all animals are "brutes". And if they had,
the confident and easy extrapolation of their results into a wholly
general view about human beings would be that much more ludicrous
than it already is. Still and all, human beings can be conditioned—to
stop smoking or to betray their countries or themselves—and Pavlov's
reflexology has been extremely influential in Russia. And in America,

John B. Watson railed against consciousness and introspection, thoughts and feelings and personality in 1913 in "Psychology as the Behaviourist Views It" and B. F. Skinner presented his version of reinforcement and operant conditioning in *Behaviour of Organisms* in 1938. These behavioural techniques that date back to Pavlov have considerable success with phobias and, sometimes, with obsessive-compulsive disorder.[19]

So we're back in the early part of the century with Freud and Kraepelin and Pavlov. And then, in 1917, Julius von Wagner-Jauregg, a Viennese psychiatrist, noticing that grand paresis did not seem to occur in countries where malaria was endemic, induced fever in nine of his patients by injecting them with malaria. In six of them, the progress of the disease was either stalled or completely halted, an achievement for which von Wagner-Jauregg received the Nobel prize in 1927. Later on, malarial therapy was replaced by penicillin. The former, however—the first really successful physical therapy for a mental disorder—was a special case. It had been known for some time that grand paresis was linked to syphilis. But in 1933, Manfred Sakel, another Viennese researcher, started giving insulin to schizophrenics on the grounds that it seemed to do some good with alcoholics and that the convulsions and the coma of the resulting hypoglycemic shock would, surely, make some sort of difference to psychotics. Like a wallop with a baseball bat but marginally less brutal. There were a number of deaths and squabbles about the efficacy of insulin—but again it appeared to help in some cases. In 1934, Ladislas von Meduna, a Hungarian scientist, mistakenly convinced of an antagonism between schizophrenia and epilepsy, caused convulsions in schizophrenics with camphor—and, later, with the chemically similar Metrazol or Cardiazol or pentamethylene tetrazol. Again there were problems—and again some success was claimed. And in 1938 in Rome, Ugo Cerletti, also interested in epilepsy and having heard of both Sakel and Meduna, began, with his assistant Lucio Bini, to produce convulsions in his patients by administering electric shock through electrodes placed at the temples. After a period of research at a slaughterhouse where the pigs, as it happened, were killed by electric shock, Cerletti decided on a little more than a hundred volts for half a second. There were problems again—but electricity is not as dangerous as insulin or as terrifying as Metrazol. Modern muscle relaxants make the risk of physical injury remote although there are the undeniable memory losses. Electroshock treatment, however, is still the treatment of choice for major depression for some members of the profession and an effective option for most of them.

In 1936, Egas Moniz, a Portuguese statesman, man of letters, neurologist and surgeon—a sort of up-market jack of all trades—performed the first prefrontal leucotomy. He was awarded the Nobel prize for his work in 1949. W. Freeman and   J. Watts imported the procedure to the United States, then came up with a more invasive, more comprehensive, version, prefrontal lobotomy.   Psychosurgery changed patients all right—and it gave rise, until the beginning of the fifties, to armies of blunted, apathetic, insensitive and sometimes aggressive or epileptic zombies. It is seldom used nowadays.

And then came the bombshell—and from out of the blue. But it was a bombshell that was not heard round the world for more than ten years. In 1948, John Cade, an Australian, discovered lithium. There was insulin, of course, and camphor—but the convulsions were the thing, not the chemicals. And there was reserpine or Serpasil, an alkaloid obtained from the bush *rauwolfia serpentina*, that had been around for centuries but was receiving increasing attention, especially in India and in spite of its heavily sedative properties and the possibility of severe depression, for its usefulness in slowing down mania as well as reducing high blood pressure. But lithium, toxic as it can be in the wrong doses, was the first drug in the field to have such an obvious and marked impact on patients with a specific disorder—in this case, manic-depression. Cade, who was investigating mania, was wondering if it might not be due to some unknown endogenous poison. He turned to guinea pigs and, injecting them with the urine of manic patients, watched for the effects of the poison. But in casting around for a convenient water-soluble form of uric acid, he had hit upon lithium urate. It was the effects of lithium, the solvent, that were surprising. Cade's guinea pigs became wonderfully calm, not sedated, not asleep, just as calm as guinea pigs could be. Cade then tried lithium carbonate. It worked too. And then he tried it on his manic patients, the donors of the nonexistent poison—aside from the fact that being injected with someone's pee can't be a very pleasant experience—who had, nevertheless and in spite of the insult, not been forgotten.   It worked. Lithium showed very good therapeutic results, according to Cade, in ten out of ten of his patients. And then—nothing much happened. A few more studies and some patients put on the drug, mostly in Australia. But Cade and lithium were largely ignored—partly because of this common mineral's unpatentability and of other discoveries that followed soon after but partly, one supposes, because it was 1948 and because it was Australia. In the early sixties, however, M. Schou, a Danish psychiatrist, made it overwhelmingly clear that lithium was pretty much what Cade had promised. It is still, for most of the profession, the most powerful weapon available against manic-depressive disorder.

The drug that did make the profession sit up and take notice was chlorpromazine or Largactil or Thorazine. It was discovered, or stumbled over, in France by Henri Laborit, an ex-military surgeon who was experimenting with some synthetic antihistamines, developed by the Rhône-Poulenc company, in an attempt to counteract surgical shock. He noticed that one of them, promethazine, had a pronounced relaxing effect. Rhône-Poulenc, impressed by this, began to produce other related antihistamines and, in 1951, came up with chlorpromazine. With this as the main ingredient of the "lytic cocktail" he administered to patients before surgery, Laborit claimed, somewhat overoptimistically, that it relaxed or quietened but did not sedate— "pharmacological lobotomy", as he put it—and he suggested that it be used in psychiatry. The antipsychotic potential of chlorpromazine was quickly confirmed by other researchers and by J. Delay and P. Deniker, in particular, with regard to mania. But as Delay and Deniker themselves were soon to realize, its primary value was to be in trying to combat schizophrenia and especially the delusions, the hallucinations and the disturbances in mood. Estimates indicate that in the first ten years after it was introduced, it was given to more than fifty million patients. It was the drug that let them out, that permitted, in the fifties and sixties, the start of the wholesale deinstitutionalization of the insane. And in 1958 in Belgium, Paul Janssen synthesized another, now common, antipsychotic, haloperidol or Haldol. What was he doing? Experimenting with derivatives of meperidine or Demerol in search of a better analgesic.

Iproniazid or Marsilid, a monoamine oxidase inhibitor and the first of the antidepressants, was developed by Hoffman-La Roche for the treatment of tuberculosis. It emerged in 1951 and 1952 that it had a stimulating effect—even, sometimes, a euphoric one. But trials on schizophrenia were inconclusive and the patients with tuberculosis were getting too excited. So iproniazid faded, for a while, from view. Then in 1956, after being tested on animals, it was tried on depression. It worked in some cases—but the side-effects were severe. Along with other monoamine oxidase inhibitors, like isocarboxazid and tranylcypromine, it has been banned at times in various parts of the world because of these effects but a number of drugs from this group are still used fairly widely. The American team of H. Loomer, J. Saunders and N. Kline confirmed the antipsychotic action of iproniazid in 1957 and, in 1958, its more specific action on depression. Kline won the Lasker Award in 1964 for his involvement. Saunders protested. Kline won again or still won. He is generally regarded as the inventor of this class of antidepressants.

Imipramine or Tofranil, the other and more important early antidepressant, is a tricyclic. Developed by Geigy, who—like Rhône-Poulenc—had been doing research on antihistamines and in response to a request by R. Kuhn, a Swiss psychiatrist, for a chemically similar but cheaper alternative to chlorpromazine, it was tested for a year on a variety of disorders with mixed results. It had been hoped, of course, that it would work with schizophrenia. Discouraged, Kuhn tried it at the end of the year—in 1956—on a few patients with depression. Their improvement was striking. Kuhn published his findings in 1957. Tricyclics or tricyclic-type drugs are still, for most of the profession, the main chemical means of controlling depression.

The minor tranquilizers, used to alleviate tension, anxiety and, sometimes, neurotic depression, were invented by Wallace in 1954—meprobamate or Miltown—by Hoffmann-La Roche in 1957—chlordiazepoxide or Librium—and by Hoffmann-La Roche again in 1963—diazepam or Valium. The first and the third of these, in this chapter of accidents, were discovered largely nonaccidentally. But then diazepam was developed from chlordiazepoxide, which was tested only as an afterthought when a researcher was cleaning out his laboratory—just as meprobamate was developed earlier from mephenesin, which was originally supposed to fight certain penicillin-resistant bacteria. More than twice as much money is spent worldwide on the minor tranquilizers as on antipsychotics and antidepressants combined.[20]

The story of the last two or three decades has been one of continuing research into drugs and the brain with a considerable increase in knowledge of the brain's chemistry but few major breakthroughs in the way of new drugs. If this is not true, it is only because there has also been a mini-story or a side-story, a background clamouring about the nature of therapy and those who might benefit from it and a louder clamouring about the good or the normal life, failure to achieve which is seen as pathology. But first, the big story.

Among the antipsychotics currently in use are the phenothiazines, including chlorpromazine, trifluoperazine or Stelazine, fluphenazine or Prolixin and thioridazine or Mellaril, the thioxanthenes, including thiothixene or Navane, the dibenzazepines, including clozapine or Clozaril, the butyrophenones, including haloperidol, the dihydroindolones, including molindone or Moban, and the benzisoxasoles, including risperidone or Risperdal. The N.I.M.H. Collaborative Study of 1964-6 reported that approximately 70% of schizophrenics showed significant improvement with phenothiazines as compared to 25% with placebos. Nothing much has changed on this front. The other antipsychotics have, at best, very similar response rates—but all antipsychotics are, in maintenance doses, of proven worth in preventing relapses. Their principal differences lie in their side-effects, which can be as debilitating as the conditions they are meant to ameliorate. These range from anticholinergic effects, such as blurred vision, dry mouth, urinary retention and constipation as well as a greater or lesser degree of sedation, on the one hand, to the so-called "extrapyramidal" effects, like Parkinsonism, assorted tics and an uncontrollable and unsatisfiable restlessness on the other. In general, the incidence of side-effects of the former group varies inversely with that of side-effects of the latter. Other side-effects are reduced blood pressure, skin and other eye problems, weight gain, excess lactation in women and ejaculatory incompetence in men, seizures, agranulocytosis, a life-threatening decrease in the number of white blood cells and neuroleptic malignant syndrome with its elevated temperature, muscle rigidity and altered consciousness. But perhaps the most bizarre side-effect is tardive dyskinesia, a usually irreversible extrapyramidal syndrome consisting primarily of sucking and smacking movements of the lips and lateral movements of the tongue and jaw. Some of these side-effects are relatively rare but the incidence of tardive dyskinesia is more than 40% in long-term users of antipsychotics and in elderly users. The "classical" antipsychotics—almost all of the above—are effective against positive symptoms of schizophrenia. But an "atypical" antipsychotic, clozapine, has some impact on negative symptoms, like blunted affect and a lack of spontaneity, interest and drive. It is also more successful than other drugs in the treatment of severe antipsychotic-resistant symptoms. Clozapine has, besides, relatively few extrapyramidal effects and is presumably much less likely to lead to tardive dyskinesia. It is, however, highly sedative and associated with a risk of an impairment of bone marrow function and a substantially increased risk of seizures and agranulocytosis. Another "atypical" antipsychotic, risperidone, appears to have even fewer side-effects—although those it has are by no means inconsiderable—and it too seems to help with negative symptoms. There is little evidence to suggest that antipsychotics have different effects on the types of schizophrenia where the types are thought of as catatonic, disorganized, paranoid and so on. There is appreciable evidence to suggest that they are effective against, not only schizophrenia, but organic psychoses, paranoia, schizophreniform disorder, schizoaffective disorder, brief reactive psychosis, mania and psychotic depression; there is some evidence for supposing that they can help with major depression, psychotic or not, anxiety, eating disorders and borderline personality disorder.[21]

Lithium, the drug of choice for manic-depressive disorder, is comparatively slow-acting. It is thus often supplemented with an antipsychotic or a sedative in the treatment of acute mania and its main value is prophylactic or in preventing subsequent swings in mood. Here, it is roughly twice as effective as a placebo, cutting the frequency of attacks of both mania and depression by about half and modifying their severity in upwards of 80% of cases. Side-effects are nausea, vomiting, polyuria, diarrhoea, weight gain, light-headedness, confusion and a fine resting hand tremor as well as thyroid and kidney problems after prolonged use. But because of its narrow margin of safety or low therapeutic index, the chief danger is lithium intoxication, which can cause seizures, coma and death. Other, less effective, drugs for manic-depressive disorder are the anticonvulsants, carbamazepine or Tegretol and clonazepam or Klonopin. Lithium is also, apparently, of some value in connection with schizophrenia, schizoaffective disorder, major depression and impulse control disorders.

The list of tricyclic or tricyclic-type antidepressants is at least as long as that of antipsychotics. It includes, along with imipramine, desipramine or Norpramin, trimipramine or Surmontil, amitriptyline or Elavil, clomipramine or Anafranil, amoxapine or Asendin, doxepin or Sinequan, trazadone or Desyrel, buproprion or Wellbutrin and fluoxetine or Prozac—although the last three are chemically very unlike the standard tricyclics. Improvement rates for major depression are in the region of 65-70% as compared to 30-40% with placebos. Common side-effects are sedation, weight gain, sexual dysfunction and, again, some anticholinergic effects, blurred vision, dry mouth and constipation. Less common are reduced blood pressure, confusion, delirium, seizures, cardiac difficulties and drug-induced mania. Of particular note is that amoxapine is one of the few antidepressants with extrapyramidal effects, trazadone has almost no anticholinergic effects and the side-effect profile of fluoxetine seems, in general, to be relatively benign. Fluoxetine has, of course, become the new opium or the new Valium of the people. While little is known about its long-term effects, it is, or so the stories go, frequently prescribed for no good nonrecreational reason. Monoamine oxidase inhibitors are employed less often than tricyclic-type antidepressants but include isocarboxazid or Marplan, tranylcypromine or Parnate and phenelzine or Nardil. They are no more effective than the tricyclics and share most of their side-effects. In addition, they can, when combined with certain foods, beverages and other drugs, give rise to acute hypertensive crises with an unbearable throbbing headache and intracranial bleeding. Antidepressants have also been used in combatting neurotic depression, panic attacks, phobias, generalized anxiety, posttraumatic stress disorder and eating disorders and clomipramine and fluoxetine have a significant effect on obsessive-compulsive disorder. No antidepressant, it should be emphasized, is any more effective against major depression than is electroconvulsive therapy.

The most widely used minor tranquilizers or anxiolytics are the large family of benzodiazepines—of which the best-known are still chlordiazepoxide and diazepam—and the azaspirodecanedione, buspirone or Buspar. Favourable responses appear to peak at around 65-75% but the response rate of anxiety to placebos is anywhere from 20-60%. Side-effects of the benzodiazepines are sedation, weight gain, paradoxical dysphoria, impairment of memory, reactions to other drugs and alcohol, psychological and physical dependence and the problems sometimes encountered in withdrawal—though these drugs are less addictive than meprobamate. Buspirone, by contrast, has few side-effects. It is slow-acting so it is not always an adequate substitute for the benzodiazepines but it does not appear to sedate or be addictive. Other indications for anxiolytics are some cases of neurotic depression, panic and phobias. Alprazolam or Xanex, in particular, a benzodiazepine, has clear antidepressant and antipanic properties and the anticonvulsant, clonazepam, another benzodiazepine, shows special promise with regard to panic and seems, again, to be an antimanic agent. Various other sedatives and hypnotics, including barbiturates, are also used, on occasion, as antianxiety drugs.

So these are the drugs. The profession has, based on their effectiveness, endorsed—more or less cautiously, more or less confidently—certain theories about the etiology of mental disorders. Briefly, almost all antipsychotics inhibit, in one way or another, the activity of the neurotransmitter, dopamine. It was thus thought for some years that schizophrenia is caused by excessive dopamine activity. But while some people in the field still accept this theory, the initial enthusiasm for it has waned somewhat. There is dopamine and dopamine—and, as the "atypical" antipsychotics have helped to make clear, other neurotransmitters, especially serotonin but also norepinephrine, acetylcholine and gamma aminobutyric acid, might well be involved. Almost all antidepressants enhance the activity of norepinephrine. There are, however, "atypical" antidepressants—and there is serotonin again and dopamine. Most anxiolytics increase the activity of gamma aminobutyric acid. But this, in turn, affects the activity of other neurotransmitters—and serotonin and dopamine seem, again, to play some role. It is generally conceded that not much is known about the biochemical effects of lithium. Theories have been suggested in terms of various neurotransmitters. But they are little more than speculation at this point. And there are, it should be emphasized, all sorts of neurotransmitters. Over sixty have, so far, been identified. And why just neurotransmitters in all cases, anyway?

A few other facts are known about schizophrenic brains from other sources—autopsies, of course, and then the computer studies and all the new imaging and scanning techniques. Thus, many schizophrenics have enlarged ventricles and slightly smaller brains. Some of them have abnormalities of the hippocampus. And many of them show reduced blood flow in the frontal lobes when engaged in certain activities. But even these results are not always duplicated—and they point, it seems, to isolated as well as very rough facts that don't, as a group, have much to do with dopamine. Even less is known, from these other sources, about the brains of those with mood or anxiety disorders—and still less about the brain in the dissociative or impulse control disorders or the personality disorders. Just what is it, for example, about the brains of the depersonalized or the antisocial? So we don't know much about the above sorts of disordered brains. We don't know anything, certainly, that we can count as a cause.[22]

And now for the mini-story or the side-story—although the numbers involved in or affected by it are enormous. It didn't all take place in California but it might just as well have done. So hey, kick back, chill out. Get your head or your shit together, get in touch or connect with yourself. I mean, find your own space. Are you hearing me? Like be happy, be rich, be cool, be real, be an asshole. Be you or the very best you you can be. And have a nice one, a really nice one. You know?

Back in the fifties, there was the incorporation or unveiling of Scientology. A sort of religion or worldview founded by L. Ron Hubbard, a former science fiction writer, and with its headquarters in Hollywood, Scientology has as its goal complete happiness, complete freedom, total mental health. It is a strange mixture of snippets of familiar psychological theories and out-and-out gobbledegook. One begins as "raw meat" or a "pre-clear", works up, with the help of the truth-meter or "E-meter" and by the "release" of psychological blocks or "engrams" contained in the "reactive" or "hidden" part of the mind, to being a "clear" and one aspires to be a "Thetan". A Thetan is not only immortal; he or she is a true "source" or "cause" and can create matter and energy, time and space. The training—perhaps understandably—is expensive, the authority of Hubbard's word absolute and the entire movement paranoid with a long history of sometimes ruthless law-suits against its critics. There was also Reevaluation Counselling or Cocounselling. Started by Harvey Jackins, a one-time labour activist in Seattle, Cocounselling is politically correct and especially popular among those on the left. Everyone is basically good, according to Jackins; indeed, everyone is an "artist" and a "genius". But we've all been "hurt" and the hurt lingers on as "rigid compulsive feelings and behaviour" instead of "useful information". So one "discharges" one's "chronic distress patterns" in order to "reevaluate". How? Share it or pour it all out while someone else listens—and then the positions are reversed. For no particular training is required and everyone is a patient, everyone a therapist. Jackins too takes immortality seriously but Cocounselling does emphasize intelligence as well as feelings. It just doesn't go very deep. A comforting chat over the backyard fence elevated to a high informal art—with the opinionated and the garrulous, as well as the lay, very much in control. It's cheap, unlike Scientology, and it's cheerful with everyone laughing and hugging and "appreciating" everyone else. And there was, of course, hovering over all this, Norman Vincent Peale and *The Power of Positive Thinking*. Get rid of all of your ills, Peale advised, by having happy thoughts, by not worrying or dwelling on negative ideas and, most important, by putting your faith in God. Millions of people, apparently, tried to achieve this grinning mindless state; they certainly read the book.

The single biggest event of the sixties for present purposes was the opening of Esalen by Michael Murphy and Richard Price at Big Sur. With its warm sulphur baths looking out on to the Pacific and influenced as much by Eastern as by Western strands of thought, Esalen quickly became the centre of the human potential movement. Activities included—apart from bathing and a fair amount of nudity—all sorts of encounter and bodily awareness groups and Alan Watts, Abraham Maslow, Fritz Perls, Aldous Huxley, Arnold Toynbee, Ken Kesey, Linus Pauling, Paul Tillich, Rollo May, Bishop James A. Pike, Carl Rogers, B. F. Skinner, Carlos Castaneda and John Lilly were all, at one time or another, in residence. No one ever accused Esalen of being narrow.

Then, at the beginning of the seventies, Primal therapy, developed by Arthur Janov, a Los Angeles psychiatrist, burst on to the scene. The cause of neurosis, in particular, is pretty much Freudian: the buried Pain—Janov insisted on capitalizing the word—the Pain of childhood but also of birth. The cure, however, is something else. The Pain has to be "unblocked" or "relived" in a Primal, a kicking, screaming, retching reenactment of birth that serves as the ultimate violent catharsis. Primal therapy is expensive, anti-intellectual and profeeling and definitely not for the faint-hearted—and therapists, the best in the world, Janov claimed, talk of "busting" a patient or not going too easy in getting him or her "back there" or "down there". Shortly afterwards, est appeared, equally hard-edged and even more of a con-job. est—Latin for "it is"—was put together by Werner Erhard. The former manager of a team of encyclopedia salesmen and influenced by bits and pieces of psychoanalysis, gestalt theory, the Bible, Scientology, the Mind Dynamics of Alexander Everett, Napoleon Hill's *Think and Grow Rich* and Dale Carnegie's *How to Win Friends and Influence People*, Zen Buddhism, Taoism and God knows what else, Erhard had a life-changing mind-blowing experience on a California freeway in 1971. The content of the experience is as difficult to pin down as the doctrines that flowed from it. Perhaps the clearest way to express it is in Erhard's own unforgettable words: "what is, is" and "what ain't, ain't". Training consists of group relaxation and various visualization, affirmation and encounter techniques—at the end of which one is supposed to "get it" or to get "it". You might be an asshole, as therapists are fond of saying, but being an asshole is not good or bad; it just is. You are perfect just as you are. A perfect asshole. The past is, the future is, life is. It is, don't you see? The training, again, is expensive and participants are routinely subjected to humiliation, sarcasm and ridicule. Neither are they allowed to use a bathroom during sessions that might go on for several hours. A full bladder is no different from an empty one; it just—well, you've got it by now. Hundreds of thousands of people have graduated from est—or from The Forum, the allegedly kinder, gentler, system that evolved from it.

There were all sorts of other mental health movements around in the seventies, although some of them started up earlier. Transcendental Meditation, Silva Mind Control, Arica, Mind Probe One, Lifespring. But the seventies also saw a phenomenal growth in the self-help book industry. You didn't have to join anything. You simply had to follow the rules laid down by some self-proclaimed expert. And for only $6.95 or $13.95, you could benefit from *Feel Free: How to Do Everything You Want without Feeling Guilty*, Pocket books, 1971, or *How to Make Winning Your Lifestyle*, Pocket Books, 1972, by David Viscott, M.D., a sort of one man psychiatric-cum-sensitivity-cum-greeting-card corporation, *How to Be Your Own Best Friend*, Ballantine, 1971, by Mildred Newman and Bernard Berkowitz, *The Psychology of Self-esteem*, Bantam, 1971, or *Breaking Free*, Bantam, 1972, by Nathaniel Branden, a former protégé and lover of Ayn Rand, about whom I will have something to say in the next chapter, *Your Erroneous Zones*, Pocket Books, 1976, by Dr. Wayne Dyer or *How to Get Whatever You Want out of Life*, Ballantine, 1978, by Dr. Joyce Brothers.

If there was a mental health movement of the eighties, it had to do with codependence and addiction and, not unconnected, with the roles of the sexes and sexual stereotypes and, of course, with sex. Codependence takes two or, as they say, a relationship. It is, we are told gravely, a matter of being affected by or concerned with someone else's behaviour and wanting to change it. Addictions? His or her crummy behaviour is an addiction and your being hung up on it is another. In fact, since everything is toxic, we're all addicted to everything: not only drugs and alcohol, but anger, power, lies, money and negativity and we're addicted to being addicted to sex. While the lessons could be learned from books—Anne Schaef's *Codependence: Misunderstood-Mistreated*, Harper and Row, 1986, for example, or Melody Beattie's *Codependent No More*, Harper and Row, 1989—there were A.A.-type or twelve-step recovery groups everywhere for those who weren't in denial. There still are. And the books kept coming and still do—and on any and all of your problems. Anne Schaef and Melody Beattie again, *Laugh! I Thought I'd Die (if I Didn't)*, Ballantine, 1990, and *The Lessons of Love*, Harper Collins, 1994, respectively, Harriet Lerner, Ph.D., *The Dance of Anger*, Harper and Row, 1985, *The Dance of Intimacy*, Harper and Row, 1989, and *The Dance of Deception*, Harper and Row, 1993, Charles Whitfield, M.D., *Healing the Child Within*, Health Communications, 1987, John Bradshaw, *Homecoming*, Bantam, 1990, *Creating Love*, Bantam, 1992, and *Family Secrets*, Bantam, 1995, Dr. Susan Forward, *Men who Hate Women, the Women who Love Them*, Bantam, 1986, Richard Carlson, Ph.D., *Don't Sweat the Small Stuff*, Hyperion, 1997, Harold Kushner, *When Bad Things Happen to Good People*, Avon, 1981, and *When All You've Ever Wanted isn't Enough*, Pocket Books, 1986, Harville Hendrix, Ph.D., *Getting the Love You Want*, Henry Holt, 1988, and *Keeping the Love You Find*, Simon and Schuster, 1992, Phil DeLuca, *The Solo Partner*, Hartley and Marks, 1996, Colette Dowling, *The Cinderella Complex*, Pocket Books, 1981, not to be confused with either *The Peter Pan Syndrome*, Avon, 1983, or *The Wendy Dilemma*, Avon, 1984, by Dr. Dan Kiley. Phew! But duty is duty. David Viscott, M.D., again with *I Love You, Let's Work It Out*, Simon and Schuster, 1987, and *Entirely Free*, Contemporary Books, 1992, Nathaniel Branden again with *Honoring the Self*, Tarcher, 1983, and *Six Pillars of Self-esteem*, Bantam, 1994, M. Scott Peck, *People of the Lie*, Simon and Schuster,

1983, *The Different Drum*, Simon and Schuster, 1988, *The Road Less Travelled*, Simon and Schuster, 1988, and *The Road Less Travelled and Beyond*, Simon and Schuster, 1997, Karen E. Peterson, *The Tomorrow Trap*, Health Communications, 1996, Ricki Robbins, Ph.D., *Negotiating Love*, Ballantine, 1995, Dr. Wayne Dyer again with *You'll See It When You Believe It*, Avon, 1989, and *Real Magic*, Harper and Row, 1992, Cardwell Nuckols, Ph.D., and Bill Chickering, *Healing an Angry Heart*, Health Communications, 1998, Megan LeBoutillier, *"No" is a Complete Sentence*, Ballantine, 1995, Dr. Ruth Westheimer and Dr. Louis Lieberman, *Dr. Ruth's Guide to Erotic and Sensual Pleasures*, S.P.I. Books, 1992, and Graham Masterton, *How to Drive Your Man Wild in Bed*, Signet, all the way back in 1976, *More Ways to Drive Your Man Wild in Bed*, Signet, 1985, *How to Drive Your Woman Wild in Bed*, Signet, 1987, *How to Make Love Six Nights a Week*, Signet, 1991—a bit of a change of pace there—*Wild in Bed Together*, Signet, 1992, and—go with what works, I guess, or what one is really good at—*Drive Him Wild*, Signet, 1993, and *How to Drive Your Man Even Wilder in Bed*, Signet, 1995. Then there's Dr. Toni Grant and Barbara de Angelis, Ph.D., and therapy on the talk-show radio as you drive home from work and on daytime TV. And then, of course, there's Shirley MacLaine. And now, now we're all into "closure".

You got a problem? You bet you do. Just look at those titles. You wanna solve it? Just read the book. But enough of this, enough of this nonsense. Let's get back or down to business.[23]

Notes

1. The question of whether psychiatry is or can aspire to be a science will be discussed in Chapter 2 in connection with the views of Szasz.

For the earlier history of the field, see, for example, G. Zilboorg, *A History of Medical Psychology*, Norton, 1967—copyrighted 1949, L. Whyte, *The Unconscious before Freud*, Basic Books, 1960, R. Hunter and I. Macalpine (eds.), *Three Hundred Years of Psychiatry*, Oxford, 1963, M. Foucault, *Madness and Civilization* (tr. R. Howard), Random House, 1965, H. Ellenberger, *The Discovery of the Unconscious*, Basic Books, 1970, J. Howells (ed.), *World History of Psychiatry*, Baillière Tindall, 1975, W. Bynum, R. Porter and M. Shepherd (eds.), *The Anatomy of Madness*, Tavistock, 1985, G. Roccatagliata, *A History of Ancient Psychiatry*, Greenwood Press, 1986.

2. I make particular use, in the following, of "A Project for a Scientific Psychology", *The Complete Psychological Works of Sigmund Freud* (ed. J. Strachey), Vol. I, Macmillan, 1964, *The Interpretation of Dreams* (tr. J.

Strachey), Avon, 1965, "The Unconscious", *General Psychological Theory* (ed. P. Rieff, tr. C. Baines), Collier, 1963, and *The Ego and the Id* (tr. J. Riviere), Norton, 1962. But also essential to an understanding of Freud are some of the introductory or more popular writings, like *Introductory Lectures on Psychoanalysis* and *An Outline of Psychoanalysis*, some of the other metapsychological papers collected together in *General Psychological Theory*, *An Autobiographical Study* and other such pieces—all these, at least, together with some of the case studies.

3. The competing claims of the various Isms in the philosophy of mind, including Interactionism and Materialism, will come up again in Chapters 2 and 3 but especially in Chapter 4.

Freud's seemingly dualistic remark in the above is from "A Project for a Scientific Psychology", p. 311. It must be admitted that what he says on this issue is sometimes more ambiguous or more perplexing. But there is no excuse for calling him, simply, a "materialist"—as Thomas Nagel does in "Freud's Anthropomorphism", R. Wollheim (ed.), *Freud*, Anchor, 1974. A rather more careful version of this view of Freud is given by R. Solomon, "Freud's Neurological Theory of Mind", also in Wollheim's collection, and an almost entirely speculative one by O. Flanagan, *The Science of Mind*, MIT, 1984.

4. See "A Project for a Scientific Psychology", pp. 308, 373, 322, 350, 296, 329, 340, 336, 322ff.

5. *The Interpretation of Dreams*, pp. 185, 606, 315ff., 211, 580, 608.

6. See, in connection with the above "difficulties" and "gaps", *The Interpretation of Dreams*, pp. 597, 653, 651, 589, 578, 592.

Freud's confusion over whether the Pcs can be known or not makes it that much easier for him to offer, as he routinely does, the "merely latent" as one of his proofs of the existence of the Ucs—and see Flanagan again for the view that the preconscious is what we are "trying to suppress" (p. 69), an echo of Freud's own ambivalence; the elements of knowledge and responsibility involved in repression are greatly exaggerated by Sartre and Szasz respectively—for which see Chapter 2; what probably lies behind Freud's many attempts to show that the Ucs is broader than the repressed is, as I hope will become clear, the worry that the notion of repression leads to a regress; and his failure to straightforwardly acknowledge that mental phenomena might be unknown as a result of mere stupidity, for example—not to mention his fairly frequent suggestions to the effect that there might be a censorship between the Cs and Pcs—points, of course, in exactly the opposite direction, to the view that the Ucs is no broader than the repressed. The number two or the number three? See my remarks in Chapter 4 on multiple personality disorder.

7. *The Interpretation of Dreams*, pp. 592, 645, 635, 640, 639, 617, 592, 606, 656, 613.

8. *The Interpretation of Dreams*, especially the last, more theoretical part, is riddled with Freud's pseudoscientific notion of cathexis. But for the more specific claims in the above, see pp. 574, 649, 593, 655, 644. Freud himself, by the way, suggests an alternative to mental topography and mental economics in *The Ego and the Id*. See below.

9. *The Interpretation of Dreams*, pp. 646, 647. Freud's overgeneralizing with regard to how many of us have a Ucs is, perhaps, as evident as it is anywhere in *The Psychopathology of Everyday Life*. And sexism has become, in this politically correct age of ours, a familiar complaint against Freud. See J. Masson, *The Assault on Truth*, Farrar, Straus and Geroux, 1984, and *Final Analysis*, Addison-Wesley, 1990, for particularly opportunistic and gossipy versions of it. But what else would you expect from Freud given his life and times? And sexism is no more ineradicable, in principle, from Freudianism than it is from big business or the government.

10. A section of "The Unconscious" is devoted to the question of which mental phenomena can and which can't belong to the Ucs. Freud's answer is not very edifying—but he does raise the question. See below for more on this.

11. See *The Ego and the Id*, pp. 7, 17, 18, 24, 16, 14, 15, 16, 28. *The Ego and the Id*, it should be noted, gives a fair amount of weight to Freud's theory of the life and death instincts—first announced in *Beyond the Pleasure Principle*. But that theory, if it is felt to be important, can also be grafted on to the Cs/Pcs/Ucs way of doing things. And the truism about the intimate connection between resistance and repression is remarked on by R. Wollheim in *Sigmund Freud*, Viking, 1971, p. 16.

12. A flurry of articles on self-deception appeared in the philosophy journals some years ago. One of the best, it seems to me, is H. Mounce's "Self-deception", *Aristotelian Society*, Supplementary Volume, 1971. The analogy with the Freudian unconscious, in particular, has been argued for by a number of people. But see Ilham Dilman, *Freud and the Mind*, Basil Blackwell, 1989, for a fairly clear version.

The ordinary continuum between different kinds of reflecting is also relevant to mental phenomena, like memories and knowledge, where the metaphor of depth as opposed to superficiality is not as entrenched; it has little or no application to sensations, images and thoughts. So it can't, for the latter, be extended to allow them to belong to the Ucs. The lower reaches of this continuum require, of course, that introspection become more and more difficult. And it is often said, though usually with no explanation, that Freud changed our concept of the mental. On the present model, the change is precisely a matter of extending the ordinary continuum for emotions, for example, or memories.

13. Many philosophers, it should be said, think there must be a straightforward answer to every question about identity, especially the identity of people—as though we could invent a method of counting for anything that worked in all cases, however strange, however puzzling.

See *An Essay Concerning Human Understanding* (ed. A. Campbell Fraser), Dover, 1959, for Locke's account of personal identity. The received wisdom is that Locke's account is exclusively in terms of memory, which he certainly does emphasize. But only the most superficial of readings would miss the fact that his concerns are much broader.

Different sensations at different times provide no reason for talking of a different person. So too for images and occurrent thoughts—unless they are influenced by or representative of background beliefs or desires or memories. The above model thus fails to make sense, once again, of the idea that mental phenomena of these sorts can belong to the Ucs. This is as it should be—for the idea doesn't make sense. Freud's writings, by contrast, frequently rely on the notion of unconscious thinking. But a stream of unconsciousness, as others have remarked, is surely absurd. Introspection, of course and whether difficult or not, is reflexive in its pure form or involves only one person. And if we want to insist that Freud changed our concepts on this model, we had better pick on Locke's concept of a man as opposed to a person. Freud changed our concept, we can say, of the enormous psychological complexity that a single man or human being is capable of, not over time, but at a time.

14. *The Ego and the Id*, pp. 45, 46, 20, 46,15. Irving Thalberg, in "Freud's Anatomies of the Self", *Freud* (ed. Wollheim), faithfully documents and predictably criticizes Freud's tendency to personalize parts of the mind. Thalberg is mostly right—but the baby disappears with the bathwater.

15. H. Fingarette claims, in *Self-Deception*, Routledge and Kegan Paul, 1969, that Freud made a major breakthrough in psychoanalytic theory in his last unfinished paper, "Splitting of the Ego in the Process of Defence". What the major problem had been we are never told. But there is nothing new in this paper. The ego proposes, the super-ego declines, the super-ego demands, the ego lacks enthusiasm, the super-ego prohibits, the id shrugs its shoulders. Here is Freud counting people again, haunted by the question of the exact right or the right whole number. All such attempts are doomed to fail.

16. *The Ego and the Id*, pp. 8, 40. Freud does just deny—see *The Ego and the Id*, p. 8, for example—that repression is repressed. But he can't help acknowledging that it is unconscious. The only way to avoid the regress is to then deny that whatever is unconscious is repressed. Freud does, to be sure, sometimes use "repression" in a narrower sense so that it is merely one sort of defence mechanism among others. This does not, however, seem to be what he is thinking of, not usually anyway, when he is discussing the present issue. And the descriptive unconscious is, of course, broader than the repressed. But again, this relatively simple point doesn't come close to explaining his preoccupation with the nature of the relation between the repressed and the unconscious. Is there a fatal regress here? It is a brute fact that the comparatively limited human mind is capable of no more than a handful of distinguishable levels—of consciousness, of knowledge more generally or of repression. For repression, at least, there's no problem; the regress peters out as our limitations set in. And as for whether cases that fall short of this rough human ceiling are genuine cases, we become—as we do with knowledge or consciousness—increasingly less certain.

17. There is thus a connection between Freudian theory and Freudian therapy—but it is not nearly as tight as is often supposed. And Freudian therapy, as Freud points out in "The Unconscious" and especially for self-analysis, might well include introspection—an extraordinary form of it to go with the extraordinary nature of the case.

J. Searle, in *The Rediscovery of the Mind*, MIT, 1992, rejects Freud's idea of the unconscious on the grounds that it is, in principle, inaccessible to consciousness. Freud does sometimes use language like this in his attempt to distinguish between the unconscious and the preconscious. But his view of introspection makes it clear that this is not his idea. Searle also talks of a distinction between a shallow and a deep Ucs. There is little evidence in Freud's writings of such a view. And Searle claims that Freud thinks of unconscious mental phenomena as conscious ones minus consciousness, an interpretation that Freud explicitly rules out. Searle's account, moreover and as he cautions us several times, is only of Freud's views as he, Searle, understands them. One wonders whether he has read Freud.

18. See E. Kraepelin, *Clinical Psychiatry* (tr. A. Ross), Macmillan, 1902. And, on personality disorders, see Kurt Schneider, *Personality Disorders* (tr. M. Hamilton), Cassell, 1958—as well as the writings of G. Allport, for example, or G. Murphy.

I will, incidentally—in what remains of this chapter and in the next—assume at least a passing familiarity with the above sort of psychiatric jargon. Any difficulties that might arise as a result of this should be cleared up in the discussion of *DSM-IV* in Chapter 3.

19. See E. Bleuler, *Dementia Praecox* (tr. J. Zinkin), International Universities Press, 1950, Kurt Schneider, *Clinical Psychopathology* (trs. M. Hamilon and E. Anderson), Grune and Stratton, 1959, *Essential Works of Pavlov* (ed. M. Kaplan), Basic Books, 1966, J. Watson, "Psychology as the Behaviourist Views It", *Psychological Review*, 1913, B. Skinner, *Behaviour of Organisms*, Appleton-Century-Crofts, 1938.

20. The above facts about developments in psychiatry during the twentieth century can be found, in one version or another, in a number of places—in many textbooks of psychiatry, for example. But K. Bender's *Psychiatric Medications*, Sage Publications, 1990, is particularly helpful in connection with drugs; E. Valenstein's *Great and Desperate Cures*, Basic Books, 1986, an eminently readable account of the heyday of psychosurgery.

21. The question of the effectiveness of antipsychotics—even against schizophrenia itself—is an extremely complicated one. James Hegarty, Ross Baldessarini, Mauricio Tohen, Christine Waternaux and Godehard Oepen claim, in "One Hundred Years of Schizophrenia: A Meta-Analysis of the Outcome Literature," *American Journal of Psychiatry*, 1994, that the success rate for treating schizophrenia reached a peak of around 50% in the 70s. This does not conflict with the figure of 70% I have given; the lower figure was obtained from follow-up studies involving all sorts of therapies and with a time-lapse of up to 10 years. But Hegarty et al. also claim that the rate over the last decade—the mid-80s, roughly, to the mid-90s—has dipped back to not much more than 35%, the level of the 40s and 50s. They cite, however, deinstitutionalization and changing diagnostic criteria for schizophrenia as reasons for the downturn.

22. See, on the pharmacological and/or the neurological aspects of mental disorders, not only Bender, but also G. Reynolds, "Developments in the Drug

Treatment of Schizophrenia", *TIPS*, 1992, R. Kendell and A. Zealley (eds.), *Companion to Psychiatric Studies* (5th edition), Churchill Livingston, 1993,H. Goldman (ed.), *Review of General Psychiatry* (4th edition), Lange, 1994, H. Kaplan and B. Sadock (eds.), *Comprehensive Textbook of Psychiatry* (6th edition), Williams and Wilkins, 1995, S. Chua and P. McKenna, "Schizophrenia—a Brain Disease? A Critical Review of Structural and Functional Cerebral Abnormality in the Disorder", *The British Journal of Psychiatry*, 1995, J. Kane, "Drug Therapy: Schizophrenia", *The New England Journal of Medicine*, 1996. And don't you wish, by the way, that you could just get in there and clean up the very small but extremely profitable industry that invents the names for new drugs? Surmontil, for example, or Asendin, Wellbutrin or Desyrel. My nerves.

23. Sources for this last section on California, the cutting-edge in the field as in so many things, are: N. Lande, *Mind-Styles, Life-Styles*, Price, Stern and Sloan, 1976, R. Rosen, *Psychobabble*, Avon, 1979, W. Kaminer, *I'm Dysfunctional, You're Dysfunctional*, Addison-Wesley, 1992—and, of course, your local bookstore. And don't you wish, by the way, that the publishing business weren't quite so sleazy? We ought, however, to be careful about generalizing here. Some publishers, clearly, are much worse than others.

Chapter 2

The Cynics

If we are going to take madness seriously, we should, sooner rather than later, clear an obstacle out of the way. The obstacle is the view that there is no such thing as madness, no such state or disorder. Two men, Thomas Szasz and R. D. Laing, have dominated the "anti-psychiatry" movement over the last thirty years or so. The movement is not against a mere subsection of the profession or a certain theory about the mad. That sort of local objection has always been around. The present one can, as well or instead, be thought of as the "anti-madness" movement. We all belong insofar as we disapprove of how madness is seen or treated or are horrified by its prospect. But Szasz and Laing call into question—though in quite different ways—the very existence of madness.

Szasz is a psychiatrist, one who is as strident as he is persistent in his criticism of psychiatry—and I will have more to say about this conflict in a while. He is also an admirer of Ayn Rand. So first, some comments about the latter.

Ayn Rand wrote—regrettably, it must be said—a number of novels. Their heroes and heroines inhabit a brave new world of intelligence, resourcefulness, courage and strength—and, indeed, of success. If there is a message here, it is: The poor and the weak and the oppressed all deserve it. This is a bleak message. The novels are tough-going in

other ways as well. The prose is heavy, the tone didactic, the characters are humourless, the plots march relentlessly on. But Ayn Rand
also wrote—and again the verdict must be that this was not a good
thing—some real philosophy. She wrote a book, a series of lectures,
called *Introduction to Objectivist Epistemology*.

It is an odd little book, more self-satisfied and preachy, even, than
the novels. There is a lot about concepts and concept-formation or
language-learning. And a great deal of noise is made about objectivity.
This despite the disclaimer, "I do not include here a discussion of the
validity of man's senses; the validity of the senses must be taken for
granted." The sceptic, the philosophical sceptic, can only be assumed
to be wrong. There is also, in Ayn Rand's book, a vaguely Kantian
doctrine about "axiomatic" concepts, like those of existence, consciousness and identity, undeveloped and hardly argued for; a view of the
mind to the effect that all mental events or processes can be split into
two aspects, "content" and "activity"—no more true in general, surely,
than Hume's view about "content" and "force or vivacity" and not
much more illuminating; some preoccupied mutterings about the
defects of Logical Analysis together, perhaps surprisingly, with strands
of Positivism where everything has to be measurable and values are
instrumental; the repeated and solemn assurance, always vacuous, that
A is A. Language-learning? It's all done in terms of the essential
distinguishing features as opposed to those that are particular or
accidental. No improvement again on Hume—or even Plato. Locke
did see something wrong here. It led him to make the impossible
demand on the abstract or general idea of a triangle or horse or tree that
it contain "all [of the particular features] and none of these at once."
Locke half-realized that his "solution" wouldn't do; he attributes our
reliance on such ideas to our imperfections, to our not having the
intelligence of angels. Locke's problem? It was very much in the
philosophical air in the fifties and sixties of this century with the work
of Wittgenstein. Ayn Rand does not discuss it.[1]

But this is to leave out what is, in a way, most important. For Ayn
Rand also wrote on ethical and political issues. In *The Virtue of
Selfishness*—another collection of shorter pieces mostly by Ayn Rand
herself—she endorses what she regards as a moral rule. It is: Do
whatever it takes to sustain your life or advance your own self-interests.
This is not just one of many similar rules, however, and selfishness is
not just another virtue. Rationality is a sort of virtue for Ayn Rand but
selfishness is the "ultimate" virtue. This raises a number of questions.

How can someone who believes that values are instrumental—
relative to some end that is not itself morally justifiable—also believe
in a "black and white"? But that is a technical question. The content of

"black and white"? But that is a technical question. The content of
Ayn Rand's morality is what should engage our attention. There are at
least three questions here. Is suicide always immoral or irrational
however severe the pain or unbearable the distress? What about
others? And what, in particular, about the helpless and the old or what
should the government do? The question about suicide Ayn Rand
brushes aside, does not face up to. With regard to others, she talks
occasionally of a "negative" rule not to inflict physical violence on
them. It's pretty minimal, not very generous—and it gets nothing like
the space from Ayn Rand that selfishness does. The poor and the
dispossessed? Nobody has any duties towards them although individuals might be willing to volunteer help—and the function of the
government is restricted to stopping us from bashing one another about.
The moral advice here is that of the novels. It is "Bugger the poor, the
hell with the feeble-minded." And all shored up by the view that love
and friendship and generosity must give pleasure and ought, presumably, to be indulged in only because of it, defended on the basis of the
patently absurd claim that there can be no conflicts among rational self-
interested men, expressed in a language where "altruism" and "sacri-
fice" and "love" of course have become dirty words and with her
opponents divided, inexplicably, into "mystics", "subjectivists" and the
despicable "altruists", all this self-congratulatory celebration of
strength and ability and turning one's back on the disadvantaged, all
this—for there is this too—this hatred of "collectivism", anything,
namely, that is not "full, pure, uncontrolled, unregulated laissez-faire
capitalism", all this barking about the individual and complete freedom
for those who can make it or make use of it. Other races, oppressed or
otherwise? The same attitude, one imagines, should apply there. Ayn
Rand is not a racist. She tells us so. She also says, however, "This
accumulation of contradictions, of short-sighted pragmatism, of cynical
contempt for principles, of outrageous irrationality has now reached its
climax in the new demands of the Negro leaders"—and she calls these
leaders "racist" and "evil". This is at least as harsh and dismissive as
the underlying moral view. She was writing of the United States in
1963.

There are some remaining philosophical questions. How can
someone who will hardly discuss scepticism about the external world
have any pretensions to moral objectivity? The emphasis on objectivity, as it is in the expression of her more central philosophical views on
concepts, existence, consciousness and knowledge, mere noise, mere
affirmations of faith in the light of the possibility of moral scepticism.
And isn't it especially easy to be sceptical about morality? An alien of

vastly different abilities and interests than ours who was largely unimpressed by problems about the welfare of human beings might, it seems, be just that and not depraved or degenerate. And aren't values unlike facts? If the only consideration were selfishness, there could indeed be a "science" of ethics and "ought" really could be derived or deduced from "is". But feelings and emotions, we all know, loyalty, trust and the ability to forgive—all these and other more spontaneous or less ponderable things—are presupposed by morality. Isn't the view that selfishness is what morality consists of nonfactual though? It is. It is about the facts all right. But it is, as I've said, a profoundly immoral view of the facts. It is—I want to be precise here so as to avoid some of the hair-splitting—the "Take Care of Number One and You Don't have to Worry about the Interests of Others or their Needs, however Dire" view. This is not a description of morality. It is an exhortation to abandon a very large part of it.[2]

I have spent some time on Ayn Rand. Our concern, however, is with Szasz. He is a shrewd writer. And sometimes he is right. Often he is wrong—on important issues. And sometimes the above vague, simplistic or dangerous views show up in his writings.

Perhaps Ayn Rand's preoccupation with concepts becomes, in Szasz, the emphasis on linguistic matters—and her "contextual definitions" are at any rate halfway towards Szasz's blatant relativism with regard to the categories of abnormal psychology. Perhaps her insistence on objectivity while barely discussing scepticism is mirrored in his claim that mental illness and madness are metaphors, accompanied, as it is, by near-silence on the subject of metaphor. Her "I know what I like" to his "I know what I don't." And Szasz shares with Ayn Rand a nostalgia for the crude days of Positivism with his "operational" definitions, the references to Reichenbach, the "promotive" or "affective" uses of language and the view that "'right' and 'wrong'... are...imperatives." But the single indisputable and pervasive influence lies in morality and social policy.

It's there in the harping on, in every conceivable context, about "freedom", "liberty" and "autonomy". It's there in the often overdone stories about the abuses of state psychiatry in what was then the U.S.S.R. and in the recommended "contract" between analyst and "client". It's there in the "heteronomous" psychiatrist, the enemy or competitor from Szasz's point of view, whose "primary duty" is the "needs of patients"—the "autonomous" psychiatrist, we are told, has "[a need] to take care of himself"—and in the talk of "institutional psychiatry" as "totalitarian" and "collectivist" and the laboured comparisons with the Inquisition. We might agree with, not much, but something in this or something behind it. And the sustained attacks on coercion and the wholesale involuntary commitment of the mad are, it should go without saying, to be applauded. But even here, the flip-side is that a lot of helpless or violent or desperate people with families who cannot cope are going to be left to their own devices. Szasz can, presumably, afford to be indifferent; he can't meet with very many such clients in his practice. And it's there too in his suggesting that all of Freud's patients are malingerers—and in the much stranger view, a consequence for Szasz, that being schizophrenic as well is not something that happens to or afflicts someone; it is something he or she does and does deliberately. The Shape Right Up School of Psychiatry, for all mental disorders.[3]

But Szasz is a magpie—and a generation younger. There were a lot of things in the sixties and seventies that could turn a man into a relativist. And there was a lot of attention to language. So we get, in Szasz, another doctrine, one about "prescriptive", "ascriptive" and "descriptive" uses of words although little is done with it; a mention or two of "semiotics" and of "iconic signs" that seem to be nothing but body language; the bizarre view that hysteria and other mental disorders are themselves "languages". We get therapy and patients' behaviour and legal disputes about the mad, everything described as "games" and thought of in terms of fairly primitive game theory with no-win situations and some truisms about choices and values. But this is window-dressing. Game theory won't tell you what Szasz's views are on morality and psychiatry, madness and neurosis. There are other things to reckon with though—metagames and meta-this and meta-that, odd bits and pieces of role theory, the vaguely Rylean suggestion, never pursued or examined, that the whole trouble is the distinction between "entities" and "processes", one or two hints, again Rylean, to the effect that the mind itself is suspect or merely an "abstraction" and a definition of therapy in its initial stages as "meaningful dialogue". "Problems in living"—Szasz's preferred phrase for what these dialogues are supposed to be about and one that is remarkable only for its calculated and chilling blandness—comes from the same stable.[4]

Despite all this baggage, Szasz is, as I say, sometimes right. He is mostly right, I think, about hysteria. His conclusion—that there is no such disorder or state—is far too quick, far too sweeping. And many of his arguments are of the typically Szaszian tub-thumping or nonexistent variety. Nevertheless, the concept of hysteria employed in abnormal or clinical psychology is, indeed, in terrible shape. Szasz is right again, I think and as I have tried to make clear, in his debunking of the Oedipus complex and the more general Freudian claim that sex is in all cases what ails us. He also scores on some easier shots. Did anyone, to reask this question, ever really understand Freud's mechanistic and implausible hypothesis about "cathexis"? And Szasz's derisive attitude towards masturbatory insanity needs no defending—though do any Freudians diagnose it these days? Most of this I have already discussed—and I will return to hysteria later on. But there are some other large questions on which we ought to listen to Szasz.[5]

Is psychiatry, as Freud very much wanted it to be, a science? This is two questions. Let's reserve the word "psychoanalysis" for broadly Freudian views. Some people in the profession don't believe in psychoanalysis. Many or most of them do—to some extent or in certain cases or they are anyway inclined to. But the people who don't believe still believe that madness can be investigated and perhaps even cured. So we have to ask: Is psychoanalysis a science?—and is trying to help the mad by other methods scientific? I think the answer to each of these questions is "No", and for the same reason. Psychoanalysis addresses the mind, the seat of free will. This is not a political matter and not, in itself, a moral matter. It is just a simple fact that most of us can, within familiar limits and depending on the circumstances, do or say or think what we please. The mad and the neurotic also have free will, often in mutilated or restricted forms. I don't mean they choose to be mad or neurotic; that is a different issue. I mean that sometimes at least they have a considerable degree of control over their actions or possible responses. But how can there be a science whose subject-matter contains this element of freedom? How can science accommodate something that might be said or done on a whim—or for no reason or not much at all? How can science accommodate something that is said or done for reasons? The difficulty is not merely that of predictability—although this can, it seems to me, be underrated. Whatever you know about someone's basic beliefs and desires, what do you know about whether he or she will pour another cup of coffee before you or make a telephone call you can't quite understand? But this, as I say, isn't really the difficulty—and we might get better at predicting. The difficulty is that the concept of freedom is an insult to science. It is an insult to the very notion of a scientific law or principle or explanation. A future science? Not one we can know much about certainly. And as for neurological research into schizophrenia, for example, it too must take account of the phenomenon of reasons and so of that of meaning and the ways in which it can break down. But how can a science hope to scientifically recognize or calibrate meaning? I am aware that large and sometimes murky distinctions are operating here. And I am aware that "science" is a term of art. I have not intended to give a definition of it.   Nevertheless, the above negative criterion having to do with freedom does answer to something deep in our picture of science.   And it does allow physical medicine to be mostly a science—but not sociology or psychology, or not yet.[6]

More briefly, more obviously and in spite of my cautions of a while ago: There has been and still is a great deal of indifference, callousness and downright brutality of one sort or another in mental institutions, more or less serious abuses of coercive and other legal powers are common and extremely difficult problems arise over what those powers should be and over insanity as a legal defence.   While Szasz doesn't solve the problems, on the legal level any more than he does on the social level, the problems are there.

And—for now equally briefly—Szasz suggests not only that the concept of hysteria is a disaster but that all of the concepts employed by abnormal psychology are.   Again, his arguments, where they exist, are often worthless.   And I don't for a moment believe that there is no such thing as madness in Szasz's sense.   But here too I think the profession has large problems, problems that will get a thorough airing in Chapters 3 and 4.

These, then, are the good points.   They do not, it will be noticed, include any of the big claims, any of the slogans that might fuel a movement.

So—mental illness and metaphor.   Szasz's only argument for the view that "mental illness" and "mental disease" are metaphors is that the words "illness" and "disease"—and, as he occasionally says, "disability" and "disorder"—were once never used of the mental even though they now are and even though there are appreciable differences. This is a bad argument for because it is not true of the general catch-alls "disability" and "disorder" or "failing", "defect" or "difficulty". But what of the more specific "disease" or "illness"?

Metaphors had better not be too close.   It's hard to imagine "knife" being used as a metaphor for a fork or one white plastic cube serving as a revealing or interesting metaphor for another.   Metaphors, like analogies, must not be restatements or repetitions.   If, in trying to explain something to you, I offer you an analogy, nothing will be achieved if the analogy reproduces exactly the features of the original. Indeed, a metaphor is an analogy expressed in a factual and usually an aphoristic form—for a running metaphor is more difficult to bring off than a running analogy.   So a good metaphor has a literary or at least a catchy dimension to it.   Metaphors are also subject to the dangers of analogy—of being tenuous, for example, or far-fetched.   And a striking analogy gives us a striking metaphor, a lame one a lame one—and so

on. So there are only two questions. How significant are the differences or how good is the analogy? And whatever answer we give to
that and just as important, what are the alternatives, in the circumstances, to metaphor?

I'll try not to take too long over the totting-up and balancing
question. The principal difference is that, in the mental case, the mind
is directly and centrally involved. Of course, if any one of Interactive
Dualism, Identity Theory or Supervenience is true—and isn't that over
most at least of the relevant territory?—there will be some sort of
analogue, related by causality, identity or a bit of both, in the brain.
Still, it's a big difference; the mind, again, is the source of free will.
The similarities? There are all sorts of similarities. In fact, *DSM-IV*
lists organic mental disorders that, taken collectively, mimic almost all
of the psychoses as well as most of the neuroses and the personality
disorders. An organic counterpart for nearly everything recognized by
the profession. And there are other more general resemblances and
connections, having to do with disability, isolation, fear sometimes or
misery and sometimes losing the will to live.

So it's a pretty good metaphor—or not a bad one. Or it's a pretty
good or not a bad—what? What are the alternatives here to metaphor?
That it's the straightforward and literal truth that...? Well, yes, in a
way, but there's more to it than that.

It is a truism that in the turmoils and advances of science, concepts
can change. One points to Einstein and Newton, Copernicus and
Darwin perhaps—and some people point to Freud. I don't think
psychoanalysis or any other form of therapy for the mad is or is yet a
science. I do think that, like economics and anthropology, like social
credit and jurisprudence, chronic optimism and the idea of democracy,
psychoanalysis carries a considerable conceptual load. But key
concepts in these disciplines or areas or doctrines can change. Did
Freud change our concept of mind? There can be no doubt that he
did—and in ways that made us see more clearly. Did he help to
introduce a new concept of mental illness? He did indeed. And
Kraepelin and the neurologists are another part of the story—and the
changes have quickened so that now we are beginning, not merely to
postulate, but to find madness in the brain. For Szasz, of course, this is
a bit of a setback. It would make the metaphor, if it were one, that
much more apt or more telling. There is, however, a great deal of
plausibility—and, I think, a great deal of truth—in the view that this
relatively self-conscious change in our theoretical language over the
last hundred or hundred and fifty years is exactly that. We don't have a
metaphor here. It couldn't be a metaphor if only because if it once

were, it would, it seems, by now be effectively dead. Everyone, as Szasz says, buys into it—although *DSM-IV* is much more circumspect. But it was, at the time, a fairly clear-eyed theoretical proposal to the effect that schizophrenia or panic disorder is more like physical illness than had hitherto been thought. So it couldn't, it seems, ever have been a metaphor because metaphors—or halfway decent ones at any rate—leave something unsaid, unrevealed or only whispered. Was it a good proposal? There can't, surely, be the slightest doubt that it was.

But perhaps this is to put things too definitively, too categorically. Perhaps there is a hint or a breath of metaphor here—for the line between what is metaphorical and what is not can be fine. I don't share Szasz's knee-jerk distaste—not to mention that of most academics and scientists—in the presence of metaphor. If there is an element of metaphor in this case, it does not follow that the phrase "mental illness" fails to refer to anything. Something that is described metaphorically does not thereby disappear. What follows, rather, is that the phrase refers to whatever it refers to in a way we can't fully document or apprehend, a way that contains a secret. For a metaphor, like a joke, ceases to exist as such when it is fully explained. We might connect this with the fact that psychiatry is not a science—or not one we can now make much sense of. Still and all, a lot of the analogy can be spelled out—and for Freud at the mental level and Kraepelin at the level of the brain as a speculative though reasoned and theoretical proposal to change our concept of madness. Insofar as it is one or can be considered as one, it continues, as I say, to work out.[7]

Szasz tries other manoeuvres in his attack on the concept of mental illness—and on those of mental disorder, mental disability, mental disadvantage, schizophrenia, obsessive-compulsive disorder and everything else. Thus, he denounces hysteria and then informs us that hysteria is "paradigmatic" of mental illness or of madness and neurosis. It isn't. Conversion hysteria, which is mostly what Szasz has in mind, did play a large part in the birth of psychoanalysis and it was, for Freud, an important sort of neurosis. It is much less central for *DSM-IV*. And the much more eclectic meaning sometimes assigned to "hysteria" these days still leaves out schizophrenia, paranoia, manic-depressive psychosis and so on. If there are paradigms of mental illness, they are to be found among these disorders and not in hysteria, however construed.[8]

There's not much else. The "medical as opposed to metaphorical" distinction is sometimes described as the distinction between "medicine and ethics and the law", sometimes even as that between "medicine and education". So is morality, in particular, metaphorical, unreal, nonexistent? This would go well with the view that moral remarks are "imperatives", the view that there can be no moral truth. And while physical disease too often gives rise to ethical problems—and legal and educational ones—only the most careless and superficial Operationalism would say they are not medical matters but, for example, ethical instead. And as for "problems in living", so are gout and a reduced income, moderate deafness and an unexciting or sporadic sex-life. There's the talk about games and the insidious effects sometimes of the model. But any serious application of game theory, as Szasz would agree, must resist turning its objects into fun. There's the talk about language—aside from the claims about metaphor—and the odd vague suggestion that it's all linguistic and therefore somehow—isn't it?—relative? If there is an intellectual disease and so, I suppose, a metaphorical one of the last two or three decades, it is surely by a large margin this. But Szasz, of course, never argues for it.[9]

It is a consequence of all this that Szasz's major complaint against the profession is quite groundless. For that complaint is: There is nothing for it to treat, to do research on, to write about. It is a complaint Szasz comes nowhere near making persuasive. He does, however, have other complaints about certain members of the profession. And this is a reflection of two different singularities in his thinking.

First, his relation to Freudianism. What relation?, you will ask. For isn't this the man who wrote *The Myth of Psychotherapy?*—and shouldn't a man be held especially responsible for his titles? It is in this book that Szasz claims that the Oedipus complex is "mythology". He also says, "The single most important term in the Freudian vocabulary is the 'Oedipus complex'." We have come across this latter sort of claim before. It isn't. Many psychotherapists who think of themselves as Freudian place little emphasis or none at all on the Oedipus complex. Szasz is one of them—as we shall see. And in the same book, Freud is lumped together with some of his predecessors, including Mesmer, as well as a sampling of the present-day lunatic fringe of psychotherapists. This is, as Szasz knows, guilt by historical and literary association. But this is only one side of Szasz. For Szasz is a Freudian. He says so. In *The Ethics of Psychoanalysis*, the views of the "autonomous" therapist are expressed in terms of "the control of the ego over...the id" and "repression" and "the unconscious". Indeed, as Szasz modestly says, "I could refer to [my theory] simply as 'psychoanalysis'." But he manages to resist the temptation. His form of therapy, then, is Freudian with less sex and a healthy injection of this Libertarian notion of autonomy. You think of the mad, the blown away and the deranged.

You think of the homeless, half of them mad or in remission or full of drugs. You look at them and you think, "Autonomy; go for it. Go for the good life." There's nowhere for them to go—or no way for them to get there or not the slightest reason to go. But the point of the story is this: Szasz is an analyst with broadly Freudian views who makes a lot of his living and almost all of his fame by denying those views.

This paradox in Szasz's thinking—in his very being, one wants to say, in his soul—comes with an added complication. In a chapter of *The Myth of Psychotherapy* entitled "Sigmund Freud: The Jewish Avenger," Szasz calls Freud an "angry" as well as a "vengeful Jew"; he attributes to him, on the basis of the fact that Freud observed certain orthodoxies, the view that "Jewish is beautiful"; he interprets Freud's awareness of his antiSemitic environment and his increasing preoccupation with it in the years leading up to the Second World War as his "venomous antiGentilism"; he suggests that psychoanalysis is itself somehow Jewish and he refers to it as "Freud's lexicon of loathing". There is a name for all this. It is antiSemitism. Szasz didn't get that from Ayn Rand. The general principle maybe—but not the target. The target here is all Szasz's own.

Having said that, I should also say that even in this flat and thoroughly unsavoury contradiction in Szasz about the legitimacy of psychoanalysis, there is a question: What is psychoanalysis exactly and how is it to be distinguished from other forms of therapy? It is a question that is not given enough attention in the literature. Szasz, I think, provides part of the answer to it, casual and off-hand as his contribution is. This should already be obvious from my examination of Freud's views in the last chapter—and the question will come up again in Chapters 3 and 4.[10]

But we have not yet considered the most puzzling and, in some respects, the most damaging defect in Szasz's views. So second, his attitude towards the brain and brain research. In the earlier books, you wouldn't know the brain existed. The occasional mention, always quickly dropped. And in *The Ethics of Psychoanalysis*, Szasz says that the "autonomous" therapist does not dispense drugs. So, you think to yourself, he's a sort of vegetarian or biodegradable type—which can't be all bad. But whatever the benefits, a theory must work. And what of the enormous strides that have been made with antipsychotics and lithium? And what of the indisputable fact that for depression, anyway, electric shock treatment often helps? Do you leave the patients hanging there with the terror or the guilt or completely catatonic, urging them again only to be autonomous?

In a more recent book, *Insanity*, Szasz devotes a few pages to the brain. He makes three points. "Some" of the so-called "mentally ill" might have "brain lesions"; discovering a correlation is not, by itself, discovering a cause; brain research will do nothing to solve the ethical, social and legal problems.

The last point is right—short of some extreme and elaborated form of Materialism. But few people would defend brain research on these grounds. The second is right too. This, that or the other brain study might establish, not the cause, but a predisposing condition or a causally necessary but insufficient factor or what seems at present to be a brute correlation. What Szasz fails to remind us is that a researcher— into the body or the mind—would and should be interested in all these things. The first point is—it's not a point. Someone makes a point only if he says something. Some Swedes have brain damage, mild or severe and sometimes unsuspected. Some Catholics do. Some adolescents display unusual brain activity, some coal miners have some atrophying of certain parts of the brain, some women suffer from blackouts as a result of neurological failure. To be able to look at the work that has been done on madness and the brain since the forties and fifties and remark that "some" mentally disordered people might, probably do, have something amiss with their brain almost defies comprehension. It does, as I've said, make all the talk about metaphor seem less threadbare. But whatever the motive, how can you possibly treat the brain as irrelevant?

Here again, though, there are questions, this time more philosophical questions. Some of them Szasz can hardly be aware of; he certainly doesn't discuss them. All this brain research can be accommodated on a number of views—Interactionism, Identity Theory, Supervenience, even old-fashioned Epiphenomenalism. Supervenience and Epiphenomenalism insist on some sort of causal asymmetry or insulation between the mind and the brain. But there are other such views— Parallelism and what we might think of as Reverse Epiphenomenalism. We know that these last two views can't be true in general; the mind just is, in many ways, influenced by the brain. Still, mightn't they be partly true? An assumption common to all of these views is that the same kind of relation holds across the board between the mind and the brain but mightn't Interactive Dualism, say, be combined with Epiphenomenalism? There is another question that Szasz is well aware of. So is everyone else in the profession. Does all this emphasis on the brain mean that Determinism is true—for both the mad and the rest of us? It is to Szasz's credit that, unlike most of the profession, he gives a clear and a forthright answer. We're free all right; just forget about the brain. The answer won't do, of course—and this question, along with some of the others, will be considered further in Chapter 4.[11]

Laing's rejection of madness is kinder. It is based in part on therapeutic concerns—though also in part on some fairly murky theoretical ideas as well as a desperate assessment of human beings.

Laing places the self at the centre of madness and neurosis. This is not an original suggestion but it is, I think, worth pursuing and I will have more to say about it later on. For now, not much more than a warning.

The concept of the self is seldom discussed by contemporary English-speaking philosophers. Personal identity is but that is a rather different matter. Questions about the self are reflexive questions about people or, if not, they are questions about the distinction between "Self" and "Not-self", as James has it, or, perhaps, about unity—and they are often put in the present tense. Questions about personal identity are usually about identity over time—and their connection with these other concerns is not clear either. So what does Laing think of the self?[12]

He does have a view, a sort of Sartrean, a sort of existential phenomenological view. In the early books where this view is sketched out, *The Divided Self* and *Self and Others*, Laing refers explicitly to Sartre only rarely. But he makes free use of the language of Sartre, the language of "bad faith" and "inauthenticity", of "anguish" and the "absurd" and "ontological insecurity", of "being-for-itself" and "being-in-itself". He also talks of "depersonalization" and a "schizoid state" and he sees the self as being composed of the mind and body in that in schizophrenia, real or so-called, "The individual's being is cleft in two, producing a disembodied self and a body that...the self looks at regarding it at times as though it were just another thing in the world." The sane self, if there is one, must have both mental and physical properties. It is, as Laing hopefully says, "a quasiduality with an overall unity."[13]

Three of Sartre's views are relevant here. One has to do with freedom, another with other people and the third with epistemology and scepticism in general.

For being-for-itself, Sartre tells us, "existence precedes essence." This means that we're free. And this means, according to Sartre, that at any and every moment we are free to think or say or do as we please independently and even flying in the face of what we have done or chosen in the past. We are "wholly free", "absolutely free". But we indulge in bad faith or deceive ourselves or at least fail to acknowledge our freedom for we are creatures of habit, weighed down by the past. With other people, Sartre thinks, there's no winning. We regard them "objectively" or treat them as "objects", lacking freedom, mere being-in-itself. And they, of course, reciprocate. We are engaged in a perpetual war of ontological denigration with the "other", that peculiarly ominous figure of Sartre's sort of Existentialism. And as for epistemology in general, Descartes takes the existence of the first-person mind or of the self as the ultimate foundation of all knowledge, the place where scepticism must stop. Sartre disagrees. The self is not "in consciousness" for Sartre; it is, rather, embodied "in the world", a world that is, however, a construct, a mere "phenomenon" Kant would have said, of mentalistic and intentional elements. So it is a mistake to think of the self as exclusively mental—and this alleged conceptual fact is somehow supposed to do away with scepticism about the external world.[14]

There is a question as to whether the second view is a view about the self, as to whether one's relations with others are partly constitutive of the self. But let's leave that aside. Before commenting on these views—however they are to be categorized or labelled—I ought to say something about Laing's strategy. Laing does take an occasional swipe at the "medical model" but he pursues this target with much less enthusiasm than Szasz. His usual approach is to try to persuade us that we're all mad—or all something pretty horrible anyway. Sometimes he seems to try to persuade us that we're all sane instead. It is the former approach that predominates in Laing's account of the morbid world of Sartre. But in either case, human beings are all of the same kind, whatever kind that is. This is fairly clear-cut, relatively no-nonsense, for Laing is, as we might put it, much less mystifying than Szasz. So we have to ask, not only whether Sartre's views are correct, but also or in particular whether they divide humanity up in this all-or-nothing way. And we mustn't forget to ask just how close the sort of morbidity or vileness we are dealing with is to madness or to madness and neurosis.

Sartre's view of freedom ignores the enormous difficulty often involved in trying to distance oneself from one's past. It also ignores the fact that any serious or informed choice—anything beyond vanilla as opposed to strawberry ice-cream—will be made in accordance with beliefs and desires, feelings, motives and so on that have been acquired or chosen, as Sartre thinks, in the past. Still, there is a disconcerting germ of truth here; the banker who takes off to paint in poverty is a trite image but this sort of behaviour is possible—and one's actions could, it seems and however much their value or importance might be open to question, be pointless or automatic on occasion or perform themselves. Does this germ of truth divide us up as Laing would wish? The trouble is, apparently, that we're not aware enough or aware constantly enough of our often very considerable freedom. Is this inevitable? We can imagine Sartre in his wanderings around Paris from café to bistro to lecture hall to hotel room muttering fiercely under his breath, "I'm free; I'm free." That, one supposes, is about as good as it gets. And many of us are more conscious of our freedom than others or have more of a sense of living on this or that edge—and Sartre himself discusses a number of examples of individuals who have more or less come to terms with their freedom. So no all-or-nothing version of this view can be found in Sartre—or, indeed, will work. Self-deception, certainly, of a genuine though ordinary kind does, as I've said, provide an illuminating model for Freudian cases. But there are all sorts of questions here—and all sorts of differences. There is, however and surely obviously, no interesting correlation between being an existentialist philosopher and being sane.[15]

Neither, of course, is there a connection between seeing others objectively, that is, clearly and accurately, and treating them as objects in Sartre's demeaning and degrading sense. In fact, one would have thought that the former might well preclude the latter. Do we all treat all others as we might a rock or a dinner-preparing robot? It's hard to know how to respond. I'm more cynical than most. I don't have the lugubrious disposition of a Sartre but I don't have an exactly sunny one either. And I come from a family some members of which are as adept as anyone I've ever met at the Sartrean withering or perishing "look". So what can I say? I go over what's out there, thinking of this business of not treating others as people. There's an awful lot of it, I think, way too much. Is it inevitable or universal? No; of course not. Don't we all know of cases where this is not so or where the deviations from an honest, nonthreatening and thoroughly rewarding relationship are minor or inconsequential? It will be said—it always is at this point— that the dehumanizing motives and the anguish and insecurity are always present beneath the surface although not, for Sartre, unconsciously, that this sort of pattern is unavoidable and not a sometime thing or a matter of degree. There is no evidence for this, none at all. And the relatively limited extent to which many of us fall victim to this dilemma of Sartre's is—unfortunately for Laing—a long way from madness and neurosis. But we have still not explained Laing's strange picture of the nonbodily schizophrenic.[16]

And so to epistemology. There are two obvious questions here. Why is the self excluded from consciousness? And what sort of world is it thrust into? Two kinds of consciousness exist, according to Sartre, "prereflective" or "nonpositional" and "reflective" or "positional". Or two levels of consciousness or, as Sartre often prefers to put it and surely oddly at least, two consciousnesses. Or one consciousness, it seems, with two aspects or faces. For, as he says more than once, "every positional consciousness of an object is at the same time a nonpositional consciousness of itself." Two kinds or levels or two consciousnesses—or only one? What is going on? And doesn't a regress threaten here? I think there is something right and important about this distinction of Sartre's—and I think he is right to dismiss the threat of a regress. Consider the hierarchy beginning, for Sartre, with a consciousness of the world, then a consciousness of that conscious-ness—and one might, of course, want to invoke still higher levels. Sartre mishandles this distinction in some ways. Thus he says that a prereflective consciousness does not know of its own existence—the thought of a consciousness with no vestige of self-consciousness is an extremely queer one—and he says that it can, nevertheless, admit to its own existence, if asked, immediately, at the drop of a hat—but this is also true, as will become clear in Chapter 4 if it isn't already, of much of the mind that is not conscious, even prereflectively. What Sartre is quite wrong about—and he sometimes sees this—is that Descartes's Cogito is reflective and therefore a different consciousness from the more basic prereflective one, its object. This is Sartre counting consciousnesses, completely arbitrarily, and refusing to allow any degree of self-knowledge into this near-scholastic notion of a single consciousness. If you are absorbed in some problem and then become more reflective, is there anything you can do with the idea that you are or have a different consciousness? With regard to the external world, Sartre does attempt to exploit our knowledge of perception and action from within. What underlies this, however—as Sartre concedes—is just Husserl again with his phantom world of phenomena. Does Sartre endorse the Kantian notion of noumena?—for that's where Husserl got some of it, with the rest coming mostly from Descartes. He certainly does although he says he doesn't—and he refers to it, with displeasure and illicitly, as a "plenum", as "solid" or "massive". For on this issue, the only one that really matters, that of things in themselves—not, or not exactly, things in themselves as opposed to human beings but genuine physical objects, what's actually out there, the real McCoy—Sartre, like Kant, has no choice but to be a sceptic. He just doesn't advertise the fact very much—any more than Kant does. So rather than arguing against Descartes's scepticism, Sartre in the end embraces it. But however we assess these views of Sartre's, they are the only ones I know of that make any sense at all of Laing's description of schizo-phrenics. The difficulty is that the alleged mistake here is a philosophical mistake shared by no more than a handful of people who follow Descartes on this point. Their opponents, the orthodox Sartre-ans, constitute another, let's say a slightly larger, handful—and the vast majority of people have never even heard of the problem. So whatever Descartes's mistake, it can't begin to show that we're all anything. And the suggestion that, in schizophrenia, this philosophical view is somehow transformed into the divorce of the self from the body is not only inexplicable; it is, quite simply, a gross misrepresentation of the phenomenology of schizophrenia—let alone of all madness and all neurosis.[17]

A note, however, on "depersonalization". Depersonalization is a condition characterized by doubts about or denials of the self's integrity or existence. The denials can, though they need not, be of delusional intensity. Sometimes the body is said to be under threat or to have disappeared. "My body is transparent and can't hold on to itself"; "It is dust, it is junk"; "It fell apart in a dream." Sometimes the mind is. "My mind is a cipher in a locked-up vault"; "Thoughts now, thoughts are for others who can barely manage." And sometimes it's just the self. "I'm dead now and have been for years"; "I spread out too easily, far too thinly"; "I once, I suppose, might have had a life." These are all ways of complaining about the self's insubstantiality or nonexistence. There is no reason for thinking that a feeling of being split off from the body dominates all such cases. And there is no reason for thinking that depersonalization, construed as above, is paradigmatic of all schizo-phrenia or all madness and neurosis. *DSM-IV* underestimates it, listing it as a "dissociative" disorder in its own right and as one of a large number of "associated features" of schizophrenia. Still, it is only one way of being mad or neurotic. There are others. Laing, I should point out, often gives "depersonalization"—as well as "schizoid state"—a much more general, much vaguer sense. But that doesn't alter the facts. No invented or technical use of these expressions, however broad, can make feeling mildly insecure about a postponed decision or even real anguish over others more like madness and neurosis than it is.

It should already be clear that the notion of the self, whatever we say of it in the end, is a very complicated one. I will, again, return to it at greater length in Chapter 4. What needs emphasizing here is that none of these views of Sartre's should persuade us that we're all mad or all neurotic or all something more or less deplorable or to be avoided. There is, however, another of Sartre's preoccupations that Laing discusses directly and in detail.

I will be brief.   In *Critique of Dialectical Reason*, published
seventeen years after *Being and Nothingness*, Sartre tries to weld
Existentialism on to Marxism. There are obvious problems. Marxism
requires that we have an awful lot to do with others. And it places an
awful lot of weight on the past. The dialectical method itself has to be
investigated and elaborated—and so we get a fair bit of Hegel. Sartre
on Hegel. And then Laing on Sartre on Hegel. For in *Reason and
Violence*, a book he coauthored with D. Cooper, Laing wrote a long
essay on Marxism and "groups" and "series" of others and the super
other or the "third" and the intricacies of dialectical reasoning. James
once remarked of "the obscurer passages in Hegel" that "it is a fair
question whether the rationality included in them is anything more than
the fact that the words all belong to a common vocabulary, and are
strung together on a scheme of predication and relation." Sartre too—
sometimes deliberately, one wants to say—can be profoundly incoherent. And Laing can't help himself. Consider, for example, the
following explosion of nonsense: "The praxis...of the militant is
constituted by the mediation of the out-group other between the in-
group individual and the group-as-object-for-the-out-group-other
interiorized by the in-group subject, and the mediation of this interiorized group-object between the in-group individual as agent and the out-
group other as object of his action." And there is the constant sing-
song of the dialectic, "The interiorization of the exterior and...the
exteriorization of the interior", "the knowledge of being and the being
of knowledge", "totalization, detotalization [and] retotalization."
Laing's essay also rests heavily on the not atypical existentialist
propensity for unforgivable philosophical hyperbole. "The meaning of
reality is the impossible, the coefficient of resistance of my praxis. The
transformation that my praxis demands is that the impossible becomes
impossible to accept. At this moment of suffocation the impossibility
of change becomes the impossibility of living." Somewhat melodra-
matic, surely, even if you're trying to replace a washer on a tap. But
there is nothing, in this talk of action and groups and ideology, that
further illuminates Laing's views on madness and neurosis. His
attention is largely elsewhere. And there is nothing in *Critique of
Dialectical Reason* that makes Sartre's position on freedom, other
people or epistemology in general any more clear or more compelling—although an ontological category, "being-for-others" or "being-
with-others", that was introduced in the second half of *Being and
Nothingness* is given much greater prominence. He too is primarily
concerned with the other, for example, or the "third" in political or
class contexts. The "look" becomes that of the other whose "needs"

compete with yours in a situation of "scarcity" or of the fellow-Marxist who nevertheless disapproves of some aspect of your theoretical stance or still, at times, of someone who has no needs or none that are pressing and doesn't disapprove, maybe a grocer or waiter, but someone who just isn't you—directed right at your back, at the fat part, the middle or least comprehending part.[18]

So that's Laing's Sartre. There is, however, a tone to Laing's essay that I have not yet mentioned. For he says that "Each of us passes his life engraving his malefic imago on other persons and on things" and he tells us that "violence is everywhere, and everywhere is terror." Which brings us to *The Politics of Experience*, published three years after the essay. This is a dark book. It's full of the anger and despair many people felt over Vietnam and outmoded or hypocritical values in the sixties. Laing, like the times, had his psychedelic side but this is, perhaps, his worst trip—and he calls us all "murderers and prostitutes". He asks if love and freedom are "possible in our present situation" and he says that "our social relations are so ugly if seen in the light of exiled truth, and beauty is almost no longer possible if it is not a lie." This is obviously overblown, nearly hysterical. The truth is more banal, much more pedestrian—sobering or even downright disconcerting as it might be. And murder and prostitution, the rejection of love or blindness to beauty, are, where they exist, not madness and not neurosis either.[19]

After *The Politics of Experience*, there was *Knots*, Laing's collection of pseudoschizophrenic poems, and then the trip to Ceylon and the six-month stay in a Buddhist monastery, then the trip to India and Japan to study Yoga and Zen. I do not propose to follow him there except to say that the later writings are more eclectic, less focused—from the conversations and poems, off-key and fictitious but somehow based on fact, of *Do You Love Me?* to the real exchanges with his own children recorded in *Conversations with Children*, from the conversations again and the memories, the diary entries and case studies, all in the interests of debunking science, drugs and behaviour modification and endorsing intrauterine experience and that of birth in *The Facts of Life* to Laing's more proper book, *The Voice of Experience*, that is full of speeches against science again and control and objectivity and speculations on the traumatic effects of life in the womb again and of birth itself. The famous views, the "radical" views, are still sometimes present. But there are too many things to do, too many distractions, too many views.[20]

I have painted a gloomy picture. But Laing is not always so negative. I said quite a while ago that he sometimes suggests, not that there's something wrong with all of us, but that there's nothing wrong with any of us—that we are, in fact, all sane. This is, once more, a much less frequent move. And Laing doesn't have his heart in it. For he straightforwardly admits that "the kernel of the schizophrenic experience...must remain incomprehensible." Nevertheless, Laing's talk of "understanding" the mad is indicative of his attitude towards them and what should go on in therapy. He says repeatedly that a patient must be treated as a "person" and not as an "object" or "organism"—and he speaks of the patient's "autonomy". He thinks of the task of the therapist as doing whatever he or she can to look at the world through the patient's eyes, to get a grip on that sort of phenomenology, and he insists that the patient's story must always be taken as seriously as anyone else's. There is the fact that the patient is usually seen by Laing as a member of a family and not in artificial isolation and the time and energy invested in Kingsley Hall, the experiment in the therapeutic advantages of communal living that Laing started in London in 1965. There is the remark, "The main agent in uniting the patient...is the physician's love, a love that recognizes the patient's total being, and accepts it, with no strings attached." Someone might feel, especially in the hustle and bustle of appointments, lectures or keeping up with the literature, that this too is overblown. Still, Laing's disagreement with Szasz over what the patient's "autonomy" amounts to couldn't be clearer. And then again, it must be said, there is all the difference in the world between this attitude of Laing's, this love, if you will, and the view that all of us are sane.[21]

So Laing doesn't really believe we're all sane. Does he believe we're all mad? In *The Divided Self* and *Self and Others*, he talks unequivocally of both sanity and psychosis but already there are relativist rumblings—sometimes pointing in one direction and sometimes the other. And by the time of *The Politics of Experience*, what was once an idea Laing had flirted with becomes official doctrine. It is in this book that Laing calls us all "mad", "crazed", "out of our minds". He also speaks of our "pseudosanity" and "collusive madness" and he wonders, even, if the psychotic might be our saviour, "the hierophant of the sacred".[22]

The view that we're all mad is not, of course, the view that there is no such thing as madness. It is, rather, the view that madness is all over the place. But it does have in common with that view the consequence that the "mad" are no worse off than the "sane", the "sane" no better off than the "mad". Laing's arguments for it, again, are not very good. And it is quite simply false. This is not because of some philosophical requirement to the effect that we need an existing paradigm or standard for each half of a distinction. Being sane is not much of an achievement for many people. One can be violent or coarse, ridiculously narrow-minded or completely lacking in humour and not be mad. There are a lot of people out there who are not mad or neurotic for that matter even though their lives might be boring or crude or marked by weakness or failure. We're not all mad. The view that we're all sane is the view that there is no such thing as madness. Laing, as I say, doesn't really believe it so he has no arguments for it— although he does let his language run away with him at times. It must seem, to most people who have ever tried to look into the eyes of a patient in a catatonic stupor or to deal with the swings of mania, not only wrong, which it surely is, but profoundly silly. The view that the mad might be "the hierophants of the sacred" could be the view that the "mad" are sane and the "sane" mad. If so, it is mistaken on two counts. It could, on the other hand, be the view that there might be some other unheard of unnameable dimension along which the "sane" would come off much worse than the "mad". There might be. It is enormously unlikely but there just might be. What, though, is Laing trying to do here? Erect a therapy for and a theory of the mad on the basis of some science fiction, some merely mystical, possibility? We are back, of course, in Ceylon and Japan—or in a dream of what Ceylon and Japan might be.

And now for one or two omissions—and then some loose ends. Maybe there is a question as to whether one's relations to others should be mentioned in a description of the concept of the self. But that's a philosopher talking. One's relations to others can certainly be of over-whelming importance. And with regard to the genesis of schizophre-nia, Laing implicates the family. In *Society, Madness and the Family*, Laing and his colleague A. Esterson try to explain the behaviour of eleven schizophrenics in terms of their place in and relations towards their schizophrenogenic families with the mother cast in a central and an especially unattractive role. They claim, in the Preface to the Second Edition, to have found the same pattern in every one of the more than two hundred cases they had by then investigated and the claim is extended even further by Laing in *The Politics of Experience*. This is not, as Laing is aware, a causal claim. And it is not incompati-ble with the results of genetic and brain research on schizophrenia. For genetics seems to be no more than part of the picture—and as Laing points out, chronic family patterns can change the brain. So we can only ask: Do all schizophrenics come from schizophrenogenic fami-lies?—and what of the families of nonschizophrenics? The second question Laing waves aside as irrelevant to his purposes. No investigator in any field can afford to be so disdainful. For while the second question is, in a sense, an independent question, the answer we give to it can make a lot of difference to the significance we attach to the answer we give to the first. The first question? No. There can be no doubt that schizophrenogenic families exist. And there can be no doubt that they sometimes play a role in the onset and nature of psychosis in one of their members. The generalization, however, is absurd. Studies have shown, one wants to say—and they have indeed. But haven't we known for as long as the disorder has been recognized that schizophrenics can emerge from the most varied of backgrounds or from the most ordinary circumstances? The denial of this is, surely, a product of Laing's passionate respect for his patients, gone awry, and an overall bitterness about all of humanity or all of the rest. On this latter question, a man who can say we are all "murderers", all "mad", all "alienated", all "fragmented"—on this question, such a man is not to be trusted.[23]

We should also notice that Laing's view of schizophrenogenic or "mystifying" families is not incompatible with, it can be grafted on to, Freud's views. But Laing is, perhaps, less committed than Szasz to Freudianism. His theory about the self and its splitting is, in a way and odd as it is, an alternative to Freud. And Laing says that "the terminology of ego, super-ego [and] id...puts unnecessary limitations on one's understanding" and he asks why it is that "almost all theories about depersonalization, reification, splitting, denial, tend themselves to exhibit the symptoms they attempt to describe?" A strange intoxicating mixture of psychological and philosophical concerns. But Laing himself employs the concepts of depersonalization and splitting—as well as those of projection and introjection, repression and the unconscious. His account of the ills the self is subject to is often expressed in terms of what is conscious or unconscious—and he applauds Freud's achievements and counts himself "a follower of Freud." Laing, we might say, is a much more giving and humane, more socially and politically and indeed family oriented Freud with a very different sense at times of how to split people into bits.[24]

As for the brain and drugs, Laing makes the occasional concession—as is evident in his disclaimer about his work on schizophrenics' families. But then there is the open hostility towards drug therapy in *The Facts of Life*, for example. And much of the time, Laing seems to agree with Szasz in wishing that the brain would go away. Perhaps predictably, he too is a sort of ecological type.

And as for taxonomy, Laing does, like Szasz, raise some important questions. But these questions, along with those about the brain and drugs, must be left until later.

That's about all. There is a theory about interpersonal perception and communication with Sartrean layers and levels. My reaction to you, for example, might be to your reaction to me—and so on and so on and all mixed up with Sartre as well as Harry Stack Sullivan. One also meets with "social adaptions", "social events" and "social facts" in Laing. But there is no serious attempt to show that madness is a social construct or that it is a somehow social as opposed to a psychological problem. There is some talk of "labelling" and, sometimes, a generalized relativism, as in "the ideal standpoint we can glimpse but not adopt." But Laing never bothers to argue for this. There are just the words—and the preoccupation about "invalidating" the patient or his or her point of view.[25]

So we're stuck with madness—and with neurosis. We can't deny the obvious facts. And this too—the existence of madness, in particular—is something we have known about for a long time now. The existence of madness, which has taken a clearer and clearer form over the last century and can be observed first-hand in any mental hospital or an acquaintance, sometimes, or someone we see on the street, the existence of madness is inescapable. We're not stuck with our concepts though, not in the same way or to the same extent. It is not easy to be objective about concepts we have grown up with. They have seeped into our very marrow, into our bones. But we do have an advantage here; the concepts of abnormal or clinical psychology have always come with something of a question mark hovering over them. The following chapters constitute a critical and an increasingly theoretical examination of our concepts of madness, neurosis and sanity. They are, if you like, an attempt to understand certain facts.

Notes

1. See Locke's *An Essay Concerning Human Understanding*, Vol. II, p. 274. For Wittgenstein's views on language and language-learning, see, in particular, *Philosophical Investigations*, Basil Blackwell, 1953—though these views had been in wide circulation for some years by then. And for the above mish-mash of views, see *Introduction to Objectivist Epistemology*, New American Standard Library, 1967.

2. The gap between "is" and "ought" is, of course, Hume's. And "a very large part", not all. Neither should it be supposed—as it not infrequently is by moral philosophers—that the other part, the self, ought to be treated no differently from anyone else. The remarks by Ayn Rand on morality are from *The Virtue of Selfishness*, New American Library, 1964.

3. I should emphasize, once again, that while the element of responsibility required by repression is what lies behind Freud's famous and self-consciously dramatic phrase, "the choice of neurosis", it is nowhere near enough to justify the view that Freudian patients just are malingerers.

For the more obviously central or otherwise significant attributions in the above, see *The Myth of Mental Illness*, Harper and Row, 1961, pp. 2, 115, 129-32, *The Ethics of Psychoanalysis*, Basic Books, 1965, pp. 104-36, 178-205, 44, *The Myth of Mental Illness*, pp. 41, 248. The word "client" as a synonym for "patient" is, by the way, borrowed from Carl Rogers—but Szasz gives it his own peculiar twist.

The only direct evidence I have for the link between Szasz and Ayn Rand is that he has for years been a Contributing Editor of *Reason*, the official voice of the Libertarian party of which Ayn Rand is the intellectual guru. I have before me now the April, 1993, issue—chosen more or less at random. It contains, as well as a not very illuminating article on suicide by Szasz and various explicit references to Ayn Rand, pieces against the left, against unions, against gun control—and an advertisement for a new free country with no taxes placed by Galt's Gulch Development, Ltd. John Galt is one of Ayn Rand's fictional heroes—and a Las Vegas address is given.

4. See *Law, Liberty and Psychoanalysis*, Collier, 1963, p. 18, *The Myth of Mental Illness*, pp. 115-63, 223-310, *The Ethics of Psychoanalysis*, pp. 62-77, *The Myth of Mental Illness*, pp. 1-2, *The Ethics of Psychoanalysis*, pp. 30, 89, 64, *Law, Liberty and Psychoanalysis*, p. 11.

5. Hysteria has, by the way, quietly disappeared from the *DSMs*—and I will have something to say about this in Chapter 4.

See *The Myth of Mental Illness*, pp. 75-110, *The Myth of Psychotherapy*, Anchor, 1978, pp. 127-42, *The Ethics of Psychoanalysis*, pp. 60-61, *The Manufacture of Madness*, Harper and Row, 1970, pp. 180-206, *The Myth of Mental Illness*, pp. 108-9.

6. Szasz—strangely, it seems to me—has no clear or settled views on whether psychiatry is a science but he frequently raises the question. Freud's wish for psychoanalysis to be a science is not, of course, unconnected with his Determinism. He is, however, mostly concerned with reasons as opposed to causes—and his Determinism, as Dilman observes in *Freud and the Mind*, is mere "philosophical froth", (p. 3). Reasons and causes? A reason is, roughly, a consideration we take as justifying or giving sense to, one we somehow approve of; a cause will have its way with us whatever we think. I am not denying that we can sometimes deflect or control causes but, even then, disapproval, by itself, achieves nothing. And if a reason is for something unconscious, it too, we should notice, will typically be unconscious. The future of science? It's everywhere these days what with Identity Theory, Eliminativ-

ism, Functionalism and Supervenience. But I suspect—and I will try to argue for this later on—that freedom, this fundamental fact of our existence, can be salvaged only by the future—of science and, one supposes, of philosophy as well.

7. The above account of mental illness and metaphor has some points of contact with that given by Andrew Collier in *R. D. Laing*, Latimer Trend, 1977, pp. 147-50.

8. Szasz discusses hysteria in a number of places but it is in *The Myth of Mental Illness* that he describes hysteria as "paradigmatic" of mental disorders. In *Schizophrenia: The Sacred Symbol of Psychiatry*, Basic Books, 1976, however, grand paresis is touted as the "model" for all mental disorders. Ah well.

9. I speak principally because with most knowledge of philosophy. But all of the humanities and all the social sciences have been in considerable relativistic or sceptical disarray for quite some time—and look at what we are here discussing with regard to abnormal or clinical psychology. We have become, at best, nay-sayers or ignorers; at worst, we are chronically equivocal with no confidence or investment in anything, ivory-tower intellectuals with no spine and less sense. Michael Williams, in his *Unnatural Doubts*, Basil Blackwell, 1991, says that "Recent years have seen a remarkable revival of this [sceptical] attitude," (p. xiii). But none of the philosophers Williams mentions, as he would be the first to admit, is an out-and-out sceptic. For this too is part of the posture. This scepticism, this nihilism, almost never presents itself as what it is.

See, for the various contrasts Szasz offers to medicine in connection with mental disorders, *The Myth of Mental Illness*, p. 8, *Law, Liberty and Psychiatry*, p. 3, *The Ethics of Psychoanalysis*, pp. 46-61.

10. There is a dilemma that haunts the profession: Freud or drugs?—or might they, just conceivably, be compatible? It is usually buried pretty deep but it does come to the surface occasionally—and the text-books contain all sorts of references to Freud and to Freudianism or psychoanalysis. You would think there would be more critical discussion of what Freud actually said. And to catch up with Szasz, see *The Myth of Psychotherapy*, pp. 133, 130, *The Ethics of Psychoanalysis*, pp. 5, 51, 58, 60-61, *The Myth of Psychotherapy*, pp. 161, 144, 147, 150, 157, 161.

11. Epiphenomenalism, traditionally, is the dualistic view that the brain can affect the mind but not vice-versa. Recently, a new nondualistic form of Epiphenomenalism has been introduced by some of the champions of Supervenience. I am, in the above, employing the label in its traditional sense—and a more detailed discussion of all of the above Isms can, again, be found in Chapter 4. Szasz's attitude towards madness and the brain are summed up in *Insanity*, John Wiley, 1987, pp. 344-9. And for his views on drugs, see *The Ethics of Psychoanalysis*, pp. 31, 114 and 183.

12. Seldom discussed? What of Dennett, say, or Flanagan or Nozick? Either negative or highly implausible—but some of the views of some of these philosophers will come up in Chapter 4. There will also be more, quite a bit

more, on the account given by James in *The Principles of Psychology*, Dover, 1950, Vol. I, Chapter X.

13. *The Divided Self*, Tavistock, 1960, pp. 174, 126. The view of the schizophrenic as bodiless, it should be said, does not appear, except fleetingly, in any of Laing's other books. *Self and Others* was published by Tavistock in 1961.

14. See *Existentialism is a Humanism* (tr. P. Mairet), Methuen, 1960, p.15, *Being and Nothingness* (tr. Hazel Barnes), Washington Square, 1966, pp. 571, 598, 711, 393-94, *The Transcendence of the Ego* (trs. E. Haldane and R. Kirkpatrick), Noonday, 1957, p. 31. And see Meditation II in *The Philosophical Works of Descartes* (trs. E. Haldane and G. Ross), Cambridge, 1975, for the allegedly purely mental affirmation, "I am, I exist."

15. The above discussion is extremely brief. For more details on the problematic nature of the will, see Chapter 4.

Many of the examples are in the novels—for Sartre, of course, wrote novels too. He isn't Ayn Rand, not by any means. But he is doomed to be compared to Camus. He has none of the grace or lightness or sureness of touch of the latter—though who does?—and the novels are sometimes dense if not impenetrable and the writing laboured. What would you expect of novels where an important part of the plot or one of the main characters is ontology? Still and all, the examples are perfectly serviceable for philosophical purposes. Whatever some of my colleagues might say about the interface between philosophy and literature, the examples in fiction have to be more concrete, more filled-in and elaborated, more revered, to put it extravagantly, for their own sakes. Shades of Wittgenstein, another writer—and Sartre sees trouble in this direction for biography and for psychoanalysis.

16. See, on the "look" and Sartre's views on psychoanalysis and the unconscious, *Being and Nothingness*, pp. 340-400 and 712-34. And the element of knowledge required by repression is, once again, nowhere near enough to make us turn our backs on Freud and return to Descartes's equation between what is mental and what is conscious.

17. The alternatives to noumena for Kant are phenomena, mere appearances of what might not even be a reality that carry the unmistakable mark of the human species. They, certainly, don't constitute reality. And I am not suggesting that the self might be disembodied. I am inclined to think—and see Chapter 4 for more on this—that it must at least be associated with a body but that the body need not be included in the self so the self would still be mental. Ryle made the problem of the regress famous—but see, for example, David Rosenthal's "Two Concepts of Consciousness," *Philosophical Studies*, 1986, or "Multiple Drafts and Higher Order Thoughts," *Philosophy and Phenomenological Research*, 1993, for a more relaxed account of consciousness than Descartes's. And Sartre's way of counting consciousnesses can, again arbitrarily, be applied to thoughts or what James calls "single pulses of consciousness"—and then his complaint against Descartes becomes rather more subtle. Finally, there is, it seems to me, a bit more to Sartre's general epistemological stance than I am here allowing. But perhaps Merleau-Ponty is

better than Sartre on the question of philosophical scepticism. For more on this question, see, again, Chapter 4.

See, for the above attributions to Sartre, *Being and Nothingness*, pp. 13, 12, 11, 401-45, 4, 10, 15, 18, 23, 9, 24, 16, 28. And for the details of Sartre's views on all three of these issues—freedom, other people and epistemology and scepticism—see *The Transcendence of the Ego* and *Being and Nothingness*, pp. 3-30, 86-116, 119-58, 301-556, 559-711.

18. See *Reason and Violence*, Tavistock, 1964, pp. 157, 105, 95, 158, 130—and compare Edgar Friedenberg, *R. D. Laing*, Viking, 1978, p. 51, on its "unintelligibility". And see *The Principles of Psychology*, Vol. I, p. 264, for James's remark on Hegel. *Critique of Dialectical Reason* (tr. A. Sheridan-Smith) was published by NLB in 1976.

19. *Reason and Violence*, pp. 119, 138; *The Politics of Experience*, Pantheon, 1967, pp. xiv, 8, xiii.

20. *Knots* was published by Tavistock in 1970; *Do You Love Me?* by Pantheon in 1976; *Conversations with Children* by Penguin in 1978; *The Voice of Experience* by Penguin in 1982.

I have, in the above discussion, arranged Laing's life according to publication dates rather than dates of composition. But whatever dates one chooses, there was clearly a gradual transitional phase. *Knots*, for example, published before the trips to Asia, is hardly the work of any sort of mainstream psychiatrist.

21. See *The Divided Self*, pp. 39 and 178.

22. *The Politics of Experience*, pp. xv, 12, 101, 47, 93.

23. *Sanity, Madness and the Family* was published by Tavistock in 1964; the second edition came out in 1971. And see *The Politics of Experience*, pp. 78 and xv.

24. See *The Divided Self*, p. 173, *The Politics of Experience*, p. 31, *The Divided Self*, p. 24.

Laing's talk of "reification" smacks of Ryle again—remember Szasz?—with his influential attempt to soft-pedal the mental in *The Concept of Mind*, Hutchinson, 1949. And now we are faced, God help us, with Eliminative Materialism, the view that there is no mind, it's all a myth, a fabrication, a story. What ship won't some people scuttle under the threat of scepticism or relativism or, simply, the future?

25. *Interpersonal Perception*, R. Laing, H. Phillipson and A. Lee, was published by Tavistock in 1966. And see *The Politics of Experience*, pp. 57, 83 and xv.

Chapter 3

The Believers

There are an awful lot of them out there. The profession in the first instance. All or almost all of those who make a living out of madness, the psychologists and psychiatrists of one sort or another, the neurologists, the pharmacologists, the technicians, the nurses—and, on the grimmer side, the legal and enforcement experts and the wardens and administrators of institutions for the insane. What is it that these people believe?

I am, for the purposes of this chapter, going to ignore the lunatic fringe of the profession; the brief discussion at the end of Chapter 1 will have to suffice for that negative way of marking out boundaries. Neither do those with more central or mainstream views agree about everything—nor, of course, should we expect them to. And in the first instance? A large number of people believe, in a more or less informal and perhaps not very detailed or somewhat dated way, what the profession believes. And many of these are people who have been there, people who have first-hand acquaintance with mental disorder in at least one of its various forms.[1]

Taxonomy will take up most of the chapter. And I am going to concentrate on *DSM-IV*. This is the latest—its immediate predecessor was *DSM-III-R*—in a series of ongoing attempts by the American Psychiatric Association to get clearer about questions of taxonomy and it is, as the cliché has it, the new bible of the profession in North

America. There is some dissatisfaction with it in other parts of the world; there was with *DSM-III-R* and some things haven't changed, at all or nearly enough. The types of schizophrenia are a chronic source of contention and the classical neuroses, it is sometimes claimed, should have been given a more prominent place. The multiaxial system of assessment employed by *DSM-IV*, is, at best, unwieldy; reliability— a sort of coherence notion of consensus among diagnosticians—is much more highly prized than validity; and an overall fussiness and an insistence on quantifying and ratings and scales mars the entire picture. More encouraging, culture-bound disorders—like the dhat syndrome of India where ill-health is attributed to the passing of semen in the urine, the brain-fag of Africa allegedly brought on by excessive studying and the anthropophobia of Japan characterized by the delusion that one is inadvertently offending others—all these disorders that went unmentioned in *DSM-III-R* are listed in one of *DSM-IV*'s appendices. And then again, there is still resentment in some parts of Europe over the exclusion of certain traditional diagnostic categories, culture-bound or otherwise—vital anxiety, for example, and degenerative psychosis. And then there are the French, the mavericks of taxonomy in abnormal psychology who do things very differently. Nevertheless and the French aside, we seem to have substantial agreement to the effect that *DSM-IV* is a new research tool of the greatest importance, one that promises, in fact, to be the wave of the future. Its only competitor is *ICD-10*, published by the World Health Organization and with a longer history, less research-oriented and still the official system in most countries. Some competitor. A number of changes introduced in *ICD-10* were precisely designed to bring it more into line with the views of the American Psychiatric Association. But the basic similarities were already there. The differences between *DSM-IV* and *ICD-10* are relatively minor—though I will return to *ICD-10* later on.[2]

DSM-IV is a labyrinth. It includes all sorts of disorders, many of which—retardation and alcoholism, voyeurism and insomnia—have nothing to do with madness or neurosis or not in themselves. The following account will be largely descriptive. I will raise philosophical questions from time to time but I will usually postpone them. So while some of the philosophical issues will start to take shape, the critical questions discussed in this chapter are mostly of the nonphilosophical variety.

A word about terminology—and a small confession. *DSM-IV* doesn't approve of "neurosis" and it wouldn't be caught dead using "madness". The former is extremely broad and smacks of Freudianism;

the latter—well, it's just not professional. *DSM-IV* does employ
"psychosis", however, and in section headings and some of its more
weighty pronouncements. It means by "psychosis" pretty much what I
mean by "madness"—with one significant qualification that will
emerge after a while. As for "neurosis", madness and what I call
"neurosis" occupy a continuous two fifths or so of *DSM-IV* except for
the "organic" disorders or disorders "due to a substance or a general
medical condition", of which more anon, and except for the insertion of
a few questionable groupings—the factitious disorders, the sexual and
gender identity disorders, the eating disorders and the sleep disorders.
Factitious disorders, or outright lies about having a mental or physical
problem that have become a career, might just count as neuroses of a
sort—but a category all to themselves? And why, incidentally, have
they been moved so that, in *DSM-IV*, they are sandwiched between the
somatoform and dissociative disorders, which, taken together, contain
most of the classical neuroses? Is the deliberate dishonesty involved in
them supposed, in spite of *DSM-IV*'s disclaimers, to somehow rub off
on what surrounds them? Sexual and gender identity disorders include,
of course, gender identity disorders—fairly good starts on a neurosis,
one thinks—but also hypoactive sexual desire disorder, female sexual
arousal disorder and premature ejaculation. *DSM-IV* does insist on
marked distress or interpersonal difficulty as a requirement in these
cases. But one could, in this way, turn anything—poverty, say, or
being crippled—into a mental disorder. And while fetishism can be
neurotic or exhibitionism a sign of mania—these entries too, it should
be noted, are provided with a similar tail-wagging-the-dog-
requirement—the American Psychiatric Association has only recently,
with the publication of *DSM-III-R*, gotten over homosexuality. Eating
disorders, again, might be construed as neuroses of an odd sort, they
just might. Sleep disorders, on the other hand, seem obviously
misplaced, or they do for the most part. These, though, are the
anomalies. The overall structure of *DSM-IV* suggests that we need a
term, relatively nonspecific and rough as it might be, for the milder or
less debilitating disorders that separate the mad from the sane. I have
used and will continue to use "neurosis" to pick out most, at least, of
this territory. *DSM-III-R* sometimes employed it. The anxiety
disorders, the dissociative disorders, dysthymia or neurotic depression,
conversion disorder and hypochondria—"hypochondriasis" in *DSM-III-
R* and *DSM-IV*—were all billed, nervously, as neuroses. But that was a
transitional move and the exorcism is now complete. I will be careful
to avoid reading into the term any Freudian views, whether warranted
or not. There is, however, not much I can do about the roughness.

Finally, *DSM-IV* also contains a list of personality disorders—paranoid, schizotypal, histrionic and so on. It has not been my intention, in talking sometimes of madness or madness and neurosis, to deny that personality disorders too are the business of the profession. What does "personality disorder" mean? A personality disorder is a disorder in the background of the mental apparatus. It need not preoccupy. One's general psychological style and way of handling oneself, one's long-term motives and basic wants and drives, seldom do. Maybe a neurosis is, or is typically, more short-lived or easier to cure but it must surely preoccupy. The thoughts and feelings or the stream of consciousness of a neurotic must, it seems, be riddled with the anxiety or uncertainty that constitutes the core of the neurosis.[3]

It will be best to begin with *DSM-IV*'s organizational framework, its guiding principles. The approach, we are told, is atheoretical. This is both a weakness and a strength. It leads to long-winded and often obsessively precise symptomatic definitions of hundreds of types and subtypes, more than twice as many as were in *DSM-II*. We should, apparently, do everything we possibly can to minimize the differences between the abnormal mind and the abnormal body—even with regard to the number of ways in which the mind and the body can break down or malfunction. *DSM-IV* thinks of these definitions as operational but this might cause confusion. If operational definitions must be expressed in terms of behaviour, verbal or nonverbal, *DSM-IV*'s definitions are not operational. In connection with schizophrenia, for example, *DSM-IV* talks of disorganized thinking and flattened affect, obsessions are construed as thoughts or ideas or images, phobias as—what else?—persistent and unreasonable fears. There is no attempt to give behaviouristic definitions of these mental notions. If, on the other hand, operational definitions must be restricted to the signs and symptoms, mental or physical, as opposed to the cause, the large majority of *DSM-IV*'s definitions are operational—and they can, as I say, be very detailed. So for a diagnosis of autism, at least six symptoms from twelve are required with at least two from a group of four, one from another group of four and one more from a final group of four. For posttraumatic stress disorder, the count is at least six symptoms from seventeen with at least one from a group of five, three from another of seven and two from another of five. And for attention deficit/hyperactivity disorder, either at least six from a group of nine or six from another group of nine; some symptoms, moreover, must be present before the age of seven, they must have lasted for at least six months, they must cause some impairment in two or more settings and clinically significant impairment in at least one of three settings. There has, it should be said, been some improvement here over *DSM-III-R* where for somatization disorder—a.k.a. Briquet's syndrome or, simply, hysteria—at least thirteen symptoms of thirty one for males and thirty four for females were required with further criteria being necessary, like seeing a doctor or altering one's life-style, before a symptom became significant. This has now been reduced to at least eight symptoms for both males and females with at least four from one group of examples, two from another and one from each of two more. But it is not just the large number of required symptoms drawn from much longer lists in these cases that is absurd; it is, rather, that any such quantification of symptoms—at least two from five, say, any two from exactly these five—any such definition makes a mockery of diagnosis and of the facts. *DSM-IV* acknowledges this by saying, in its Introduction, that the diagnostic criteria "are meant to serve as guidelines to be informed by clinical judgement." Then why express them with this sort of pseudoprecision? *DSM-IV* is clearly able to speak good plain English. It simply refuses to do so in formulating its operational definitions. Still, *DSM-IV* is obviously right in its atheoretical unwillingness to endorse any overall etiological view of madness and neurosis. Freudian diagnoses are, once again, strained and implausible in many cases. And while there have been important breakthroughs in the neurology of schizophrenia and manic-depressive disorder, for example, we are, once again, not even close to neurological etiologies.[4]

Another general feature of *DSM-IV*, another weakness and another strength, is its multiaxial system of diagnosis. There are five axes. Axis I contains almost all of the disorders mentioned in *DSM-IV*, including the psychoses, the neuroses and the childhood or developmental disorders. The exceptions, listed on Axis II, are the personality disorders and mental retardation. Sweeping as it is, the distinction seems reasonable in some respects—though see below. Axes III-V, however, are another example of overkill. They have to do with physical disorders that might be relevant, psychosocial and environmental stressors—one of the few remaining vestiges of the psychobiological views of Adolf Meyer that permeated *DSM-I*—and, finally, a global assessment of functioning. A competent diagnostician will automatically comment on any relevant physical disabilities or any traumatic events in a patient's life and might well be in the habit of offering a line or two in summary together, perhaps, with some indication of whether this represents a turn for the worse. There might be room for more than two axes—but five?

The distinction between Axes I and II is a part, a relatively small part, of *DSM-IV*'s answer to a very queer question: Which mental disorders can and which can't occur together? That's why the axes are separated, to encourage joint diagnoses. But another, much larger part of the answer is provided by *DSM-IV*'s "hierarchies" or, more generally, its "exclusion criteria". The question is queer because you would expect the answer to be that any two disorders can occur together— with the exception of certain special and obvious cases. So of course one can have gout and measles or angina and diabetes though not high blood pressure and low. But for *DSM-IV*, perhaps predictably, the issue is much more complicated.

First, however, for a sort of exclusion criterion that doesn't, or doesn't unproblematically, exclude although *DSM-IV* clearly wants it to. In an early section entitled "Use of the Manual", we are informed that where "particularly difficult...diagnostic boundaries" exist, "the phrase 'not better accounted for by [X]' is included to indicate that clinical judgement is necessary to determine which diagnosis is most appropriate." Such a criterion is satisfied if either of two things is true: if the symptoms in question are worse accounted for by X or if they are equally well accounted for by X. But if the former is true, X is, trivially, the wrong diagnosis and the criterion is vacuous. *DSM-IV* compounds this confusion by saying, in the differential diagnosis section for attention-deficit/hyperactivity disorder, that this diagnosis "is not" made "if the symptoms are better accounted for by" an anxiety disorder and, in that for brief psychotic disorder, that this diagnosis "cannot be" made "if the...symptoms are better accounted for by" a mood disorder. Well of course. It will be objected that the criterion, misleading as it is, still has some content because of the specific value given to "X" in different cases. But even that disappears for personality disorders where one of the diagnostic criteria is: "not better accounted for as a manifestation or consequence of another mental disorder." Of course. And for almost all of the sexual dysfunctions, the criterion reads: "not better accounted for by another Axis I disorder (except another sexual dysfunction)." These disorders, apparently, can be correctly diagnosed even when a better diagnosis is available. The problem this time is not about good plain English; it is a problem about making even the most elementary kind of sense. So all we are left with are those situations where symptoms are equally well accounted for by at least two diagnoses. Then the diagnoses will be equally correct. And, indeed, *DSM-IV* says that "both diagnoses might be appropriate." But it also insists that the above form of words constitutes an exclusion criterion and that its point is to "discourage multiple diagnoses." What is a clinician supposed to do? Toss a coin?[5]

And now back to hierarchies. In the classical view, "organic" disorders head the list. Behind them, the "functional" disorders—or "primary" disorders, in the idiom of *DSM-IV*—are ranked as follows: schizophrenia, manic-depressive disorder, neuroses and then personality disorders. Why does one disorder come higher up than another? According to *DSM-IV*, it is because the first disorder is more "pervasive" than the second. What is implied by saying that one disorder is higher than another? The first "preempts" the second so that you can't have both. If the two sets of diagnostic criteria are satisfied, you have the preemptor, not the preemptee. You can't, for example, on the classical view, have both schizophrenia and manic-depressive disorder.[6]

How much of the classical view does *DSM-IV* accept? While the American Psychiatric Association has, for some time, been trying to distance itself from this view, much of it still remains. Take schizophrenia, for example. Like the great majority of the disorders in *DSM-IV*, it is not diagnosed if the symptoms are organically based. As for its relationship to manic-depressive disorder, a word, first, about schizoaffective disorder and mood disorder with psychotic symptoms. They differ in that, in the former, psychotic symptoms must be evident in the absence of mood symptoms for at least two weeks whereas, in the latter, psychotic symptoms must appear exclusively during the disturbance in mood. Don't ask about psychotic outbursts that last less than two weeks without mood symptoms. The point I want to make is that neither of these disorders involves a joint diagnosis of schizophrenia and a mood disorder. Such a diagnosis is thus largely precluded, not by exclusion criteria, but by the invention of these two separate disorders. Still and all, *DSM-IV* does allow for a joint diagnosis of schizophrenia and a mood disorder. Not bipolar I or bipolar II disorder, however—while each of these disorders includes major depression or does usually, bipolar I has a manic or mixed manic-depressive component and bipolar II a hypomanic one—and not major depression. Rather, schizophrenia is allowed to coexist with bipolar disorder not otherwise specified or depressive disorder not otherwise specified. The main purpose of these N.O.S. waste-basket categories—*DSM-IV* has them all over the place—is to accommodate unclear or out of the ordinary cases but they are here invoked to prevent a joint diagnosis of schizophrenia and a straightforward mood disorder. As for the neuroses, both cyclothymia, a combination of hypomania and minor depression, and dysthmia or minor depression are preempted by schizophrenia. All of the other important neuroses are contained in the groupings of anxiety, somatoform and dissociative disorders. These groupings, taken together, comprise more than twenty separate disorders. In only two cases—obsessive-compulsive disorder and somatization disorder—is there an explicit acknowledgement to the effect that a joint diagnosis with schizophrenia can be made. In one or two cases, there are no guidelines of any sort. In all of the rest, such a diagnosis is ruled out or advised against, either in the differential diagnosis section or the diagnostic criteria and either in a firm no-nonsense tone of voice or more tentatively and sometimes with one of *DSM-IV*'s "not better accounted for by..." clauses. And as for the personality disorders, there are no guidelines for five of the ten listed by *DSM-IV*. For the other five, a joint diagnosis with schizophrenia is ruled out—though we are assured that a paranoid, schizoid or schizotypal personality disorder may be a "premorbid" antecedent of schizophrenia.[7]

And now for some exclusion criteria that are even more puzzling. There has, again, been improvement here over *DSM-III-R* where—perhaps most remarkably of all given the official view—attention-deficit/hyperactivity disorder somehow managed to preempt organic personality disorder. But intermittent explosive disorder, kleptomania, pyromania and pathological gambling all belong, in *DSM-IV*, to the same grouping. And yet antisocial and borderline personality disorders preempt intermittent explosive disorder, the former but not the latter preempts both kleptomania and pyromania and neither preempts pathological gambling. This is all done with a "not better accounted for by..." clause or its absence—but consider the ordering. If you're still thinking in terms of hierarchies, you're liable to get dizzy. In the sections on the pervasive developmental disorders, it is claimed that autism preempts all forms of schizophrenia except for those with prominent delusions or hallucinations but that Asperger's disorder is preempted by schizophrenia, period; childhood disintegrative disorder is also preempted by schizophrenia though only with a "not better accounted for by..." clause and, for Rett's disorder, there are no guidelines. In the section on schizophrenia, however—for clinicians, presumably, who like things a bit simpler—all pervasive developmental disorders are said to preempt all forms of schizophrenia except those with prominent delusions or hallucinations. In the section on undifferentiated somatoform disorder—a low-level cousin of somatization disorder—we are told that it is preempted by the adjustment disorders—another remnant of Meyer's psychobiological views. But under "Adjustment Disorders", the suggestion is that these disorders are preempted by all other Axis I disorders. And while social phobia and acute stress disorder are preempted by the direct physiological effects of a substance or a general medical condition, the specific phobias and posttraumatic stress disorder, apparently, are not. All these precipitates, these little hard deposits, these little nubs or knots left over from *DSM-IV*'s committees.[8]

So I don't think much of *DSM-IV*'s hierarchies—and I don't think much of its exclusion criteria. And while the distinction between Axes I and II is not entirely unreasonable, joint diagnoses can also be made within Axis I and within Axis II just as there are exclusion criteria that operate across the divide. The childhood or developmental disorders obviously deserve a special place. They were, in *DSM-III-R*, coded on Axis II along with the personality disorders and retardation but simply moving them to Axis I has created as many problems as it has solved. They don't fit any more comfortably with the psychoses and neuroses than they did with the personality disorders. Perhaps they should, along with retardation, be given an axis of their own—*DSM-IV* does, after all, have three other axes that presently serve little purpose—and their connections with adult disorders be allowed to emerge on the basis of more straightforward empirical investigation. On this point, *DSM-IV* seems nowhere near empirical enough. But whatever is done here, *DSM-IV*'s multiaxial system needs tidying up—and it needs to be cleansed of the mostly pernicious effects of hierarchies.

There are, to be sure, instances where each of two diagnoses should not be made. So conduct disorder is likely to contain all of the features of oppositional defiant disorder but it must contain others besides and somatization disorder is similarly related to undifferentiated somatoform disorder. Conduct disorder and somatization disorder are, we might say, more "pervasive". And some disorders are, not more pervasive, but more severe versions of others, like major depression and dysthymia. *DSM-IV*, once again, disagrees with this example—as though a severe case of mumps and a mild one could be diagnosed at once. But there is no sense of the word "pervasive" in which organic disorders are more pervasive than schizophrenia. Neither is there a sense of the word in which schizophrenia is more pervasive than manic-depressive disorder. Schizophrenia is, to be sure, more serious than the neuroses and the personality disorders. Is it more pervasive? And why on earth can't one have schizophrenia and bipolar I or bipolar II disorder? Why can't one have schizophrenia and anything else or, for that matter, any two disorders together—unless there is a good specific reason for thinking otherwise?[9]

Which brings us to the organic disorders. These are Axis I disorders in their own right and not, or not necessarily, the possibly relevant physical disorders that are supposed to be reported on Axis III. They give rise to both general problems and more local ones. *DSM-IV*, as I've indicated and unlike *DSM-III-R*, doesn't use the word "organic". But the concept—due to the direct physiological effects of a substance or a general medical condition—is the same. And *DSM-IV* does use, not only "primary", but also "mental", a near-synonym for "nonorganic" in this context. Look, for example, at its title. This completely ignores, according to *DSM-IV*, the problem of there being "much [that is] 'physical' in 'mental' disorders." The problem, however, "has been much clearer than its solution." It has indeed. In *DSM-III-R*, the organic disorders were separated off from the functional or primary disorders even though the former contained symptomatic counterparts for almost all of the latter. In *DSM-IV*, some of these disorders are still separated off—"Delirium, Dementia, and Amnestic and Other Cognitive Disorders", "Mental Disorders Due to a General Medical Condition Not Elsewhere Classified", which include catatonic disorder and personality change, and "Substance-Related Disorders". The rest are distributed throughout the other groupings. So the grouping of schizophrenia and other psychotic disorders has an entry for psychotic disorder due to a general medical condition and one for substance-induced psychotic disorder; that of mood disorders has an entry for mood disorder due to a general medical condition and one for substance-induced mood disorder—and so on. But there are a number of exceptions. The somatoform disorders do not have such entries and neither do the adjustment disorders. These, of course, are special cases or they might be thought to be; the somatoform disorders are mostly defined as disorders with physical symptoms that are not explicable in terms of the organic condition one would naturally expect and the adjustment disorders are defined as being due to a psychosocial stressor. But the dissociative disorders have no such entries and neither do the impulse control disorders not elsewhere classified. And while most organic personality disorders can be coded under personality change, the personality disorders don't either. On the other hand, many—though not all—of these exceptional cases do carry an exclusion criterion of the "not due to a substance or a general medical condition" variety. Then there's the odd way in which catatonic disorder is singled out along with personality change. So what is going on here? This is *DSM-IV*'s solution—although it can't, it says, do anything about its title. But what, exactly, is its problem?

Committees—of course. But *DSM-IV* still clings to the idea that organic disorders preempt nearly everything else. This is quite indefensible. Hasn't *DSM-IV* heard of the possibility of overdetermination for any set of symptoms? There is also the question that came up in the last chapter of whether those with organic disorders are free. This, however, is a philosophical question and I am, again, going to shelve it until Chapter 4. More important for *DSM-IV* is another question that arose in the last chapter, that of just how many disorders are organically based. This, let me repeat, has nothing to do with the debate between Interactive Dualists and Identity Theorists, for example—and nothing to do with the organic condition one might or might not expect or, indeed, the presence or absence of psychosocial stressors. It is simply the question of whether any of the functional or primary disorders are independent of the brain or different in kind from organic disorders. *DSM-IV* is more keenly aware of this worry than was *DSM-III-R* but the above hodge-podge of organizing principles and exclusion criteria is surely not meant as a response. So will the province of psychiatry remain intact while that of neuroscience expands?—or will the authors of *DSM-V* and *DSM-VI* be writing their own obituaries? I will, again, have something to say about this question as well in Chapter 4.

Finally, *DSM-IV*'s organic disorders amount to a queer collection even on their own terms. Delirium and dementia of one sort or another, amnestic disorders done fairly briefly, a cognitive disorder N.O.S. listing, the mental disorders due to a general medical condition not elsewhere classified, then the substance-related disorders—and then the organic disorders that are counterparts of the functional or primary disorders. There is no mention of the cases to be found in books on clinical neurology, the aphasias, the agnosias, the body-schema disturbances; there is little interest in the effects of brain tumours or gun wounds or car wrecks; there is no real interest in the various and sometimes crippling amnesias. *DSM-IV* does look at the brain from its own blinkered point of view.[10]

We can now turn to the details of *DSM-IV*'s taxonomy. The first of *DSM-IV*'s nonorganic groupings—apart from the childhood or developmental disorders—is "Schizophrenia and Other Psychotic Disorders". And the most important of these is, of course, schizophrenia, the dark prince or the heavyweight, the most outlandish and the most savage, the major disorder of thought or of reason. To be distinguished, it is claimed, from the cross-sectionally identical schizophreniform disorder on the grounds that it must have persisted for at least six months and have a relatively poor prognosis; the prognosis for schizophreniform disorder is, by contrast, so good that there is a logical guarantee of cure or remission within six months. A further criterion for schizophrenia is that an "active phase" of at least one month's duration must have been observed. And *DSM-IV* is atheoretical?—for this reeks of some unstated theory. Symptoms required for the active phase are any two or more of delusions, hallucinations, disorganized speech, grossly disorganized or catatonic behaviour and negative symptoms, that is, affective flattening, alogia or avolition. A disturbance of thought or reason is obviously central to the first, third and fourth of these and impossible to separate completely from the second and fifth. These symptoms have different diagnostic implications, however, in that only one is required if delusions are bizarre or hallucinations are of a "voices commenting" or "voices conversing" sort and negative symptoms are of greater significance than the rest for the nonactive phase. The types of schizophrenia are paranoid, disorganized, catatonic, undifferentiated—a highly questionable type that means not paranoid, not disorganized and not catatonic—and residual. And residual schizophrenia is, surely, no more a type of schizophrenia than burned-out leprosy is a type of leprosy. Simple schizophrenia, characterized largely by negative symptoms without an active phase and a possible future entry according to *DSM-IV*, is shunted aside to schizoid or schizotypal personality disorder or smuggled into residual schizophrenia. So there are really only three types—though perhaps we should add simple—and catatonia is underplayed in the diagnostic criteria as compared with the types. Also of note with regard to schizophrenia is that a considerable overlap exists with the symptoms of autism—and inappropriate affect, depression, anxiety, depersonalization and derealization are mentioned as associated features. And what is this theory about an active phase? Is that when the virus is at its most devastating?[11]

Other psychotic disorders in *DSM-IV* are, not only schizophreniform disorder with its upper time limit of six months, but schizoaffective disorder, delusional disorder, brief psychotic disorder, induced psychotic disorder, psychotic disorder due to a general medical condition, substance-induced psychotic disorder and the seemingly obligatory N.O.S. listing. Schizoaffective disorder is, again, simply a combination of schizophrenia and a major mood disorder—although the at least two weeks' period of psychosis without a disturbance in mood that is used to distinguish it from mood disorder with psychotic symptoms can, oddly, be manifested only in delusions or hallucinations. Couldn't someone with half of a mood disorder, as it were, have, when its symptoms are in abeyance, other psychotic symptoms? Delusional disorder or paranoia is marked off from paranoid schizophrenia on the basis of *DSM-IV*'s murky distinction between nonbizarre and bizarre delusions and a less noticeable background scruffiness—and the main types are erotomanic, grandiose, jealous, persecutory and somatic. One has to wonder, of course, just how different it is. Brief psychotic disorder can be cross-sectionally identical to any psychosis—or, at least, any psychosis that satisfies one or more of the first four positive symptoms of schizophrenia—but it must be brief, lasting no longer than a month. Shared psychotic disorder or folie à deux occurs when a typically dominant partner draws the other weaker or more gullible one into his or her psychosis. Psychotic disorder due to a general medical condition and substance-induced psychotic disorder are psychoses with an organic base that, once again, preempt all other psychoses and they must, again and again oddly, involve delusions or hallucinations. And psychotic disorder N.O.S. is just that—any other psychosis.[12]

And then come the mood disorders. Then? Isn't manic-depressive disorder—bipolar I or bipolar II disorder—a psychosis? And isn't major depression?

DSM-IV offers us three definitions of "psychosis", more or less broad, more or less narrow. Insisting on three is yet another example of unnecessary complication; it's perfectly all right to rely on a single broad definition and allow it to cover all relevant cases, however specific they might be. But more to the point, none of the three is at all helpful. For they are all definitions, if that is what they are, by mere enumeration of symptoms—from the broadest, in which "psychotic" refers to any of the positive symptoms of schizophrenia, to the narrowest, in which the word refers only to delusions. So mood disorders are ruled out as candidates for psychosis arbitrarily, for no reason. Enumerating, after all, never makes explicit its own rationale. And yet isn't mania, with its hurry, its excitement and its inflated or distorted self-image, almost as much a paradigm of psychosis as is schizophrenia? And isn't mania often linked, as a matter of fact, with major depression? As for the latter, a man might believe he is being punished by God for having betrayed the universe and all insurance salesmen in particular; a woman that it's not worth it, nothing is worth it, nothing is worth anything. Is the first belief a sign of, not major depression, but mood disorder with psychotic symptoms? And isn't the second equally unrealistic?—and mightn't it be equally incapacitating? Think of the stupor, sometimes, of major depression and the stupor of catatonia. And *DSM-IV* itself mentions psychotic symptoms of one sort or another as associated features of both major depression and mania. It is silent, however, on just how often these symptoms are manifested.

So the American Psychiatric Association is, I think, quite wrong to depart from the tradition on this issue. It has no arguments, certainly, no reasons. But the mood disorders do, of course, include—along with bipolar I disorder, which, incidentally, is turned into six different disorders by *DSM-IV* depending, largely, on the nature of the most recent episode, bipolar II disorder, which is not, strictly speaking, manic-depression but hypomanic-depression, and major depression, psychotic or otherwise—the two minor disorders, cyclothymia and dysthymia. They are rounded out by mood disorder due to a general medical condition and substance-induced mood disorder, which preempt all of the rest, and, not merely the predictable mood disorder N.O.S, but bipolar disorder N.O.S. and depressive disorder N.O.S. as well. The diagnostic criteria are almost all done in terms of those for a manic episode, a major depressive episode, a mixed episode and a hypomanic episode; there is, curiously, no space given to the criteria for an episode of minor depression. They are of the one plus at least three, or four in certain circumstances, of the following seven for at least one week variety—this specific formula is employed in connection with a manic episode—but their content seems sound enough. Thus a persistent and highly elevated, expansive or irritable mood is strongly indicative of mania whereas a pervasive—or let's say a chronic, a chronic and extreme—depressed mood is particularly significant for major depression as is a marked loss of interest or pleasure and so of desire. Mood disorder with psychotic features must, again, involve delusions or hallucinations although a mood disorder can also present with catatonic symptoms, there is a special malignant kind of major depression, melancholia, that responds well to drugs, a mood disorder can exhibit a seasonal pattern or have its onset during the postpartum—and cyclothymia and dysthymia are, of course, less severe than bipolar I and bipolar II disorders and major depression. But there are a number of questions here.

Some of them are small questions. Cyclothymia and dysthymia both carry an "of at least two years' duration" tag—except in children and adolescents where the requirement is one year. Why classify the milder mood disorders of less than two years' duration as N.O.S. cases? Perhaps, one can't help feeling, to have something to put there. And a hypomanic episode, unlike a manic, a major depressive or a mixed episode, must be observable by others. Why pick out hypomania in this strange and puzzling way? More importantly, there are two obvious asymmetries among the mood disorders. While hypomania and major depression go together to produce bipolar II disorder, cases of mania together with dysthymia apparently never occur—although if cyclothymia has a manic or mixed episode superimposed on it, both cyclothymia and bipolar I disorder can be diagnosed. And while either major or minor depression can exist on its own, things are not nearly as clear with regard to mania and hypomania. There are diagnostic criteria for major depression with a single episode and for recurrent major depression; there are such criteria for mania with a single episode but none for recurrent mania. There is no entry at all for hypomania by itself. So what is this ambivalence about unipolar mania and unipolar hypomania? If they are rare as compared with major depression and dysthymia, that should tell us something interesting about the brain. But if they don't exist at all, the emotional switch in the brain will have to be very remarkable indeed. And what of other moods or emotions? What of pathological hatred or homicidal rage or unreasoning terror? What of completely indiscriminate affection or mindless content-ment?—and what of indifference, indifference to everything? Aren't these disorders of mood too?[13]

And so to the "anxiety" disorders. Panic disorder comes with or without agoraphobia, agoraphobia can exist without panic although it is defined in terms of a fear of it, the other phobias are divided into social phobia and the various specific phobias, then there's obsessive-compulsive disorder—a bit of an anomaly in this context—posttrau-matic stress disorder, acute stress disorder, generalized anxiety disorder, anxiety disorder due to a general medical condition or to a substance—which preempt all of the others except, again, for the specific phobias and posttraumatic stress disorder—and anxiety disorder N.O.S. These disorders are usually thought of as neurotic or relatively mild. This is true as a rule—but panic or terror can, of course, be extreme and obsessions and compulsions totally disabling. And the role of anxiety in obsessive-compulsive disorder differs from that of the mood or emotion in the rest of these disorders. It arises, characteristically, from not wanting to give in to what might well be seen as a senseless and even dangerous action, for example—a compulsion for *DSM-IV*. There is thus as much reason for classifying the disorder with the other impulse control disorders, like kleptomania and pyromania, as there is for listing it with the anxiety disorders. Still, this is by no means a straightforward or an uncomplicated matter and *DSM-IV*'s way of doing things can hardly be thought of as wrong. Then again, *DSM-IV* is operating here—as we all must—with our not very precise notion of mood or emotion or feeling. The above disor-ders, which turn on panic, anxiety and fear, are as much mood disorders as manic-depression, say, or dysthymia. Or does *DSM-IV* know something about moods or emotions, and on the symptomatic level, that we don't?

The anxiety disorders are followed by the somatoform disorders, somatization disorder, undifferentiated somatoform disorder, conversion disorder, pain disorder, hypochondria, body dysmorphic disorder and somatoform disorder N.O.S.—in all of which the body plays an important role. Body dysmorphic disorder is peculiar in its concern about cosmetic considerations; it is a preoccupation with an imagined or exaggerated defect in appearance. And perhaps conversion disorder, the classical neurosis in which apparent blindness or paralysis, for example, is not explicable in the physical terms one might expect, should also be separated off from the others. The apparent deficits, after all, are pretty special and pretty bizarre. But there is no very clear distinction among somatization disorder, undifferentiated somatoform disorder, pain disorder and hypochondria. All four involve complaints about a physical problem that are not borne out by examination. In somatization disorder, there is a greater emphasis on symptoms, in pain disorder on pain and in hypochondria on a more or less specific disease. Someone who is feeling grumpy or hellish enough to complain about all three has, according to *DSM-IV*, three different disorders. And while somatization disorder must extend over a period of years and involve complaints about multiple symptoms, undifferentiated somatoform disorder can be much shorter in duration and a complaint about a single symptom is sufficient. Finally, although there are no entries for somatoform disorder due to a medical condition or to a substance, *DSM-IV* does give what it sees as a physical exclusion criterion for each of the somatoform disorders. But it does so in a variety of ways. For somatization and undifferentiated somatoform disorders, the complaints can't be "fully explained by a known general medical condition or the direct effects of a substance"—the insertion of the word "known" in this sort of context is unusual in *DSM-IV*; for conversion and pain disorders and as relatively rare exceptions to its atheoretical policy, the explicit claim is that "psychological factors" are important in the etiology; for hypochondria, the "preoccupation persists despite appropriate medical evaluation and reassurance" and, for body dysmorphic disorder, the defect in appearance is, again, "imagined or exaggerated". *DSM-IV* also says, however, that none of these disorders is "fully explained by a general medical condition [or] by the direct effects of a substance." Let me put this once more and as clearly as I can. Given Interactive Dualism or Identity Theory, Functionalism or Supervenience, all mental disorders are explicable in terms of the brain whether the details of the explanation are known or not and whether or not a psychological explanation can be offered as well. We now know or think we know that one of these theories is at least largely correct for most mental disorders. We don't know of any mental disorders for which all of them are simply mistaken. And since any set of symptoms can be overdetermined, no physical exclusion criteria are ever legitimate, even for the somatoform disorders and even for body dysmorphic disorder—unless, indeed, they are formulated in terms of what is known or in terms of specific physical factors that have been eliminated.[14]

After the somatoform disorders come the factitious disorders, about which I have no further comment except to say they are forms of pathological lying, something that ought, surely to be listed in *DSM-IV*—it doesn't appear—as an impulse control disorder or, perhaps, a personality disorder. And then come the dissociative disorders, dissociative amnesia, dissociative fugue, dissociative identity disorder, depersonalization disorder and dissociative disorder N.O.S. The central theme in these sections is allegedly "a disruption in the usually integrated functions of consciousness, memory, identity, or perception of the environment." But this is hopeless. Most of the disorders in *DSM-IV* fit that description. Dissociative amnesia and dissociative fugue both involve loss of memory and they are both, like posttraumatic stress disorder and acute stress disorder, reactions to "traumatic or extremely stressful events" or they are usually. Connected with this, in the thinking of *DSM-IV*, is that both are preempted by disorders due to a general medical condition or to a substance—as, indeed, are dissociative personality disorder and depersonalization disorder. The distinction between dissociative amnesia and dissociative fugue is handled awkwardly by *DSM-IV*, with the "predominant feature" of the latter being, along with the memory loss, "sudden, unexpected travel away from home or one's customary place of work." This is "accompanied by", *DSM-IV* tells us, "confusion about personal identity or assumption of a new identity." Perhaps we can count two disorders here. But the better split would seem to be over problems about personal identity with the fugue being given a less prominent position. Dissociative or multiple personality disorder is, of course, a matter of having several different personalities at once. *DSM-IV* speaks of them as "recurrently" taking over and thus tries to side-step the difficult but unavoidable problem of "coconsciousness". Depersonalization, for *DSM-IV*, has, as an associated feature, derealization, "the sense" that the world is "strange or unreal". By contrast, depersonalization is "a feeling" of "detachment or estrangement" from one's self, not that the self is unreal or does not exist. In both depersonalization and derealization, moreover, "reality testing" is supposed to remain intact as though this sense and this feeling could not reach delusional proportions. But *DSM-IV*'s views aside, dissociative personality disorder and depersonalization disorder are, I think, among its more interesting entries—and I will have a fair bit to say about them in Chapter 4.[15]

And now we are really in the back alleys of *DSM-IV*. After the sexual and gender identity disorders, the eating and the sleeping disorders, we get the impulse control disorders that are "not elsewhere classified": intermittent explosive disorder, kleptomania, pyromania, pathological gambling, trichotillomania, the inability to stop oneself pulling out one's own hair, and impulse control disorder N.O.S.— although not, once again, pathological lying. A physical exclusion criterion of one sort or another is given for intermittent explosive disorder, kleptomania and pyromania; none is for pathological gambling or trichotillomania. Perhaps these disorders are all right as a group of antisocial or self-destructive neuroses. Perhaps they should be regarded as special, more easily intelligible, subtypes of obsessive-compulsive disorder, in particular. Or perhaps they might, again, be treated as narrowly focused personality disorders—as, indeed, might some of the sexual disorders and the eating disorders. But however they are classified, it should be noticed that this is the only place in *DSM-IV* where the will enters into the taxonomy in any very explicit way. Next are the adjustment disorders, a ragged little group of disorders that are, by definition, reactive. There is no mention of physical exclusion criteria here, presumably because *DSM-IV* thinks that being a reaction to a psychosocial stressor is incompatible with being organically based. One might expect a reactive counterpart for most, at least, of the major neuroses and psychoses. Apart from one or two adjustment conduct disorders, however, the disorders in this "residual category" all have to do with mood.

And now, finally, for the personality disorders. There are—not counting the N.O.S. listing—ten of them, divided into three clusters. The first cluster is paranoid personality disorder, "a pattern of distrust and suspiciousness such that others' motives are interpreted as malevolent", schizoid, "a pattern of detachment from social relationships and a restricted range of emotional expression" and schizotypal with its "acute discomfort in close relationships, cognitive or perceptual distortions, and eccentricities of behaviour." The second is antisocial, histrionic and narcissistic—which are pretty much self-explanatory— and borderline, "a pattern of instability in interpersonal relationships, self-image, and affects, and marked impulsivity." The third is obsessive-compulsive—pretty much self-explanatory again—together with dependent and avoidant where, just as dependence is on other people, avoidance is of other people. The distinction between avoidant

personality disorder and social phobia is thus, as *DSM-IV* acknowledges, tenuous at best.

The first cluster seems fairly natural—though why isn't borderline
included here? It too can be thought of as a psychosis at the level of
personality disorder if it is such a disorder at all. The others, however,
are more artificial. What does being narcissistic have to do with being
antisocial?—or being dependent with the rigidity and overconscien-
tiousness of obsessive-compulsive personality disorder? *DSM-IV*
concedes that its clusters have "serious limitations". So why does it
insist on them? And can't there be erotomanic or jealous paranoid
personalities? How different really are histrionic and narcissistic
personality disorders? Doesn't the inclusion of antisocial personality
disorder presuppose a moral view? What of the hermit?—or the
misogynist? And aren't there other personality disorders? *DSM-IV*
mentions two, depressive and passive-aggressive, as subjects for further
study—and *DSM-III-R* had two more, sadistic and self-defeating. Then
there's the secretive, the automatically hostile, the fundamentally
personally dishonest, the suffocatingly and unknowingly smug. But
these are not, it seems to me, points of major or overall importance.[16]

DSM-IV's personality disorders are all provided with a "not due to
the direct physiological effects of a substance or a general medical
condition" exclusion criterion. Joint diagnoses of personality disorders
are, by contrast, usually encouraged and their diagnosis in children is
also permitted—part, presumably, of what lies behind the relocation of
most of the childhood disorders to Axis I. The single clear exception is
antisocial personality disorder. This can't be diagnosed in children but
it has a childhood analogue, conduct disorder, which is, in fact, a
prerequisite for the adult disorder. A similar relationship is hinted at
between dependent personality disorder and separation anxiety
disorder—and avoidant personality disorder should, it is claimed, be
diagnosed in children only "with great caution". Two personality
disorders, moreover, but only two—schizoid and schizotypal—are
preempted by pervasive developmental disorders.

There are personality disorders corresponding to two or three kinds
of schizophrenia. There are none for manic-depressive disorder or
major depression—although *DSM-IV* does, again, regard depressive
personality disorder as a possible future entry. There are for obsessive-
compulsive disorder and, arguably, some of the somatization disorders
in histrionic and narcissistic personality disorders. There are none for
the other anxiety disorders, none for the dissociative disorders. Is this
more of *DSM-IV*'s arbitrariness? I'm not sure. It is hard, certainly, on
conceptual grounds—and *DSM-IV* is aware of this—to separate

depressive personality disorder from dysthymia. But to recognize a personality disorder for schizophrenia, say, or obsessive-compulsive disorder is to make a contribution to etiology. What is endorsed for some cases, in *DSM-IV*'s austere atheoretical pages, is the idea of a predisposing factor. It might be correct. It might be that dissociative fugue and depersonalization disorder, for example, are not made more likely by any preexisting personality disorder. Whether or not they are, at any rate, seems to be mostly an empirical question.

How do personality disorders differ from psychoses? Untreated, personality disorders are typically long-lived. Psychoses—and neuroses—vary. And as neuroses are milder or less severe than psychoses, so, one might think, personality disorders are, in the main anyway though with a great deal of overlap, less disabling than neuroses. They are, there can be no doubt, less disabling than psychoses. But a psychosis, like a neurosis and even more obviously, must preoccupy; the unintelligibility, the delusions or the hallucinations, the terror or the all-encompassing flatness must dominate the stream of consciousness. A personality disorder, again, need not, and very often does not. That personality disorders and psychoses can lie on a continuum should not, of course, be taken to imply that they are not of different kinds. The incoherence or the grotesque inappropriateness of mood in madness is of a different dimension, a quite different modality of experience, from anything that might be found in a personality disorder—even schizoid or schizotypal or borderline.[17]

That's the end, the end of *DSM-IV*'s sections on psychosis, neurosis and personality disorder. These sections give us a fairly detailed—in some respects, a far too detailed—taxonomy. But underlying this taxonomy are large assumptions, many of which have begun to show up on the surface. *DSM-IV* is a state of mind. I hope the broad outlines are clear.

ICD-10's taxonomical system exhibits significant disagreement. The organic disorders, preempting everything else, are still separated off on their own—and *ICD-10*'s listings are rather different from *DSM-IV*'s and they contain, in particular, organic counterparts for the somatoform, dissociative and personality disorders. There is also a separate category of substance-induced disorders although these do not, apparently, exclude the functional disorders.

Schizophrenia has a few extra types, including simple, which does, arguably, deserve to be mentioned, and postschizophrenic depression, which certainly does not since it is more depression than schizophrenia. Latent schizophrenia, a type of schizophrenia in *ICD-9*, *ICD-10*'s previous incarnation, has been dropped as a type.   Schizophrenia waiting to explode or take over is, after all, not a type of schizophrenia; it is schizophrenia waiting to explode or take over.   It reappears, however, under schizotypal disorder, elevated by *ICD-10* to a diffuse sort of nonschizophrenic psychosis from the ranks of the personality disorders. The other principal difference from *DSM-IV* with regard to the nonschizophrenic psychoses—apart from the organic and/or substance-induced varieties being located elsewhere—is that brief psychotic disorder is, with good reason, eliminated in favour of a whole family of acute and transient psychotic disorders, one of which, incidentally, is schizophreniform disorder.

The differences with regard to the so-called "mood" disorders are slight. *ICD-10* does not make the fuss that *DSM-IV* does over the distinction between bipolar I and bipolar II disorders and the subdivisions for manic-depressive disorder and major depression turn on the nature of the current, not the most recent, episode. *ICD-10*, unlike *ICD-9* and persuaded, presumably, by the American Psychiatric Association, thinks of these disorders as nonpsychotic although, like *DSM-IV*, it recognizes mood disorder with psychotic symptoms. It does, however, explicitly acknowledge the possibility of both mania and hypomania without depression in either a single episode or a recurrent form. It insists, nevertheless and paradoxically, on classifying these disorders as bipolar.

ICD-10 retains the neuroses—except for cyclothymia and dysthymia, which are listed with the "mood" disorders—as a single large group. Body dysmorphic disorder and multiple personality disorder are downgraded by *ICD-10* as compared with *DSM-IV*, the former being subsumed under hypochondria and the latter assigned to a category of "other" dissociative disorders. Conversion disorder, by contrast, is split into several disorders. The adjustment disorders, understandably, are listed here. And additional entries include mixed anxiety and depressive disorder and trance or possession disorder—both subjects of further study for *DSM-IV*—as well as the more traditional neurasthenia with its characteristic fatigue, irritability and anhedonia.

The personality disorders in *ICD-10* are very much what they are in *DSM-IV*.   The only noteworthy differences are that schizotypal disorder, once again, becomes a psychosis and narcissistic personality disorder is relegated to a mopping-up category.

Then there are the childhood disorders, done somewhat differently—and then the odds and ends: the factitious disorders, the impulse control disorders, the eating disorders, the sleep disorders and the sexual and gender identity disorders.

Finally, *ICD-10* does, like *DSM-IV*, have a multiaxial system—although the axes are not the same; it has hierarchies and exclusion rules—although they are less tangled and arbitrary than *DSM-IV*'s; and it has fairly detailed diagnostic criteria—although, and here we should all be thankful, they are expressed clearly and straightforwardly with none of the absurd overquantification manifest in *DSM-IV*'s.[18]

So the differences between *ICD-10* and *DSM-IV* are significant. The similarities, however, are more fundamental. The organic disorders—whether or not they are grouped together—preempting everything else, schizophrenia—give or take one or two types—as the major psychosis of thought, then delusional disorder and the other psychoses, then the severe but allegedly nonpsychotic "mood" disorders and the milder variants. The neuroses, or the other neuroses, are not referred to as such by *DSM-IV* and the most important of them are scattered across three categories. But they are there and they are largely the same with pretty much all of the classical ones intact. And the agreements over the personality disorders are much more marked than the disagreements. Perhaps schizotypal disorder is confusing but look at the broad overlap in types. And then the childhood disorders—and the odd or less familiar entries. The similarities—seen from this point of view or on this scale—are much more striking.

That's what they believe then—more or less and most of them any-way—about taxonomy. But what about cause or etiology, cure or therapy?

Most of them believe in drugs—whether as the main or only ther-apy or some sort of adjunct or back-up and especially with regard to psychoses. A lot of them believe in electroconvulsive therapy for mood disorders and major depression, in particular. And many of them believe in behaviour modification for the phobias and for obsessive-compulsive disorder. Other physical therapies, like insulin shock, psychosurgery and, it seems, multivitamins, have gone the way of the shackles and the alternating hot and cold baths. And then a lot of them believe in Freudianism—despite its recent decline and in some sort of role at least, not usually for psychoses but for neuroses, certainly, and sometimes for personality disorders. These are the dominant views; we must not lose sight of that. There are, however, a number of other schools or therapies I want to take note of in this last section. They are not exactly orthodox or widely accepted—though all of them have their supporters. They are, rather, distinguished by the fact that, for many of the profession, they are quite acceptable and, for most of them, not totally kooky or completely beyond the pale. A sense of them thus provides for another perspective on the mind of the profession. I will, in this brief account, be both selective and partial.[19]

The interpersonal approach derives from Harry Stack Sullivan's sometimes pragmatic attempt to weld Freud's views on to a version of Adolf Meyer's view of mental disorder as a product of one's environment and, in particular, one's relationships with others.   Other interpersonal influences here are Adler and Karen Horney, a contemporary of Sullivan's.   Anxiety is placed at the centre of things as are questions about "biological needs", "security needs" and "self-esteem"—a notion borrowed from Adler—and close attention is paid to the mother-child relationship. The effect on Laing of all of this should be obvious. For Sullivan, as for Freud, mental disorder is a regression to or a fixation at a very early stage of development. The stages are "prototaxic" or prelinguistic, "parataxic" with private or autistic symbolization and "syntaxic" characterized by communication. There is, however, some talk about "oral" and "anal" stages although less about sex in general than in Freud—and the self engages in various "security operations", including "selective inattention", relatively easy to remedy, and "dissociation", the equivalent, in Sullivan, of repression. Correspondingly, therapy—with its "participant observer" and "consensual validation"—is the two-way process of trying to undo the largely unknown results of one's early relationships with others. It's all interpersonal, outgoing if you like, but it's basically Freudian. Some of Sullivan's interpersonal techniques and his concern with logic and rationality in connection with the syntaxic stage have, on the other hand, since been taken over by some nonFreudians.[20]

And so to cognitive theory or therapy—much more eclectic in spite of the fact that reason lies at its heart. The general claim that emotions are nowhere near as nonrational as is often thought is both right and important. But the cognitivists go overboard. This is the theory or therapy for MENSA types with its overrationalizing of emotions in the unwarranted insistence that they are preceded in the mind by "automatic" and usually unknown thoughts, its almost exclusive emphasis on mistakes in cognition or in "beliefs", "assumptions", "interpretations" and "strategies" and in its "assignments" and its "homework". There is a hint of Freudianism already—and other Freudian elements are the attempt to overcome the extreme difficulty at times of getting a patient to admit to certain mistaken assumptions and an analogue for Freud's "primary process" and the "reality testing" of the "secondary process"—and Leon Saul, one of the main influences on the cognitive movement according to Aaron Beck, its founder or chief proponent, has more or less orthodox Freudian views. But cognitive theory or therapy is just that, the cognitive treatment of problems that are themselves seen in cognitive terms, sweet reason applied to unreason. And it is mostly about the "here and now". There are numerous references to "information processing" and "problem solving", the therapist is a "Socratic guide or questioner" and therapy a "learning experience". Cognitive defects include arbitrary inference, overgeneralization and dichotomous thinking—the sort of thing discussed in Informal Fallacies 101. And Beck suggests different "schemas" or mistakes in cognition for different disorders: "I can't do anything" or "Nothing brings me pleasure" for depression, for example, and "It is my responsibility to protect my own life and the lives of my family" for obsessive-compulsive disorder. Then again, cognitive theory is phenomenologi-cal—which seems to mean little more to much of the profession than that the patient's point of view is important—and Beck thoroughly approves of the "warm", "nonjudgemental", "client-centred" attitudes of Carl Rogers to therapy. Another influence on cognitive doctrines is Albert Ellis whose Eleven Basic Irrational Thoughts include "One should be quite upset about other people's problems" and "Some people are bad, wicked or villainous and therefore should be blamed and punished." Cognitive therapy, unlike Sullivan's interpersonal therapy, is comparatively short-term and recommended only for the neuroses and personality disorders, some cases of major depression and some eating disorders. It employs a wide variety of techniques, the keeping of diaries, graded tasks, imaging, activity scheduling, role playing—and sometimes, even, Freudian techniques. But always the focus is on what is cognitively right and cognitively wrong. These matters, as should be evident, are often construed pretty crudely, pretty simplistically—although it should be pointed out that this is not inevitable. And those who can't respond in any normal way to reason are those for whom the therapy is "not indicated". Still, we all know people who make lists—and we all know people who make wrong lists, disturbed or threatening or fragmented lists. What we should notice, however, is that we have created a broader clientele—and I use the word advisedly. Many people have fundamental beliefs or ways of looking at the world that are somehow unsatisfactory or could be improved on. And Beck speaks of treating patients "who have suffered their first myocardial infarction" or "who have physical injuries". Depressed and in need of counselling as such people might be, they are often not clinically depressed at all. The same theme, the same broadening, runs through Rogers's earlier talk of "self-actualization"— as, indeed, it does Maslow's and Goldstein's and Sullivan's talk of "self-esteem". We have been witness here to the birth of the promise of American psychiatry for the masses. Not just because of those who have fallen through the cracks in the system and been denied therapy. What should be noticed, once again, is that many people have problems that have nothing to do with madness or neurosis or even personality disorder in any very strict sense. Dale Carnegie time or, more charitably, Kurt Vonnegut territory, people whose lives would be made appreciably better by taking Vonnegut's advice, which he was prepared to offer for a modest fee and a guarantee that it would be followed.[21]

A word is in order at this point about behaviour modification. Behaviour modification, based on Pavlov's and Skinner's work, had been around long before the cognitivists came on the scene. In the opening paragraph of this section, I placed it among the physical therapies. And it is, with its "desensitization", "flooding" and "aversion" and its reliance on biofeedback, a therapy that concentrates on behaviour. Some dogs are too stupid to learn to salivate however—and some learn much faster than others. These are cognitive considerations. And in the much more complex world of human beings and their varied and sometimes unpredictable reactions to rewards and even distress of one kind or another, reasons and logic and problem-solving loom large. The above behavioural techniques have, as I say, considerable success with some disorders. They do—with their emphasis on reasons and rewards, however elementary or apparently desirable—have their cognitive side. And cognitivists tend to be good empiricists and to seize on anything that seems to work or to help. So the shingle sometimes reads, not "Cognitive", but "Cognitive-Behavioural".

And then there are the existentialists and—a rather wider group, one would have thought—the humanists. But there are also the existential-humanists and the humanist-existentialists. They talk about the patient's concrete everyday existence, the choices and the obstacles, the anguish and the autonomy, the phenomenological feel of it all and the nonmechanicalness and even irrationality—and they treat him or her as—well, you know, human—but with all, whatever it is, that is thereby implied. They rely on Sartre or Kierkegaard, Heidegger or Jaspers, they have debates with one another about whether God is dead and what that means or the unconscious as an intellectualist plot or the intentionality of anxiety or how to become a "third force" in psychiatry and they sometimes quote Nietzsche or Plato or Dostoevsky. They are, it should go without saying, a mixed bunch. Maslow, with his humanist as opposed to the sciences reading of "humanism" and the importance given to morality, beauty and authenticity and the striving for self-actualization again and his hierarchy of needs; Fromm, much more Freudian and more philosophical and concerned about individuation and freedom, isolation and the paradoxes of life, "productive orientation" and "productive love"; Rogers again with his views about the self and its possible rifts with experience and a therapy marked by "genuineness", "accurate empathy" and "unconditional positive regard"; Perls with a sort of existential marriage between Freud and gestalt psychology; and room should be made here for Binswanger and May—and, to be sure, for Laing. Existential therapy, as should be obvious, is sometimes Freudian but it is often as diffuse and certainly as various as the doctrines that lie behind it.[22]

There's ego psychology where one half of one of Freud's theories is highlighted—because Freud's views of the id are thought to be wrong or incomplete or just not as interesting. And here belong Hartmann with his "conflict-free ego zone" and "adaptive" and "synthetic" functions, Erikson and his "eight stages of man" and "ego-identity", Anna Freud's work on defence mechanisms and childhood analysis.[23]

There's transactional analysis, invented by Eric Berne. Each of us is a "child", an "adult" and a "parent". The Freudianism, of course, is transparent—though the child, in Berne, is creative and by no means to be despised. But each of us is his or her relationships with others as well and these relationships are expressed in a number of stereotypical "games" we all play—my adult and my parent or my child and your adult. So we get "pay-offs" and "gimmicks", "strokes" and "scripts"—and the breakdowns occur when the barrier between the parent and child is breached or when the adult and child can't be fused. The broader clientele should, again, be obvious. We can all be immature or too moralistic, not relaxed enough or complete toads. Transactional analysts are encouraged to resolve issues quickly and often make use of group therapy. This, along with individual transactional therapy, is mostly good clean pop Freud with a bit of a party flavour.[24]

There are all sorts of other "talking cures", many of them Freudian in some way or to some extent. One researcher, with a perfectly straight face, counts over four hundred therapies in all. But I have said nothing of Jung's "collective unconscious" or Adler's "organ inferiority", nothing of Melanie Klein, Otto Rank, Jacques Lacan. There is also group therapy to consider and family and couples therapy—doing it, whether or not it is Freudian, to more than one person at once so that therapy itself becomes, apart from the role of the therapist, significantly interpersonal. There is crisis therapy, especially designed for emergency cases and making relatively little use of Freud. There is, we are now told, supportive or supportive-expressive therapy—largely or often Freudian—in which the principal aim is not to change people but merely support them. The therapist is available, open and predictable—and those who are psychologically healthy but who are, often temporarily, unable to cope or suffering from physical problems are, again, as good candidates as anyone else. There is integrative therapy—doing everything or whatever the therapist considers valuable or worthwhile from any other psychotherapeutic school. As if the cognitive approach were too confining. One version concentrates on what is common to all therapies. Another researcher, with an equally straight face, found that this is predominantly a matter of a trusting relationship with the therapist and a healing setting, a rationale or conceptual scheme and a therapeutic ritual. That's therapy. Fill in the details yourself. And a day will come, of course, when the various integrated therapies that will no doubt continue to emerge will themselves cry out for integration. There is psychophysiological therapy where the patient's heart rate and blood pressure are constantly monitored during regular therapy, often Freudian. And there are brief forms, lasting for no more than months or even weeks, of all the "talking cures", including Freud's own.[25]

With regard to such cures, it should be emphasized that good, sound, sensible advice and, let's say, an understanding and a sympathetic ear would help a lot of people. It has nothing to do, in itself, with Freudianism. And to suppose that it conflicts with any other sort of therapy or that it is a science or remotely like one or that we can all be trained to do it well—or, indeed, that the dull-witted, indifferent or disturbed Freudian therapist is simply a myth—all this is absurd. And with regard to Freudianism, it must not be forgotten that there are, nevertheless, continuities—between good, sound, sensible advice through intermediate cases to genuinely psychoanalytic procedures. How can the latter themselves be scientific?

A further observation about Freudianism is in order. Almost all of the above therapies give rise, in one way or another, to a question that came up in Chapter 2: What is psychoanalysis and how does it differ from other sorts of therapy? In fact, the above therapies, if and when they are at all plausible, usually owe a large debt to psychoanalysis. So now that we have some idea of the competition, we can put the question more aggressively. Why is it that Freudianism, in whatever guise, constitutes the only alternative to physical methods that shows much promise? I will return to this question in the penultimate section of the final chapter.

Notes

1. There is an often pathetic but sometimes enormously brave and brutally honest subgenre of literature: the autobiographies, full-length or fragmentary, of the mad. Some of them are written while still mad or half-mad; some of them with memory as an uncertain guide to a reality that can't, in the end, be described, not very well, not very adequately. See, for example, B. Kaplan (ed.), *The Inner World of Mental Illness*, Harper and Row, 1964. But see also C. Landis (ed.), *The Varieties of Psychopathological Experience*, Holt, Rinehart and Winston, 1964. Landis suggests, explicitly and by some of his arrangements into chapters, that these first-person accounts might have conceptual implications for psychiatry. I am not sure that the idea of writing the present book didn't first formulate itself while reading Carney Landis a number of years ago.

2. *DSM-I* was published by the American Psychiatric Association in 1952; *DSM-II* in 1968; *DSM-III* in 1980; *DSM-III-R* in 1987; *DSM-IV* in 1994. The *ICD*s had their origins more than a hundred years ago in *The International List of Causes of Death*. *ICD-8* was published by the World Health Organization in 1968 to coincide with *DSM-II*; *ICD-9* in 1975; and *ICD-10* in 1992. The new bible is one thing; the new cash cow is quite another. *DSM-IV* is, of all the *DSM*s, the first to have its title trade-marked. I admit to being naïve enough to think that this must already have been covered by some other law. And the dust-jacket of *DSM-IV* lists no less than eight different spin-off publications, ranging from the *DSM-IV Study Guide* to the *DSM-IV Casebook*. You are urged, in one instance, to make sure you have enough copies to provide for all of your "staff members". Then there are the publications that are flooding the market on all the research that was done in putting *DSM-IV* together. Fortunes are being made here—fortunes and high-powered and fail-safe careers.

The French just are different in some ways—and one of them has to do with the taxonomy of mental disorders. A bit more detail on this can be found in Chapter 4.

3. All of the disorders in *DSM-IV* must cause clinically significant distress or impairment. But the tail does not, in general, wag the dog. On the contrary, such requirements are—wonderful phrase—"somewhat tautologous"—"*DSM-IV Meets Philosophy*", Allen Frances, A. Mack, M. First, T. Widiger, R. Ross, L. Forman, and W. Wakefield Davis, *The Journal of Medicine and Philosophy*, 1994. Frances, by the way, was the Chairperson of the Task Force on *DSM-IV*. And the only philosopher mentioned by name in this article—and, indeed, with approval—is Ryle. One should be reminded of Szasz and Laing. And one should remember that it was getting on for fifty years ago that *The Concept of Mind* came out. A lot has happened in the philosophy of mind since then.

As for roughness, I was brought up as a Wittgensteinian and roughness in concepts is, for Wittgenstein, as tolerable, even as desirable at times, as it is inevitable. But roughness is not incompatible with definition and there is more on the definitions of key psychiatric terms at the end of Chapter 4—although it must be acknowledged that the roughness here at issue is of relatively unusual proportions.

4. There are no behaviouristic definitions in *DSM-IV*. But *DSM-IV* does say, in connection with schizophrenia: "Because of the difficulty inherent in developing an objective definition of 'thought disorder', and because…inferences about thought are based primarily on…speech, the concept of disorganized speech…has been emphasized in the definition"—p. 276. Practical or heuristic considerations are cited—but are we headed back towards definitions that are operational because behaviouristic? And see Chapter 4, again, for more on Freudian and neurological etiologies.

5. Part of the problem here, but only part, is the alleged distinction between categorical and dimensional methods of classification and *DSM-IV*'s admitted preference for the former. See note 17.

6. *DSM-IV* criticizes, on p. 165, the use of "nonorganic" and "functional" because it implies that the relevant disorders are "somehow unrelated to physical or biological factors or processes." A few lines later, it says: "The term 'primary mental disorder' is used [in *DSM-IV*] as a shorthand to indicate those mental disorders that are not due to a general medical condition and that are not substance induced." And this is progress? Both *DSM-IV* and *DSM-III-R*, on p. 6 and pp. xxiv-xxv respectively, maintain, without actually using the word "pervasive", that disorders due to a general medical condition or a substance preempt primary or functional disorders. In both cases, however, all other hierarchical orderings are expressed in terms of a greater or lesser degree of pervasiveness—although in *DSM-IV*, the peculiar "not better accounted for by X" exclusion criterion is allowed to muddy the issue.

7. While schizophrenia can coexist with the N.O.S. mood disorders, delusional disorder or paranoia can't. Interestingly, delusional disorder itself then becomes psychotic disorder N.O.S. This strange relationship, or lack of one, between delusional disorder and the N.O.S. mood disorders is mimicked by that between bipolar I disorder, bipolar II disorder and major depression, on the one hand, and psychotic disorder N.O.S. on the other. And while cyclothymia and dysthymia are preempted by schizophrenia, cyclothymia is, oddly, not preempted by bipolar I or bipolar II disorder—though the second of this pair is preempted by the first—and dysthymia is not preempted by major depression.

8. Some of these examples might be no more than simple mistakes or oversights—but they can't all be. And neither should the potential for squabbling within or between *DSM-IV*'s committees be underestimated. The Task Force had thirty seven members; there were thirteen different Work Groups and two other major committees that called upon all sorts of other people in the profession; and *DSM-IV* proudly announces itself as "a team effort" with more than one thousand individuals contributing overall. See, for example, David Shaffer—himself a member of the Task Force—"A Participant's Observations: Preparing *DSM-IV*," *Canadian Journal of Psychiatry*, 1996, for one version of the inside story. *DSM-IV* is also proud of its empirical stance and it talks of "a three-stage empirical process" that includes literature reviews, data reanalyses and field trials. Some of this, of course, is to be applauded—although

empiricism has its limitations. See, for example, Kenneth Kendler—another member—"Towards a Scientific Psychiatric Nosology," *Archives of General Psychology*, 1990.   But one meaning that *DSM-IV* sometimes gives to "empiricism"—and this is reflected in the instructions to Work Group members to act as "consensus scholars"—is head-counting among colleagues and the more the merrier. Empiricism and democracy might both be good things; they are certainly not the same good thing.

9. Organic disorders—for which see below—must bear much of the blame for hierarchies.   Separated from and given precedence over the nonorganic disorders since not long after the beginning of the last century, they put the idea in the profession's head.   It would hardly occur to a family doctor or a specialist in tonsils or the stomach.

10.   Interactive Dualism, it should be emphasized, allows for causal connections between the mind and the brain and in both directions. So it allows—indeed, it insists—that the physical can intrude into the mental. But what lies behind *DSM-IV*'s list of organic disorders is not this philosophical concern—or any other. Those that are included are just those that have happened, over the years and for one reason or another, to catch the professional attention of psychiatrists.

11.   Sensory abnormalities are often linked to schizophrenia. But it is not easy to know what to make of this. Part, anyway, of the explanation for the link is that the diagnostic criteria themselves guarantee a high incidence of such abnormalities. Paranoid schizophrenia has, of all the types, the best prognosis. Catatonic schizophrenia, once common, is becoming increasingly rare.   And over 50% of schizophrenics attempt suicide at some point or another; around 10-15% succeed. For these figures, see H. Kaplan, B. Sadock and J. Grebb, (eds.), *Synopsis of Psychiatry* (7th edition), Williams and Wilkins, 1994.

12.   Brief psychotic disorder is much broader than its *DSM-III-R* counterpart where a "reactive" requirement was included. Folie à deux opens the way for group disorders; not only mass hysteria but also mass psychosis—as is sometimes seen in the more bizarre religious cults, for example. And while the culture-bound psychoses in *DSM-IV*'s Appendix I can be coded under psychotic disorder N.O.S., this trivializes a legitimate question.   Can all culture-bound psychoses be accommodated within *DSM-IV*'s classification or do some of them, at least, suggest taxonomical differences?—and a similar question, of course, arises about nonpsychotic culture-bound disorders. *DSM-IV*'s N.O.S. categories could swallow anything.

13. The metaphor of a switch in the brain is almost unavoidable here—and it seems to point to something right. But there are switches and switches—as well as mixed manic-depressive states and all these other moods or emotions. Kaplan, Sadock and Grebb say, in their discussion of mood disorders, that these disorders should not be regarded as affective disorders—a distinction between different kinds of emotion, one thinks—but they then define "mood" as "internal emotional state" and "affect" as "external expression"—so manic-depression, one thinks, doesn't have an expression? They put the figure for suicide attempts among people with major depression at roughly two thirds—higher, as one would expect, than for any other disorder since the threat of

gher, as one would expect, than for any other disorder since the threat of suicide is almost definitional for major depression—but that for successful attempts, a little oddly, at around 10-15%, the same as for schizophrenics. And they note the increased risk of depression among the elderly with some studies claiming a rate of as high as 50%.

14. The situation is not helped by views that are superficially similar to the one I am suggesting but completely unintelligible. Thus Kaplan, Sadock and Grebb say of pain disorder, in particular, "Purely physical pain can be difficult to distinguish from purely psychogenic pain, especially because they are not mutually exclusive." Anxiety disorders, by the way, come with a considerably increased risk of alcoholism. And somatoform disorders are reported considerably more frequently in women than men. See Chapter 4 again for more on hysteria and women.

15. Coconsciousness—and Dr. Strangelove. And multiple personality disorder is diagnosed much more often in women than men. But this is different. There is lots of evidence of childhood sexual abuse in the victims. And the French just are better at depersonalization and derealization, these bizarre delusions of theirs of negation.

16. A borderline condition has been around in psychiatry for a long time. It started as a disorder between the psychoses and the neuroses, it has resurfaced, periodically, under various names, with different symptoms, sometimes psychotic, and often seen from a Freudian perspective and it has now settled, not very comfortably, into one of *DSM-IV*'s clusters of personality disorders. And I am not trying to downplay the importance of the fact that moral concerns are involved in the occasional diagnostic category. But this is not, in general, a problem.

17. A not very edifying debate rages in the profession over whether a taxonomy should be categorical or dimensional. The categorical approach, we are told, favours clear divisions between disorders and homogeneity within a disorder whereas the dimensionalists like continua, grey areas and heterogeneity. A completely categorical taxonomy? Don't be so daft. A completely dimensional one? What can you be thinking of? So the obvious right answer is some of both—but look, of course, before you leap. I don't expect this simple truth to have much effect on the debate. For what we are dealing with here is a contrast between the anal, the quantifiers, the black and white no-nonsense merchants and the more laid-back and imaginative or dreamy or woolly-minded. A conflict, as one might put it, of personalities.

18. Although *ICD-10*, it should be said, comes in different versions. It is the version for clinicians, not that for scholars, that is relatively free of overquantification. Clinicians, apparently, are much less literal-minded, more sensible, than researchers, much less concerned with reliability or agreeing with their colleagues. But *ICD-10* for clinicians is, in many ways, a friendlier place than *DSM-IV*. Not the least of them is length. The mental disorders section of *ICD-10* is 77 pp. long. *DSM-IV* is a bloated 886 pp., up from the 119 pp. of *DSM-II*. *ICD-10* is, as I say, widely used in many parts of the world other than North America—and it is getting some attention even there. See, for example,

R. O'Connell, Editorial: "Psychiatric Classification and Publication," *Comprehensive Psychiatry*, 1995. But this last, of course, is at least in part the result of the increasing North Americanization of the *ICD*s.

19. The distinction I am making here between legitimate or anyway not illegitimate forms of therapy and those that are obviously worthless or pretty much so involves judgement calls. Of course.

20. See, for example, Harry S. Sullivan, *The Interpersonal Theory of Psychiatry*, Norton, 1958, and *The Fusion of Psychiatry and Social Science*, Norton, 1964.

21. See, for example, Aaron Beck, *Depression*, Staples Press, 1967, and *Cognitive Therapy and the Emotional Disorders*, International Universities Press, 1976—as well as Aaron Beck and A. Rush, "Cognitive Therapy," *Comprehensive Textbook of Psychiatry*, 6th edition (ed. H. Kaplan and B. Sadock).

And compare G. Berrios, "Phenomenology and Psychopathology: Was There Ever a Relationship?", *Comprehensive Psychiatry*, 1993—although Berrios's concern is with Karl Jaspers, not Beck—on the lack, often, of any very specific or technical meaning for "phenomenology" in psychiatry.

Vonnegut's prescription for self-improvement is contained, as I recall, in one of his prefaces or forewords; I have looked but cannot locate it. And Beck and Vonnegut in the same breath. But Beck not only inherited populism in psychiatry; he embraced it. So while cognitivism is for the elite among the masses, as it were, it is also for the great unwashed and the great troubled—as long as they do or can be made to think rigidly or militaristically enough.

22. I give, perhaps arbitrarily sometimes, no more than one work here for each of the writers I have mentioned: Abraham Maslow, *Toward a Psychology of Being*, Van Nostrand, 1962; Erik Fromm, *The Art of Loving*, Harper and Row, 1962 (copyrighted 1956); Carl Rogers, *Client-centred Therapy*, Houghton Mifflin, 1951; Fritz Perls, *Gestalt Therapy*, Dell, 1951; and Ludwig Binswanger and Rollo May, *Existence*, Basic Books, 1958.

23. With parsimony again in mind, see, for example, Hans Hartmann, *Ego Psychology and the Problem of Adaption*, International Universities Press, 1958; Erik Erikson, *Identity and the Life Cycle*, International Universities Press, 1959; and Anna Freud, *The Ego and the Mechanisms of Defence*, International Universities Press, 1946.

24. See, for example, Eric Berne, *Games People Play*, Grove Press, 1964, and *What Do You Say After You Say Hello?* Grove Press, 1972.

25. Other sources for this section on therapies are as follows: I. Yalom, *Existential Psychotherapy*, Basic Books, 1980, E. van Deurzen-Smith, *Existential Counselling in Practice*, Sage Publications, 1988, A. Nicholi (ed.), *The New Harvard Guide to Psychiatry*, Harvard, 1988, N. Polansky, *Integrated Ego Psychology* (2nd edition), Aldine de Gruyter, 1991, R. Kendell and A. Zealley (eds.), *Companion to Psychiatric Studies* (5th edition), A. Stoudemire (ed.), *Clinical Psychiatry for Medical Students* (2nd edition), J. B. Lippicott, 1994, Kaplan and Sadock (eds.), *Comprehensive Textbook of Psychiatry* (6th edition).

Chapter 4

The Anatomy of a Concept

This last chapter, the second half of this book, is in the form of a long philosophical essay on madness. Philosophers describe concepts, the very general and fundamental pictures we employ in our attempts to understand reality or get at the truth. The concept of madness differs from most in that it is partly theoretical or quasitechnical. Because of this, the voices of the experts have to be given prominence although not necessarily, of course, and not always the final word. Concepts move slowly by and large—like a loris or a glacier or the observed position of a star. But the concept of madness is, as concepts go, still in its infancy or on the newish side—even, as one might put it, immature and almost inevitably so. I confess to being on the wrong side of fifty five and I began to acquire the broad outlines of this concept roughly fifty years ago, a half of its lifetime ago or a half of its more or less clear and intelligible lifetime. It does, to be sure, have roots that extend back much further but they need not detain us. And it has changed a lot during its comparatively brief period of existence. While the underlying concept of mind has also changed, the concept of madness has changed even more. And the field, as I've said, is exploding. The concept of madness—along with those of neurosis and personality disorder, schizophrenia, agoraphobia, conversion disorder and so on—is, as concepts go, flashing past us at an exceedingly high rate of knots. Intertwined with all this is what sometimes seems to be the fundamen-

tal mysteriousness of the mind and, even more, the brute unintelligibility of madness or true madness. We ought not to be surprised if our
concept of madness contains paradoxes or problems we cannot
resolve—and we will have to try to catch it, so to speak, on the wing.[1]

Philosophers have not paid much attention to madness—or not
much direct or undivided attention. There are a handful of books, a
somewhat more generous scattering of articles and quite a few more,
both books and articles, in applied or related areas such as the philosophy of law and social and moral philosophy. These latter almost
always assume or fail to consider the claims and issues we are going to
examine. That there has been so little philosophical interest in this
topic ought to shock our complacency. Intriguing or unusual cases,
counterexamples, perhaps, to a pet theory, and overwhelmingly obvious
but seldom noticed concerns and questions. Completely incomprehensible facts, on occasion, the distorted images of indisputable and
timeless or near-timeless truths. For what we are about to discuss is the
concept of a state of mind that is a degraded state, a concept of a kind
or part of reality whose very fabric or medium and whose laws of
operation and integrity have been destroyed. Not broken down merely
in the way an internal combustion engine or a computer modem might
be. A parody, rather, an absurd pathetic mockery of the normal healthy
human mind. A fool or a grotesque or a monster perhaps—a sort of
freak.[2]

A hobby-horse of Wittgenstein's: Differences, in philosophy, are
the order of the day. A hobby-horse of various other people's as well.
So each concept has its own particular shape, its distinctive signature.
It will therefore be important, at times, to take note of idiosyncrasies.

I suggested, quite a while back, that the concepts of abnormal
psychology have always been relatively easy to distance ourselves
from, relatively easy to turn traitor on. We shall see how we go.

Abnormality and Scepticism

We should first look at the mad against the background of their
brothers and sisters and cousins. The mad are among God's blasphe-
mies or, as I say, nature's freaks. Or they are, instead or as well,
mutants produced by a hostile environment, human or otherwise. They
are not only different from the rest of us but an insult, a disturbing
affront, to things we hold dear. The notion of a norm or standard is, of
course, presupposed by this. It will be best, however, to begin with
some examples, to mark out our territory with cases.

There is a form of retardation, the Lesch-Nyhan syndrome, in which
one and two year olds eat their own lips and the soft tissue of their

mouths from the inside out, another, cranium bifidium occultum or exencephaly, in which some of the brain has oozed from the skull and spread across the eyes and face, yet another, the Happy Puppet syndrome where the formidable list of physical symptoms includes frequent and prolonged laughter—one of those private jokes, apparently, that is lost on everyone else. There are Siamese twins like Chang and Eng who learned, towards the end of their lives, to despise each other, there are microcephalics, the knockabout pin-heads of midways and side-shows, the stupendously fat, the sickeningly thin, the unnervingly hairy or scaly and those two-headed boys with one bodiless head attached to the crown of the other and three-armed or three-legged girls and then those who are both blind and crippled or deaf and mute and people with sexual abnormalities of the most bizarre kinds. Some of the latter have a penis and vagina, often rudimentary; others have a penis and two female breasts or a vagina and four breasts or no sex organs at all. There is Victor, Itard's wild-boy, who was discovered in the forest at the age of eleven or twelve, grunting like an animal. There are Amala and Kamala, the wolf-girls of Midnapore. And how many other Victors are out there or Amalas and Kamalas or Kaspar Hausers, how many people who, as children, had to fend for themselves or were confined to cages and forced to lie in their own excrement? How many, for that matter, who were horribly beaten or systematically sexually abused? There are dwarfs and giants, women with no faces, babies with a single central eye. Babies. Boodly-boo, koochy-koo. And who can forget the Elephant Man, the incredibly deformed, indescribably dignified, figure of John Merrick?

A mixed collection. I have not tried, particularly, to tidy it up. But the point about kinship can be made more specific—and in a number of ways. One of them is as follows. The retarded are—or so the statistics say—three to four times likelier than the nonretarded to be mad. And while some schizophrenics are intelligent, it is difficult to tell how many of them are at least mildly retarded, impossible to tell how many of the profoundly retarded are paranoid or depressed. I know of no studies on the incidence of madness among Siamese twins or among autosites, the hosts of sometimes marginally conscious parasites; one would expect it to be high. Giants, more nearly normal than most of the above, often die young, plagued by anxiety and hypochondria—and dwarfism can hardly be the surest recipe for mental health. Depression among those with sexual abnormalities or the more seriously disabled victims of thalidomide with not much more than a head for a body? It doesn't bear thinking about. Someone brought up in the dark and fed like a dog as suffering from delusions? Personality disorders among the blind and the paralysed or the blind and the deaf? What are the chances? Agoraphobia or social phobia among the enormously fat or enormously thin? The chronically tortured or sexually abused and dissociative disorders? And the prison population, that natural home of the psychopath or sociopath, has more than its fair share of the retarded, the sensorily impaired, the halt and the lame—as well as of homicidal and sex maniacs, of paranoiacs and alcoholics and deeply religious axe-murderers.[3]

So the mad have close ties with others who are often treated as objects of revulsion or awe. They thus represent and owe allegiance to a broader constituency. Back in the old days, back in the much darker days of the first half of the nineteenth century, they were still being exhibited in lunatic asylums for the edification and amusement of the paying public. The mad, however, or the mad and neurotic have their own peculiar style or character or cast.

There are the cases that somehow manage to be both exotic and trite at once: conversion hysteria, psychogenic fugue, multiple personality disorder. Then there are the odd or unusual cases: the puzzlingly approximate answers of Ganser's syndrome, the second, hallucinated self of autoscopy, the atypically clouded dreamy consciousness of oneiroform schizophrenia—as well as cases like those occasionally reported from England or Poland of low I.Q. twins who rarely go out, communicate with each other in mysterious ways and are psychological clones, a sort of autism of two. And autism itself is pretty odd. It was, again, one of Bleuler's four symptoms of schizophrenia—and, indeed, one version of one of *DSM-III-R*'s eight characteristic symptoms although it is, in this connection, deemphasized by *DSM-IV*. It is also, of course, a disorder in its own right. It can be detected at five or six months of age, is presumably present at birth and can, as even *DSM-IV* admits, be extremely difficult to distinguish from childhood schizophrenia. But is it madness—or even neurosis? And what of Tourette's? The cruellest, in a sense, of all the disorders with those in its grip sometimes outrageously and involuntarily filthy-mouthed. Isn't this, though, a neurological disorder? But how, one thinks, can a part or a system of the brain specialize in filth? Then, one thinks, it just can; something in the brain simply must. Schizophrenics too—and there's a strange state—have abnormal brains. And if schizophrenia isn't madness, nothing is. This is psychosis. This is the three Christs of Ypsilanti and Nijinsky with his awful mad diary and his final harrowing performance at Suvretta House, his marriage to God. It is Hölderlin in his tower writing complete gibberish in the end and signing it "Scardanelli" or "Buonarotti". It is Nietzsche spending the last years of his life, sometimes comatose, sometimes bellowing unintelligibly, dressed in white Brahmin robes in the upstairs of the villa purchased by his sister for the Nietzsche Archives with the royalties from his books while she entertained the leading lights of European culture and society in the lavishly decorated salon below. Or maybe—this is improbable, to be sure, but it can't be dismissed— maybe that really was grand paresis instead. So what?, you might think. It's still you rotting, brain first, like a delicious-looking piece of fruit that has travelled enormous distances to get to your table and is, as a consequence, turning into a thick brown liquid from the pit outwards. Schizophrenia, though, or schizophrenia proper is believing that one is dead or the Messiah—a not uncommon theme—or that the telephones are an international conspiracy, that one has sired thousands of children through atomic impregnation or that women are depraved and need to be cured of their lust through a meat-free diet. It is having one's thoughts broadcast or stolen to expose one to ridicule. It is hallucinations, terror, incoherence, stupor, a mind-numbing silliness, voices in the head, a bright glaring flatness with all the colour and sound drained out of everything. It is being a plaything of the Devil, the cause of everyone's grief, tormented by ghosts. And then there is manic-depressive disorder. Here as well we get the famous cases, from Oliver Cromwell to Robert Schumann to Virginia Woolf—all incapacitated and then energized at times by the unpredictable swings between mania and depression, between depression and agitation or an intoxicated excitement where anything seems possible. An acquaintance of mine, an intelligent man but a very lazy one, once said, sprawled across the couch in my living-room, that he wished he were hyperthyroid. So it is, for some people, with mania—or just the right touch of it, at any rate. And there is, of course, major depression—pure stark disabling misery, pure self-loathing, total hopelessness. No one—or no more than a few of the most desperate souls, perhaps—ever wished that he or she were depressed. And there are those who are straightforwardly paranoid or consumed by panic, the driven impelled obsessive-compulsives, the immobilized agoraphobics, the allegedly uncompli-catedly depersonalized, the kleptomaniacs, the pyromaniacs, the hypochondriacs, the anorexics. And again, we mustn't leave out those who have disordered personalities: the schizoid and schizotypal with a kind of attenuated schizophrenia, the histrionic and the narcissistic, the avoidant, the dependent, the antisocial and so on.

We will have to talk later on about frank neurological cases. We can think of them as brain cases. They are directly relevant to our

principal concern. But mostly we will look at the mad, the madman or
the madwoman or mad sexless or voiceless human being.

I said there is the notion of a norm here. Indeed, there are several
different kinds of norms. The point I want to make, however, is a
simple one.

A norm is a device or an algorithm for grading—and, very roughly
and crudely speaking, from "Good" or "Satisfactory" or "Acceptable"
to "Bad" or "Useless". So norms involve values. And values are
unlike facts. How, exactly? According to a familiar and not entirely
implausible view, facts are located in the world and thus can be objects
of knowledge whereas values are imposed on the world and therefore
cannot be such objects—any more than they can be determinants of
truth. The point is that this view is false. A brief detour will be
necessary, a detour into the heart of epistemology.

Philosophical scepticism maintains that we can't know some or all
of the most fundamental and elementary things we ordinarily think we
know—about other minds, about the past and the future, about external
reality itself. It is often argued for by describing a counterpossibility,
one that provides an alternative explanation of the apparent facts but is
beyond the abilities of human beings to address and rule out. With
regard to external reality, for example, a suggestion of Descartes's is
that there might be an evil genius, incomparably more intelligent and
advanced than we are, who is behind this whole elaborate and seamless
but illusory show. And, of course, there might, there just might be. So
how can we know that this is a hand or that a book? And since, given
our limitations, there are always these sorts of counterpossibilities, how
is it that we can ever know anything?

A particularly virulent and underdiscussed form of scepticism is
scepticism with regard to reason, considered either as a human faculty
or as a body of rational or supposedly rational principles. Hume does
discuss this form of scepticism and what he says about it is disturbing.
One way of dismissing it is to insist that it cannot be legitimately
argued for. Any such argument would inevitably employ the very
faculty or the very principles at issue—it would, after all, be an
argument—and so would be self-defeating. Decisive as this way of
proceeding might seem, Hume disapproves of it; he calls it "the
expeditious way". And he goes on to remark that the sceptical
arguments and what he here refers to as the "dogmatical" arguments are
"of the same kind". For any argument against this form of scepticism,
any attempt to defend reason, would, equally inevitably, be question-
begging. It too would be an argument. And it follows from this that
the most powerful argument for scepticism with regard to reason is

significantly different from what is, perhaps, the more common counterpossibility sort. It is, again, that any argument for the opposite position will and must be question-begging, not worth anything, anything at all.[4]

Hume is, it seems to me, obviously right about this. I am not recommending scepticism with regard to reason. Neither am I claiming that there is nothing to choose between it and its opposite. I am claiming, rather, that there is nothing to choose on the basis of argument between it and its opposite. And this conclusion can now be generalized. To say that a counterpossibility is beyond the abilities of human beings to address and rule out is just to say that we cannot argue against it. We cannot gather evidence or come up with reasons to establish that it does not obtain. All we can do is insist that it cannot be. And sceptical counterpossibilities can, once again, be described for any area. Indeed, the evil genius hypothesis will always do the trick. Perhaps an evil genius has so contrived appearances that while we think.... As an alternative, Hume's scepticism with regard to reason can always be invoked. If we can't trust reason, after all, we can't trust anything. So if we are going to be antisceptical as we surely ought to be, we have to pay a price. We have to beg the sceptic's question. We have to—for any and every form of scepticism—give an affirmative or a positive answer to the sceptic's question without being able to argue for it.

It will be said that an indirect argument might be available to us—even, Heaven help us, a transcendental argument—where some other fact is alleged to presuppose that we know what the sceptic doubts. This obviously won't work. Unless an argument, a direct and specific one, rules out the sceptic's counterpossibility, endorsing this other fact or putative fact will beg the sceptic's question. There's no way around this. And, again, any argument, indirect, transcendental or whatever, will, as will the understanding of even the baldest and least complicated of assertions, necessarily rely on reason.

So there are only two options—and this is what it is difficult to get straight about. We can be sceptics. Or we can, instead but at the expense of begging the sceptical question, embrace what is as plain as the nose on our face—that here is a hand, there a book, that we are surrounded by others who think and feel and dream, that we were each of us born and will just as certainly die. In doing this, we will, of course, be downplaying the role and the importance of argument in philosophy as compared with the requirements entrenched in the tradition. But we clearly cannot argue for everything we philosophically say, argumentatively dot every i and cross every t. Almost no one is a Foundationalist in epistemology any more. This, however, this willingness to waive, in key epistemological situations, the need for argument, is what antiFoundationalism amounts to.[5]

I have approached the fact/value distinction from the wrong side. But the moral is that we must adopt a much less grand, a much more common-sensical and piece-meal, attitude towards knowledge than has usually been fashionable in philosophy. And the moral is the same for norms; I now come to my simple point. Take the example of retardation. We have a notion of abnormality, one that doesn't carry much of a sting, where all that is involved is belonging to a minority. This is not, however, the only one we have. And whether the retarded constitute a minority or not, we have another notion in terms of which they deviate—and negatively—from a norm. The retarded labour under a deficit or a deficiency, a marked falling-off from a natural and comparatively clear standard, the optimal intellectual functioning of not especially gifted human beings. That this is so is as evident as any truth I know of. The retarded can't do certain fundamental and indispensable things that the nonretarded can. Just that, that undeniable fact. So we do have at least one robust and nonnumerical norm that is objective or out there in the world—although the same point can easily be made with the deaf, the crippled, the obese and so on.

Bad or useless? Of course not; I said that was crude. Ethical norms? They are not the subject of this book. The norms associated with madness? They are, in a way, what this entire chapter is about so the verdict on them must wait. Still and all, it should be emphasized that what I say in this chapter owes nothing to scepticism—or, for that matter, to relativism, its softer and typically less forthright ally. Relativism is the view that there is no single plain unvarnished truth—about anything or in connection with some more specific target—and often because different cultures think differently. Such differences, of course, are irrelevant as long as a notion of a mistake is provided for. But relativists sometimes make use of more powerful sceptical arguments. For these two views have in common a refusal to acknowledge whatever is at issue as the plain truth, the literal and clear truth. I want to separate myself from both of them—and I want nothing to do, certainly, with, what is not an argument, but the mindless question "True for me?"

Freaks? The word is a graphic one, with a bit of the dramatic to it. And it does, I suppose, express outrage—and, if you like, a kind of moral outrage. The outrage seems to me to be justified even if it is directed at something as impersonal as the universe itself.[6]

The Mind in Philosophy

The results of this survey will be uneven, to say the least, but we have to give philosophy a chance. I begin with Descartes. The mind, the first-person mind, is, for Descartes, inextricably tied up with the attempt to show that scepticism is misguided. Starting with the alleged indubitability of the Cogito—the claim or argument "I think, therefore I am or exist"—starting with this as foundation, the idea is that all knowledge—of external reality, for example, or of mathematics or logic—can be anchored to it in a way that is immune to scepticism, the way, according to Descartes, of deduction, of necessity, of entailment. There are several things wrong with this. Two of the more obvious are as follows. The Cogito is not indubitable if only because in some cases of depersonalization, the existence of the self is doubted if not straightforwardly denied. Neither are there deductive connections between the Cogito and what it is meant to support. So I will do what I can to keep these two preoccupations of Descartes's—the first-person mind and the attempt to undermine scepticism in general—insulated from each other. A few more remarks on the Cogito, however, are in order.

The strength of the Cogito's premise has to do, of course, with its being first-person, present tense and psychological. But Descartes also makes it clear that he doesn't care whether what he thinks is mistaken—or, indeed, whether he is mistaken about what he thinks. To put this last feature of Descartes's procedure differently, his use of "think" here is about as broad as it could conceivably be. Doubting, understanding, willing, feeling and perceiving as well as a number of other mental states or processes are all forms of thinking. So "I think" is roughly synonymous in this context with the nearly vacuous "I am somehow conscious." It is, certainly, hard to see how that could be mistaken. And the inference involved in the Cogito is not simply an instance of the general schema "X thinks, therefore X exists." If it were, the case of Hamlet might, as some philosophers have maintained, create a problem. But the inference too depends on and is strengthened by its being made in the first-person. The Cogito does, then, have a rather special epistemological status even though it is not indubitable. Nevertheless, it is little more than a philosophical curiosity. The premise, again, has almost no content so nothing follows from an account of it about the nature or the epistemological credentials of any other first-person present tense psychological statement. And again, nothing follows deductively, or nothing very interesting anyway, from the bare existence of the self.[7]

But influenced, perhaps, by his fascination with and treatment of the Cogito, Descartes takes all first-person present tense psychological statements or assertions to be indubitable. Or, not equivalent but at least as extreme, he assumes that if such a statement or an assertion is true, it must be known by the person concerned to be true. And this is no ordinary kind of knowledge since its object, for Descartes, is part of the stream of consciousness and so must be presently impinging on the attention. Descartes never makes this wholly explicit. He doesn't, lacking any clear sense of an alternative, have the resources to—which is exactly the point. Descartes never clearly recognizes what I referred to, in discussing Freud and borrowing from him, as the "merely latent". So not only do we know of all our memories, desires, beliefs, emotions and sensations; they are all at all times "present to our consciousness". The noise would be terrific. And then again, Descartes says, we can be "ignorant" of our "beliefs", "confused" about our "ideas" and not "feel" a "slight pain". But there is no pattern to these exceptions, no way of reconciling these contradictory claims. It is just that while Descartes is very much inclined to adopt an extreme view on this question, every now and again, for this or that local reason and sometimes, it seems, for no reason at all, he allows for an exception.[8]

How do we know, if and when we do, about our own mental phenomena? This is, according to Descartes, a direct kind of knowledge in that it is independent of and bypasses speech and behaviour. The mental is what is known by "contemplation" or "reflection", it is that which is "present to the mind" or of which we are "directly aware". Descartes does not employ the word but I will call this ability of ours "introspection". "First-person telepathy", in spite of the oxymoron, will do for a definition. So as far as definitions go, there is no more commitment to infallibility or comprehensiveness and no more need to restrict this ability to the stream of consciousness than there is with telepathy.[9]

With regard to others, Descartes's view should, of course, be that the best we can achieve in the absence of telepathy is indirect knowledge. But Descartes says very little about other minds apart from one rather famous remark to the effect that the clothed figures he sees from his window might, for all he knows, be "automatic machines". Maybe he is being sceptical and suggesting that we can never know. Or maybe he is aware that what he says is compatible with knowledge given the merely unlikely event of an outbreak of public nudity. But whatever we make of it, this is Descartes's only contribution to the problem of other minds.[10]

A further view of Descartes's, his view of the self, is dictated by epistemological considerations. The view is that the self is exclusively but indiscriminately mental. Descartes sometimes flirts with here, only to seemingly resist, a notoriously invalid epistemological argument: I know I exist but I don't know whether I have a body so a body can't be essential to me. The invalidity is obvious in the light of certain parallel arguments. For example, I know this is a right-angled triangle but I don't know whether the square of the hypotenuse is equal to the sum of the squares of the other two sides—a familiar predicament in high school—so their being equal can't be essential to its being a right-angled triangle. Even Euclid or Euclid in particular would have known that this is a bad argument. And on those occasions when Descartes's view of the self is announced in official and solemn terms, he tells us that he has a "clear and distinct perception" of himself without a body as a "complete being". This too is an epistemological though a quite unsupported claim.[11]

Descartes's views on the ontology of the mind are, by contrast, largely independent of epistemology. He believes, first, that the mind is real or, as he puts it in his quaint seventeenth century way, the mind is a "substance". Second, he believes that the mind and the body are very different substances, that they belong to very different kinds of reality. He has several reasons for this: the mind is indivisible, the body is not; the mind can think, the body cannot; the body is in space, the mind is not. Only the last of these reasons for Dualism seems to have some vague connection with epistemology. And, finally and for most mental phenomena, Descartes is firmly committed to, not only Dualism, but Interactive Dualism. The mind and the body but especially the brain can exert a causal influence on each other in either direction or both.[12]

Thus Descartes. He does have other views about the mind, the most significant of which for our purposes is that it is made up of various faculties. But Descartes is sloppy about this. The list in some passages is the "understanding...imagination, sense, and memory"; in others, it is both reduced and augmented, with no explanation, to the "understanding" and the "will". Then there is the view that we all have "innate ideas", the view that "choice or...free will" is as critical to belief as it is to action, the view that wonder is the most singular or "first" of the passions because its object is, "not good or evil", but what is "rare and extraordinary" so that it "has no opposite". These, however, are peripheral or idiosyncratic opinions with no connection to the more central views.[13]

And now, briefly, for some more history, this time the history of the philosophy of mind. For nearly three hundred years and culminating with the writings of James towards the end of the nineteenth century and Broad in the early part of the twentieth, some version of Cartesianism was, with few exceptions, endorsed by everyone. This was true, even, of Freud with his unhesitating reliance on introspection. But then, suddenly, came the Behaviourists. Initially, the view was that a one-to-one correlation—whether as a matter of the methodology of psychology or of straightforward truth—obtains between a mental happening or process and some item of behaviour. That this view is misguided or false is shown by such banal facts as those of pretending or stoicism or simple reserve. Alive to this problem but still convinced of the importance of behaviour in an account of the mind, Ryle argued that mental phenomena are dispositions or tendencies to behave, Wittgenstein that behaviour is, in a technical and difficult sense, a criterion of mental phenomena. And so Logical Behaviourism was born, the fashionable view of the forties, the fifties and, in some places, the sixties. Beliefs, emotions, desires, sensations?—or the mental or the inner itself? Ryle systematically soft-pedalled it or tried to brush it aside; Wittgenstein claimed, in a not uncharacteristically opaque formulation, that it was "not a something" and "not a nothing" either. But Ryle's sleight-of-hand failed to satisfy as did Wittgenstein's obviously evasive language. What was it that was being brushed aside, what were these mysterious inner half-somethings? The Australians, great believers in the concrete and the tangible, thought they knew. They were, they said, not mysterious at all, they were states of the brain. This view, Identity Theory, emerged in the fifties and began to take over in the sixties. But who were these tone-deaf Australians? For the inner here surely didn't mean just in or inside the body. Nevertheless, the view prevailed—it was so scientific or at least hard-headed—but it too was quickly superseded although not discarded. Science and the promise of artificial intelligence were in the air and the Functionalists maintained that the mental is nothing in itself, it is simply what it does or produces and what is done to it. So we were treated to descriptions of the mind in terms, not only of neurological models or electric circuits or plumbing devices, it sometimes seemed, but inputs, programmes and flow-charts, receptors and levels and print-outs, black boxes, no less, and human hardware. We still are by some people. Functionalism, it should be noted, is compatible with Identity Theory, of the token kind as opposed to the type, and it is often linked, as is Identity Theory, with Eliminative Materialism, the view that the mind is a myth, that all statements about beliefs and desires and memories are and must be mistaken. We have made up the mind. This—Functionalism, Identity Theory, Eliminativism—is where most philosophers were well into the seventies and even the eighties. They were pretty bleak times. For what is common to these views—and, indeed, to Behaviourism of whatever form—is that the mind, understood in any Cartesian way, does not exist. Or, only slightly more misleading or more contentious, the mind does not exist period. So for more than fifty years, it was, in philosophy, as though there was no mind. But while some of the above views continue to attract their supporters, two strange things have happened over the last fifteen or twenty years. The first is a reemergence of interest, among philosophers and scientists, in consciousness. Not in introspection itself but it is not easy to be interested in consciousness without noticing the fact of introspection—and, indeed, without stumbling over the unconscious so that even Freud's name has become respectable again in some quarters. The second is a growing disenchantment with Monism. Not in support of Dualism, or not exactly, but under the banner of an odd metaphysical hybrid, Supervenience, that seems as much in favour of Dualism as it is of Monism, as much opposed to Monism as it is to Dualism. So let's go back to Descartes.[14]

While we're at it, we can try to get some sense of how the above two issues might be related. But let's not go back to the Cogito and not to indubitability in the first-person and scepticism in the third. Let's go back, initially, to telepathy, then back again to introspection. Few of us, if any, have telepathic powers. And those who believe they do usually lay claim to them in a relatively modest form: one just knows, sometimes, that it's her on the phone or one dreams, perhaps, of a cousin calling out for help at the moment of his death. Researchers at Duke University also tell us that some people can identify a playing card picked at random and shielded from sight significantly more frequently than can be explained by chance. But this is pretty small beer compared to our introspective powers. Sit in a chair and think about something for a minute or two. Close your eyes, if you like. When you have finished, try to write down, making allowances for the vagaries of memory and maybe the odd murky or absent stretch, what it was that you thought. You probably weren't behaving in any especially revealing fashion. And if you were, it wouldn't have made the job any easier. Do you have a fairly good idea of what you thought? Or do you draw a complete blank as you almost certainly would with someone else? But don't bother to go through with it; you already know the outcome. So there is no question that we have introspective powers. The only question is that of how impressive they are and what they can be expected to discover.

We have this notion of the stream of consciousness: the thoughts that more or less continuously occur to us, the images and sensations of one kind or another—and all shot through with perceptions or the deliverances of the external senses, sometimes predominating and sometimes not. Do we have introspective knowledge of, not only our thoughts, but also our images and sensations? There can't be any doubt. Of what we receive through the senses? Of course. It is impossible to quantify any of this at all precisely. But if you had such knowledge of another's stream of consciousness, you would make, and legitimately, the front page of the *Weekly World News*.[15]

The stream of consciousness, however, is only one part, a small though an extremely important part, of the mind. I return to the merely latent. Consider your beliefs, your desires, your memories, your emotions, your intentions. You believe, let us say, that democracy is not all it's cracked up to be, you want to paint the house before the end of the fall, you remember the most inconsequential events from your childhood, you are contemptuous of your brother-in-law or proud of that shrewd investment and you plan to spend a few weeks next summer in Hawaii or the south of France. But at any given moment, these items of your mental furniture—along with literally millions of others—do not concern you in the slightest, they are the farthest things from your mind. Do you have introspective access to them?

We have been through some of this before in discussing Freud. Suppose I ask you if that's what you really believe. You might—you need not but you might—go over the evidence and reaffirm to yourself for the umpteenth time this obvious truth. Is that what you want? You might go over your reasons and be surprised, perhaps, by your eagerness to get started. Do you remember? You might set out on the sometimes tricky business of deliberately recalling, of bringing back to mind, as we say, those distant events and you might well succeed. Do you have such feelings or emotions? You might think of your brother-in-law and the chronic self-satisfied smirk or of the investment that, improbable as it seemed at the time, turned out so profitably and be filled again with contempt or with pride. Is that what you intend? You might think of the constant daily grind but also of the money you can put away and find that you can almost feel the warmth of Hawaii or taste the wine and the food of France. Yes it is, you think; it is indeed. These are familiar facts. They involve the voluntary translating or dredging up of what was not part of the stream of consciousness—or, at any rate, some surrogate or representative of it—into the stream of consciousness. And with more detail and examples, all equally familiar, they provide us with an account of the kinds of introspection appropriate to much of the large area of the mind that lies outside the stream of consciousness.[16]

You can, once again, introspect casually or hastily or, instead, more seriously, more diligently and at greater length. So you might be mistaken—for some mental phenomena are merely latent while others are latent though hardly merely. But however painstaking your efforts, you won't, given that you stay within ordinary limits, gain entry to your unconscious—if, that is, you have one. Nevertheless, there is, again, an extraordinary form of introspection here, enormously difficult to employ, that fits the extraordinary nature of the case.[17]

Indubitability, again, or infallibility? Of course not—even with regard to the stream of consciousness. And we have, it should be emphasized, departed from Descartes in other ways as well. But without introspection—and it is by no means clear that this is even close to being possible—our lives would be unrecognizable. If anyone had this sort of acquaintance with the mind of another, it would, once more, be truly astonishing. And yet this, the direct, fine-grained and comparatively comprehensive access that each of us has to his or her own mental states or processes, is what most of the Isms in the philosophy of mind have no place for—or anyway ignore if not despise.[18]

As for others, the situation can, notoriously, be desperate. And what knowledge I have of them, certainly, is of the indirect variety. With a few, just a few, the ones I've been around longest and have most to do with, I know quite a lot. After that, things, for me, taper off sharply. But with enough interest and a reasonable amount of intelligence and good sense, a fair bit can often be learned about total strangers. We all know this; it is absurd to deny it. So even though the first-person position is superior to the third and manifestly superior, a general scepticism about others is quite unwarranted. How we know, how we can know—these are other and in some ways more difficult matters.[19]

And as for the self, I am going to discuss it in some detail later on. But the most obvious, the most initially plausible, alternative to Descartes's view that the self is the mind is the view that the self is public with both physical and mental properties. All I want to point out here is that this latter view can easily accommodate the most robust of introspective accounts. For if the self has mental properties as well as physical ones, why not introspective properties, in particular?

And now for ontology. Is the mind real? This is simply the question of whether it is true that we all—or the vast majority of us, at any rate—have beliefs, for example. I believe that it is. The Eliminative Materialists, I have to report, believe that it isn't. Case closed, you would think. But the Eliminativists continue to believe this nonsense with no more excuse than a fear of the presently unimaginable secrets that some future science might reveal about the mind together, at times, with a background and seldom explicit scepticism or relativism. We are so stupid, so primitive, so rock-bottom dumb that we must have got it wrong and in the most basic of ways although these far-off descendants of ours might one day get it right. This intellectual faintheartedness, this prostration before the chasm of the future and the unknown is what, not infrequently, passes for philosophy these days. We are not even supposed to acknowledge that we believe and think and feel. So let's not bother any more with the Eliminativists.[20]

A second and more interesting ontological question is that of whether the mind and the body or the mind and the brain constitute different kinds of reality. Descartes's serious competition here is twofold: Monism, or, in its contemporary guise, Identity Theory, and Supervenience, which might, although rather oddly I would have thought, be presented as a form of Functionalism. We are back with the future of science. Identity Theory always saw itself as being in the prediction business. The view is, after all, that some much more advanced science of the mind will, if we stay around and in the maybe very distant but essentially unspecifiable future, weld the mind and the brain together as lightning is electricity or this table a whirling constellation of atoms and molecules in great reaches of empty space. And since the advent of this view, everyone has jumped on the band wagon. Everyone—whether an Identity Theorist, a Functionalist or a believer in Supervenience—will insist, given the occasion or opportunity, that the view he or she is presently expressing is only the barest sketch of what will some day be endorsed by a mature science or science-cum-philosophy of the mind. Connected with this is the idea that the coming of age of Identity Theory, say, or Supervenience will, like other revolutions in science, change some of our most fundamental concepts. And connected with this is the fact that a peculiar advantage can be claimed by these views. Any problems, conceptual or otherwise and however baffling, can be waved away as handleable by those much smarter guys somewhere down the road. The most blatant contradictions, the grossest falsehoods, can thus be set aside. If the concepts don't fit, they can be made to fit. These philosophers, apparently, have discovered a weapon of enormous polemical power. This seems fair enough, given the nature of their views—and yet it doesn't seem fair. If only, you think to yourself, you had a view with that sort of elasticity, that automatic immunity to pretty much any objection.

Well, let's invent one. For why can't we rely on the future as well? We can conceive of a view that is exactly like Identity Theory and

Supervenience—as theoretically high-powered and based just as firmly on all sorts of evidence we don't yet have—except that it prefers the language of duality and good old-fashioned two-way causal interaction between the mind and the brain. We can call it Mutual Mapping Theory; it always helps to have an official-sounding name. This theory too is still only a dream. But what we have to recognize is that the competitors here are Identity Theory, Supervenience and, not or not exactly Cartesianism, but Mutual Mapping Theory.

The arguments? We already have Descartes's arguments for Dualism: the mind is indivisible, the body isn't; the mind can think, the body can't; the body is in space, the mind isn't. The first of them needs cleaning up. A kind of indivisibility or unity is a must only for a normal or healthy mind. But this, it turns out, hardly matters. For as we learned shortly after Identity Theory appeared on to the scene, these arguments, however decisive they might appear at the outset, are useless. The same thing is true of the observation that the mind is the realm of qualia and of freedom, meaning and reasons whereas the brain doesn't seem to be. It is precisely these differences or alleged differences that might be wiped out in the coming conceptual upheaval. There are two arguments against Dualism, the same two arguments repeated by all of its detractors and in favour of Identity Theory or Supervenience: Occam's razor or the need for the universe to be simple and the thought that it would be very odd indeed if the mind were the only part or aspect of reality that is immune to the laws of physics. There is a supposed internal difficulty as well, the question of how two kinds of reality, being so different, could have causal relations with one another. Occam's razor? I take it back; this isn't an argument. It is, again, the need or the hope for the universe to be uncomplicated, a brute preference for the number one over the number two. Look and see, one wants to say. We know of some unities that could serve as models—but also many dualities. If you can't see, however, suspend judgement. And Mutual Mapping Theory locks the mind into the brain and the brain into the mind as tightly and as naturalistically as any other theory. The relations between the mind and the brain are said to be causal. So the mind is, on Mutual Mapping Theory, as much subject to the laws of physics as it is on any other account. To put this in different terms, all of these views would make brain cases of us all. The causal problem? It will be solved by those much smarter guys somewhere down the road, presumably with the aid of a richer and more refined concept of causality—just as the analogous problems of the causal powers of light and of gravity will be solved. And it isn't always or only causes for reasons too operate within the mind. Maybe they operate between the mind and the brain. And if what follows from all this is that the brain has to be no mere physical object but a very remarkable one indeed, isn't this what we should have expected? The brain, after all, is the only naturally occurring physical object—apart, perhaps, from the body and then by extension—that sometimes dances to the tune of reason. What certainly follows from all this is that the arguments are quite indecisive, that the best that can be said for either Identity Theory or Supervenience is that one of them might just be true. But then so, of course, might Dualism.[21]

The models? The Identity Theorists' favourite model is a paradigm of physics, the relation between this book or that table and its atomic counterpart. So they have two views: this paradigm of physics is an example of identity and so too, and similarly, is the relation between the mind and the brain. These believers in Supervenience have two views as well. The first is that this same paradigm of physics is an example of, not identity, but supervenience. The second is that the mind is, in a similar way, supervenient on rather than identical to the brain. But what is this relation of supervenience? It is time to get into some details.

Supervenience is asymmetrical; the table supervenes on its atomic representation but not vice-versa, the mind supervenes on the brain but not the other way round. So supervenience can't be identity for that relation is symmetrical. And Dualism, well, everyone knows that Dualism is mistaken without even thinking about it. So Supervenience is as unhappy with the number two as it is with the number one. The "One-and-a..."—this is cheap, I know, but it's hard to resist—the "One-and-a-halfists." The mind is allowed to be the brain—it is sometimes repeatedly said to be as though this were a kind of insult—but the brain is not the mind. The brain has, instead, a fixing, determining and often causal influence on the mind. But not vice-versa. The mind cannot control or affect the brain. A two-way causal relation, surely, would call for some sort of Dualism. Supervenience is thus sometimes thought of as a new form of Epiphenomenalism. And, finally—if this is not already clear—Supervenience insists on a principle of explanatory priority. The book or the table can be explained in terms of its atomic make-up but not the other way round; the mind can be explained by the brain but not the other way round.[22]

All this leads to further worries. First, however and as far as Identity Theory or Monism is concerned, what I can't help asking is, "How can the mind and body, being so different, be identical or the same?" An internal problem? I don't think so. The differences, again, might one day disappear. But still, one wants to say, our present concepts of the mind and the brain are concepts of a duality. So Dualism is—right now and as a matter of fact, as it were—the philosophical truth. And as for Supervenience, it is, it seems, just false. We can all think of as many apparently straightforward cases of the macro affecting the micro or the mind the brain as we can of the micro affecting the macro or the brain the mind. It is, perhaps, incoherent. Identity is incompatible with causality. Supervenience employs half of the language of identity and half of that of causality. Is this enough to make the incompatibility evaporate? Maybe some of the above cases can be chivvied away at and maybe half an incoherence—or should it be a quarter?—is just barely intelligible. What is really puzzling about this view is its stance on explanatory priority. Idealism, of course, and various sorts of antiRealism would have things in the reverse order. And it might be that we simply have to accommodate ourselves to a mixture of cases with explanations sometimes going in one direction, sometimes the other. What needs emphasizing here is that this is a substantial philosophical issue. The truth—whether supervenient or otherwise—has to be argued for. No argument is required for taking the micro to be more basic than the macro; it's smaller—and that's the end of it. But the brain is not smaller than the mind. Whatever else, not that, that mental phenomena are larger than neurological phenomena. Mereol-ogy? The parts of the mind might be the stuff that dreams are made of. They certainly are if those parts are neurons—or anything very like them. So the situation, I think, is worse for Identity Theory and Supervenience than fifty-fifty. But I'm going to leave it like that and insist, only and again, that Mutual Mapping Theory has as much chance of being true as does any of its competitors.[23]

Back to models—and this will help with the question of competitors or alternative views. Both Identity Theory and Supervenience, as I say, favour the model of a regular common or garden physical object and the atomic quantum level version of it. They disagree as to how that model is to be construed. What, though, of the mind and the brain as antimatter and matter, tachyons and tardyons or particles and waves or waves and particles, as energy and matter or as different kinds of charge? I am, of course, aware that these various dualities are not all, not always causal. But what would Occam have to say about them?— this allegedly scientific view, this belief that God is into numerology and the number one, in particular. And, by contrast with these examples anyway, the official model, the physical object/atomic level paradigm, seems like an instance of identity. We should also think of other examples or apparent examples of unity or identity. But that generations of philosophers, espousing various Isms, should have been

fascinated by one particular model to the exclusion of other, equally
and maybe more illuminating, models fairly boggles the mind. It helps,
once again, with the question of competitors or options. It doesn't help
a bit with the question of arguments. The arguments are as indecisive
with regard to the models as they are with regard to the Isms.

There is a third ontological question to consider, that of whether we
should be antiRealists about the mind. AntiRealists in the sense of
believing that the human mind carries the stamp of the human point of
view, the bat's the bat's and so on—with the result that sometimes
enormous and largely unbridgeable gulfs exist between species. Of
course we should; one can't have the slightest doubt here. But this has
always been known in abnormal psychology. It has always been
known that the truly mad are strictly unintelligible to everyone.
There's antiRealism for you—for the mad are separated from, out of
touch or out of tune with, even themselves. Should we be antiRealists
about the physical universe? Should we believe that out beyond Alpha
Centauri, out into the far reaches of the universe, the name of humanity
looms large? Even Ptolemy had fewer pretensions.[24]

And now for bringing some of the strands of all this together and a
few odds and ends. It ought to be made clear that both Identity Theory
and Supervenience are compatible with an introspective view. All that
has to be done is to concede that the brain is the only physical object—
apart, perhaps, from the body—that is introspectible. But we already
knew that the brain is queer. No view, Identity Theory or whatever,
can be considered an advance if it involves the denial of obvious facts.
And what could be more obvious than the fact of introspection?[25]

I am not going to try to give a direct answer to the question of how
Supervenience is connected to all this recent talk about consciousness.
I will try, rather, to answer a closely related question: What is the
connection between Supervenience and introspection? Supervenience—unlike Identity Theory but also unlike Functionalism—has a
positive reason for being uncomfortable with Eliminativism. The very
asymmetry of the mind/brain interface is, it seems, enough to confer on
the mind a genuine albeit an inferior existence. Having said that,
Eliminativists have been known to endorse introspection. And
nonEliminativists have, notoriously and not infrequently, dismissed it
or downplayed it. So while Supervenience can live with an introspective view, there is not much of a connection between them—except for
a generalized and an indiscriminate nostalgia, a nostalgia for the direct
access views as well as the antiMonism of Descartes. And maybe
Supervenience is right in maintaining that the mind and the brain don't
constitute a clear one or a clear two. Not one and a half, of course, but

neither unproblematically one nor unproblematically two. There's a good Wittgensteinian thought for you—and, perhaps, one that can be employed to the advantage of an enlightened Cartesianism. For think, again, of all of the possible models. We have come full circle.

I have said quite a lot about Supervenience, not much at all about Functionalism. But Functionalism too, it should be noted, must get used to the fact of introspection—and so, indeed, to qualia. Functionalism, the view that the mind is only what it causes and what is caused by it, has, with the recent growth in popularity of Supervenience, quickly disappeared from the philosophical landscape. Maybe Supervenience is a kind of Functionalism but the only worthwhile kind so that there is no point in discussing Functionalism in general. Maybe what many Functionalists, anyway, had in mind differs from the peculiar relation of supervenience—the effect is the cause?—so there's no point in bringing up Functionalism of any kind. Ah, such is philosophical fame. For a while there, beginning in the late sixties, going right through the seventies and even into the eighties, almost everyone was a Functionalist. But it is no more than right that Functionalism should have become so unfashionable—although what has succeeded it is hardly an improvement; the effect is the cause? The causal or functional properties of a brick are not, of course, independent of its intrinsic properties. And yet no one would claim that a brick is merely some sort of functional matrix. Its intrinsic properties—its shape, its size, its weight and so on—are so evident to simple inspection. But the intrinsic properties of a sensation or of a belief or the occurrent affirming thought that is its representative in the stream of consciousness are equally apparent to introspection. So there is no reason for distinguishing between the physical and the mental here. And even if we can tell a brick from a feather by its functional properties, we can't, by these means, tell one brick from another. Their functional properties are identical. And yet there the individual brick is in all its truculent being or thinghood. This too is evident to our senses—just as the existence of this or that pain or feeling or thought is an immediate datum of introspection, the pain, for example, there, undeniable, intrusive, overwhelming even, in all its individuality. The rhetoric—not the substance but the rhetoric—of Existentialism enough, by itself, to undermine Functionalism at this point. Moreover, even if everything intrinsic about a brick did have a functional analogue—which, it seems to me, it plainly doesn't—what sort of intellectual eccentricity is it that would insist on the functional and dismiss the intrinsic rather than the other way round?—or, better, than insisting on both? Functionalism, let me repeat, cannot be the whole truth about the mind.

But even as a partial view, it must, like Identity Theory, give introspection its due. It must also learn to take qualia seriously; qualia, after all, are simply the appearances of the mental to introspection. And if it can't do this, the issue decides itself. So much the worse for Functionalism.[26]

The same thing is true of Logical Behaviourism, which is often thought of as a kind of Functionalism. Philosophers have, it seems to me, offered good arguments for this view—although it has to be qualified, as do most views in the philosophy of mind, to apply to only normal human beings. We can't just assume that there are, for aliens or for the mad, the links between the mind and behaviour that there are for us. But Wittgenstein's half-somethings and half-nothings must be exorcised for the metaphysical fictions they always were and we have to recognize that the mental is governed by two criteria, one behavioural or outer, the other psychological or inner. This will, of course, give rise to conflict cases. But these cases do exist, pathological as they might be. A philosophical view ought to allow for such cases, not try to deny them.[27]

Epistemology and ontology don't exhaust the mind. Think, for example, of the self. Or think of meaning, the will, memory, desire. While epistemological and ontological questions do arise over these topics, they are not, simply, topics in the epistemology or ontology of the mind. But some of them will be discussed at length in this chapter—and the broad categories of epistemology and ontology do constitute a framework for the sort of general overview I have tried to provide in this section.

So what have we learned from this excursion through the major Isms in the philosophy of mind? What are we to retain, what can we take with us, in our thinking about the mad? Not much, it must be admitted. There is the epistemological side of Cartesianism, of course, although this view too must be bracketed. For what do the mad know, what must they know, about their own minds? And Identity Theory or Supervenience might be true—but then so, instead, might Mutual Mapping Theory. This is an in-house philosophical issue with no prospect of a resolution in sight. There's Logical Behaviourism— although it's no more than part of the truth, at best, and it is, again, of no use outside of normal parameters if only because the relevant connections can be influenced by what is believed to be appropriate by the person concerned. And while the causal properties of the mind might well be significant, neither will Functionalism work by itself. Nor is much space devoted, on any of these views, to certain key issues in the philosophy of mind, issues that are, again, going to preoccupy us for much of the rest of this chapter. There is, for example, no official much of the rest of this chapter. There is, for example, no official account, on Logical Behaviourism, Identity Theory, Functionalism or Supervenience, of the self or of the faculties or basic building blocks of the mind and no account of the will—not even for normal cases. Descartes does have something to say here but even Descartes is not always clear or, indeed, very interesting on these questions—and the connection between them and his more central concerns is, again, sometimes pretty tenuous, to say the least. And madness has, once more, seldom been addressed by philosophers of any persuasion. So we are, not invariably but most of the time certainly, on our own. We will have to approach the mad with not a lot that is given.

The Kinds of Madness—and Some New Perspectives
We should start with *DSM-IV*. The schizophrenias, the four or five types, followed by paranoia, the bipolar and unipolar mood disorders and panic, anxiety and obsessive-compulsive disorder, then the less debilitating or the odder cases. For *DSM-IV*, schizophrenia with its various kinds, including paranoid, lies at the centre of psychosis. We should start with schizophrenia.

In Chapter 3, I brought up the question of just how different paranoia is from paranoid schizophrenia. Let's decide. Let's think of it as a kind of schizophrenia. This is not, for our purposes, a terribly important matter but it will make the discussion easier and paranoia does, after all, have a great deal in common with paranoid schizophrenia. Then I mean by "schizophrenia" what *DSM-IV* means by "schizophrenia" and "paranoia". So schizophrenia really is the thought disorder—with, if you like, two paranoid types. I have argued against *DSM-IV*'s view of it in close to the ground and relatively minor ways. But suppose I could invent a quite different five kinds of schizophrenia—or a quite different three. Suppose I could invent forms of schizophrenia you've never heard of and I could point to their victims.

I have two sorts of arguments for believing I can do this. The first is fairly abstract. Despite the increasing success of research into the brain, we are, as I've said, a long way from a neurological etiology for schizophrenia—and Freudian diagnoses are, again, often suspect, especially with regard to the psychoses. So we're pretty much stuck, like *DSM-IV*, with the symptoms, the thoughts, the behaviour, the speech. Two disorders could display indistinguishable symptoms; one could, in various types or unusual circumstances or with advancing age, display different symptoms. But I hope, like *DSM-IV*, that we can still see some of the main outlines. Take, then, any self-respecting computer, suitably programmed, and feed into it the five "characteristic symptoms" of schizophrenia listed by *DSM-IV* or the eight listed by *DSM-III-R*. Add the dozen or so "associated features" mentioned by both *DSM-IV* and *DSM-III-R* together with some information, for both symptoms and features, on their incidence, mutual correlations and degrees of severity. What information, exactly? Well, use your judgement but you obviously have a considerable amount of leeway here. Throw in one or two principles of organization, like "Concentrate on the fragmentation or the loss of the self" or "Give a prominent place to emotion or desire." You obviously have a lot of choice here too. Then ask for five categories or three with not too many loose ends. For the most that can be required of such an exercise is a reasonably good fit; a mere handful of recalcitrant or apparently anomalous cases can always be accommodated somewhere else in the system. The computer could do the job in a minute. And if the point is not yet clear, feed these five or these three patterns of schizophrenia back in, make some alternative suggestions as to how, on theoretical grounds, the material is to be organized and top them off, if you want, with some more information about symptoms and features, then set it to work on how the patterns might be manifested or construed in other recognizable ways. The computer could easily do that as well.

The other sort of argument is simply a concrete version of the above. For example, the self is important in schizophrenia. A "disturbance in the sense of self" is one of *DSM-III-R*'s eight symptoms and what we might think of as the two paranoid types are usually described as being dominated by "delusions of self-reference", delusions in which some real or imagined aspect of the environment is perceived as directed at or of somehow particular relevance to the self. Or perhaps we have—we haven't decided this—only one paranoid type with a more or less dishevelled or refined face. But that aside, *DSM-IV*'s and *DSM-III-R*'s varieties are erotomanic, grandiose, jealous, persecutory and somatic, all turning in on the self. The self is important then. So the splitting or the disappearance of the self must also be important.

Consider, first, depersonalization. Here, the self doubts and sometimes denies itself—an improbable and a terrible wrench in the self's dealings with itself. Out of mind does not mean out of existence, of course—but the self's opinions of itself do have to be accorded special significance. And then, in catatonic stupor, the self has gone or gone to sleep in an outlandish sort of waking coma, the body immobile often, the mind switched off—or so it seems. In hebephrenia, the extreme and malign form of what *DSM-IV* calls the "disorganized" type, the self is masked or it is shattered by a web of total unintelligibility. For there is no centre, no focus, to be discerned in the "word-salads" of the hebephrenic. Paranoid schizophrenia and paranoia are, maybe not or not so much divisions within the self, but breakdowns in the critical barrier between the self and the rest of the universe, rips or haemorrhages through which the self oozes or explodes. What of autism where, by contrast, the self, absorbed in itself, seems blind to itself? It is, surely not unconnected, more or less unaware of or oblivious to others too. And should multiple personality disorder, in which the self is split into discrete but comparatively homogeneous parts, be thought of as a kind of schizophrenia?

There are two connected questions here. What have I included of *DSM-IV*'s conception of schizophrenia? What have I left out? We can begin with the latter.

I have left out the residual type. It should, again, never have been there in the first place. I have also left out the undifferentiated type. Another absurd excuse for a category. It is the category of "Some type—but we have no idea what." Of the three remaining categories, I have left out half of the catatonic and some of the disorganized. One possibility open to us is that we can keep things like this and allow them to be absorbed into other areas of the taxonomy. But what is the relation of catatonic excitement to catatonic stupor? I mean, what are the facts? Are there unipolar kinds of catatonia and, if so, how common are they?—is there something comparable here to melancholia?—and are the symptoms of stupor negative symptoms? Still and all, for bipolar catatonia, as it were, catatonic excitement can, if we choose, get in by piggy-back. Then unipolar catatonic excitement, insofar as it exists, can be let in as a kind of courtesy. And most of the outstanding cases of the disorganized type can easily be seen in terms of some sort of, maybe lesser, affliction or disfigurement of the self. Being overattenuated, for example, or not readily available or completely in control.

I have therefore included at least most of the ground covered by the three acceptable categories. Depersonalization is included too—as I think, in its extreme form, it should be. It is, after all, one of the most bizarre disorders that we know of. Autism, again, is hard to distinguish, symptomatically, from childhood schizophrenia—and the fact that autistics are or appear to be brain cases doesn't seem to help. Finally, the question about multiple personality disorder does need asking, the fragmentation then, whether along a continuum or with isotopes, a matter of differences of speed or of scale. These breakdowns or absences in or of or around the self are, moreover, of various kinds. So if we insist on a number of types of schizophrenia, we already have them at our finger tips.[28]

Or think now, not of the self, but of the will and desire. *DSM-IV* doesn't make a great deal of fuss about these two notions. Hume did. He took desire, which he thought of as a "passion", to be one of the more important "influencing motives of the will". And of course he was right. If one wants to do something, this certainly makes willing that much easier—and if one has no desire, willing and the production of action are, trivially, much more difficult if not impossible. *DSM-IV*, once again, groups obsessive-compulsive disorder, in which there is an obvious impairment of the will, with the phobias and anxiety disorders, traditionally regarded as neuroses—and it has a forlorn little section, "Impulse Control Disorders Not Elsewhere Classified", that contains kleptomania, pyromania, trichotillomania and so on. It does, however, give "avolition", characterized by "an inability to initiate and persist in goal-directed activities", as one of its negative symptoms of schizophrenia and it mentions "anhedonia" or a "loss of interest or pleasure" as an associated feature. No interest, no pleasure—so not much, if anything, in the way of desire. *DSM-IV* also suggests, as does *DSM-III-R*, that these sorts of deficits are most often found in the residual type.[29]

Maybe these sorts of negative symptoms are—to stick to the official story—most frequently observed in the residual type. But a generalized failure or conflict of initiative and motive and an inability to get things done are present in a lot of disorganized patients too. Then there is catatonic stupor and, in particular, waxy flexibility—that unprotesting robotic response to having a limb moved by someone else of keeping it in place, however uncomfortably as one is inclined to say, sometimes for hours. And we can include catatonic excitement upfront this time. For behaviour there is frequently so intractable and with such potential for annoyance, outrage or even physical mayhem that forcible restraints must be employed. Many paranoiacs and many paranoid schizophrenics can partly see through their delusions—just as many schizophrenics with hallucinations can, in some ways or to some extent, see them as hallucinations. This is becoming more common with all the new drugs but these cases that are rather less extreme than the paradigms or the stereotypes have always been around. And there is, in them, a struggle between what is dimly or only sometimes recognized as rationality and various other instincts and preoccupations. It is a struggle that mostly goes on in the mind but it is, nevertheless, a struggle of the will. And perhaps some cases of obsessive-compulsive disorder, the more severely disabling ones where cleanliness, for example, is an all-consuming passion and the hands and lower arms are raw and bleeding from being washed a hundred times a day, perhaps some of these cases did ought to be classified as schizophrenic. And here as well, of course, we have a number of types.[30]

There are two questions again. They call for a more or less careful accounting, wondering what has been missed and trying to balance it against what has been added. I trust their answers, in general import, at least, are fairly clear but I won't attempt to give these answers, not even in a rough form. For a further and by no means unrelated problem has come to the surface—although it could easily have been raised earlier on. A lot of disorganized patients... ? Many paranoiacs...? Behaviour is frequently...? So it too is a counting problem, a problem about counting heads.

Different kinds of studies are done on counting heads. Some are on the chances of having schizophrenia if it's in the family, some are on the recurrence rate, given a bout of major depression, within a period of two years, others are on the likelihood of a panic attack being followed by a heart attack. All reasonable and obvious concerns. But what of the counting studies that are not being done? The results of such studies, it should be noted, are seldom clear-cut or decisive. You get a somewhat increased risk if you are a young adult male, say, or belong to a certain socioeconomic class or an associated feature is elevated, perhaps, to a symptom. And how are low correlations to be interpreted? As a sign of changing therapeutic techniques, maybe, or a shift in culture or the chemical environment? But the point I wish to emphasize is that which heads are being counted is nearly always determined, explicitly or otherwise, by taxonomical considerations. And as for the above questions about disorganized, paranoid and catatonic patients and their difficulties with the will or the will and desire, I don't have any firm statistics. I suspect that no one does. The questions are not official counting questions.

But we were discussing alternative ways of conceiving of schizophrenia—together, almost inevitably, with bits and pieces of the surrounding territory. Are there any others?

There are indeed. So think, more quickly now, of clinical neurology and all the work being done on the aphasias and agnosias, the dementias, the disturbances of body-schema, emotion and the senses, the amnesias and the various motor abnormalities. And think of looking at schizophrenia through the filter of these sorts of linguistic, psychological and behavioural deficits or excesses. I am not claiming that this is an easy or a straightforward thing to do. The topic of schizophrenia and language, in particular, has been a minor industry in the literature for several decades now without much consensus and, not infrequently, perverse or doctrinaire approaches to language. But many schizophrenics exhibit symptoms that are remarkably similar to those of some neurological patients. Indeed, *DSM-IV* itself points out that the disorganized speech of schizophrenia can resemble that of receptive aphasia. Some research, perhaps, is being done on this. It is a large question, it seems to me, as to whether enough is being done.

Or think of the voices of schizophrenia, the voices and the hallucinations. Voices or hallucinations of one kind or another occur in about one third of schizophrenics. They must surely be linked to the sensory parts of the brain. And since this taxonomy business is never very precise, aren't voices in the head, one finds oneself wondering vaguely, the heart or the soul of one of the most striking forms of schizophrenia? This seems to be *DSM-IV*'s view for it maintains, once again, that the single symptom of voices conversing or commenting can do duty for any other two symptoms in diagnosing schizophrenia. But are the voices always auditory hallucinations, the voices of others, or are they sometimes images, as it were, of speaking oneself? That sort of hallucination. And what work is being done on that large group of schizophrenics who don't suffer from voices or hallucinations, what work is being done on them as a group?

Or think, instead, of schizophrenia as an emotional illness. *DSM-IV*, as I've said, has strange views about emotions. It does, however, list affective flattening as one of its negative symptoms of schizophrenia and flat or inappropriate affect as a requirement for the disorganized type. Then there is the silliness of catatonic excitement and the rigidity and stiltedness, often, of paranoia and paranoid schizophrenia—and depression and anxiety are extremely common in schizophrenia. The emptiness of catatonic stupor and the flatness, again, of the disorganized type, in particular—and mania can overlap with or be difficult to distinguish from schizophrenia. Mania, to be sure, along with major depression, would assume much greater importance with this way of carving up the landscape. But then why not? And most cases of schizophrenia could easily be accommodated within a mood-centred taxonomy with other, nonemotional symptoms being treated as secondary or somehow derivative, part of the background of the disorder rather than the foreground. How much work is being done on schizophrenia as a disorder of the emotions? Not much, one can safely say, not much at all.[31]

New types of schizophrenia? We already have quite a few. But there is also or in particular the "No One Home Syndrome": Catatonic stupor and catatonic excitement if the babbling is purposeless enough, hebephrenia with its complete incoherence and grossly deranged behaviour and, of course, depersonalization. Then there is "Emotional

Dwarfism": Catatonia again, much of disorganized schizophrenia again, paranoid schizophrenia and paranoia if the austerity or distance is especially marked and, of course, autism. And so on and so on.

I have been reinventing schizophrenia. Why? And do we have any solid neurological evidence for these taxonomical alternatives?

Not really or none to speak of—which is hardly surprising. The alternatives I have spent most time on, those having to do with the self and the will, are special. For the key notions involved, that of the self and that of the will, are not respectable, they are certainly not favourite, objects of study for neurologists of any kind. More importantly, however and like epidemiologists, neurologists who are interested in psychiatric disorders almost always accept the official taxonomy. How could they do otherwise?, it will be said in their defence. But whether this counts as a defence or not, the fact of the matter is that *DSM-IV* or something like it is very much taken for granted by neurologists. So of course there is little or no neurological evidence for any competing taxonomy. Still and all and equally, neither is there any evidence for *DSM-IV*'s sort of thought versus emotion taxonomy. The alternatives I have mentioned are precisely that—alternatives. They simply don't enter into the thinking of your average neurologist. An opposition, however, takes two. And without an opposition one has—what?—a truism, an inherited assumption, an intellectual reflex almost. Who needs evidence?[32]

So why all the alternative taxonomies? The concept of schizophrenia is central to psychiatry and, indeed, to neurology. It is, as the above exercises in taxonomy—and the empirical evidence or the lack of it—make clear, a concept that is in considerable disarray. It can be viewed in quite different ways than the received wisdom indicates with quite different affinities and implications. I will come back to this more than once before this chapter is over. But I want to take a few moments here to mention some other problems about schizophrenia—partly as a kind of update.

Although a great deal remains to be done, schizophrenia is unique among forms of madness in the number of authoritative results from studies of the brain. It thus raises, in a particularly urgent fashion, three questions, of which two are familiar while the other is becoming increasingly difficult to ignore. The first is that of which of the currently fashionable Isms in the philosophy of mind—Identity Theory of some form or Supervenience—is correct. I have argued that there are no grounds whatever for preferring either of these theories to Mutual Mapping Theory—although we have not yet addressed the issue of scope that arises for all of them. The second is that of whether schizophrenics are free or determined—a question that is of equal importance for everyone else. I leave it until a later section of this chapter. The third question has to do with other sorts of defective brains. How can we distinguish between schizophrenics and brain cases, the victims of car wrecks or of known and fairly well-understood diseases of the brain? I think the answer is that, in one sense, we can and, in another that is critical to our attitudes, we can't. I think that, on this point, our concept of schizophrenia—along with that of madness itself—contains a prejudice, a mere relic or an echo of the past. I will have more to say about this later on as well.

And now, much more quickly, for the rest of the taxonomy: madness or madness and neurosis or madness, neurosis and personality disorder—but minus or over and above schizophrenia. Let's begin, anyway, with the self and the will. Multidimensional taxonomies could, of course, be considered. The official one, again, turns mostly on the twin notions of thought and emotion. But my concern here is not to give an exhaustive account of the possibilities; it is to sketch certain broad alternatives. And those based on the self and the will or the will and desire have further consequences for the rest of the taxonomy, consequences I have not yet remarked on. There are two outstanding questions. Haven't I taken away some cases? And haven't I relocated or suggested different slants on others?

Some of the changes at least would be minor. Subtracting autism from the developmental disorders and depersonalization and multiple personality disorder from what is an ill-defined and surely an ill-assorted group to start with, the dissociative disorders or those disorders, again, in which there is "a disruption in the usually integrated functions of consciousness, memory, identity or perception of the environment." There is, perhaps, an oblique reference to the self in this but *DSM-IV* says nothing about what this woolliest of phrases might mean. Or, instead, subtracting the more extreme cases of obsessive-compulsive disorder from the rest of the pack. And maybe we can include extreme cases of phobia and panic along with them—for these too might be thought of as involving a kind of deficiency of the will. We need not worry about how, exactly, we might deal with any of the resulting stresses or strains.

But there are other sorts of changes—and there are broader as well as more detailed concerns. In induced psychotic disorder, for example, the self is abandoned or set aside to take on, not merely the beliefs, but the psychotic beliefs of another. In mania, the self can disintegrate into a blur of whim, impulse and momentary distraction—and in depression, we are sometimes left with little more than the empty shell of the body.

Psychogenic fugue presents us with a self that is merely fictional or constructed. Body dysmorphic disorder might, perhaps, revolve round the belief that the body does not exist. What of gender identity disorders and self-image? And isn't the personality a part somehow of the self? So what of personality disorders—and what, in particular, of the paranoid, the schizoid, the schizotypal, the borderline and the dependent? Should any of these disorders be regarded as schizophrenic? No—or not necessarily. There are other differences between them and schizophrenia—even when the latter is construed as an abnormality of or within the self. And the will is obviously crucial to the category of "Impulse Control Disorders Not Elsewhere Classified". So trichotillomania is a kind of neurosis of the will and kleptomania a sociopathic aberration of it. Tourette's, we might insist, is partly a question of the will for its exercise can make a marked difference—and in some eating disorders, like anorexia and bulimea, the will itself has become voracious. The will has lost its grip or its edge in all of the phobias, including the milder ones; it does, as I've said, play a role in conversion disorder and it is often paralyzed in depression by an absence of desire. And there are, of course, the cases of obsessive-compulsive disorder that are less severe as well as those of obsessive-compulsive personality disorder. They merge gradually into the pointless, repetitive and potentially annoying rituals that most of us indulge in from time to time. And again, there are differences or other differences between all these cases and schizophrenia, however the latter is thought of.

Are these suggestions and questions a blueprint for large-scale changes? They do—there can be no doubt—give us new or alternative ways of looking at madness, neurosis and personality disorder. And there are, moreover, other ways; there are always other ways.

For consider mood or emotion again. *DSM-IV* believes that there are only two emotions or only two for taxonomical purposes, depression and euphoria or excitement. It does, on the other hand, recognize emotional flattening or inappropriateness. So two emotions, which can themselves be pathological in intensity and two potentially more general defects that they are subject to. Isn't panic an emotion? Isn't anxiety? Isn't fear, the emotion that is central to the phobias? Isn't self-loathing or jealousy, blind rage or crippling remorse? And aren't there more pleasant forms of madness? Apart from the exhilaration, tense and ragged-edged as it might be, of mania and some kinds of paranoia, aren't there demented states that come close to pure bliss or that give one a good and pretty frequent chuckle at the world together with a chronic sense of well-being? Aren't there such states of peace and contentment or perpetual orgasm?—and couldn't one be in love, or something like it at least, for the whole of one's life but always with someone new? More shifts in the larger territory of psychiatry and even beyond. So we might see depression and mania as important examples of a broad range of mood disorders that also includes, not only much of schizophrenia, but much else besides. We might redo our taxonomy in that way.

Are these brief and sometimes free-wheeling suggestions about emotion an invitation to make major changes? Of course. And when the changes to schizophrenia, construed emotionally, are also empha-sized, of course they are. So too and equally if not even more obviously are the changes associated with the self and the will, without schizophrenia but also and especially if we take it into account. Alternative taxonomies will be with us for the rest of the chapter but I will try to keep things simple from now on and confine my attention to those that have to do with the self and the will. The imagined changes, however—of course and again and this is the point here—the imagined changes, in each case but also multiplied or cross-bred for possibilities, of course they are major, far-reaching, of great import. There can be no question.[33]

I want to turn now to a quite different sort of concern, a concern about certain more specific examples. And I am going to begin with multiple personality disorder.

Multiple personality disorder is a matter of one personality taking over or controlling or being—I am struggling for a neutral way of putting this—a particular person for some time and then being replaced by another and then another or maybe the first again. But cases differ over whether two or more personalities can be on stage at once or "coconscious" as well as over the total number of personalities involved, the amount they know about one another and whether and to what extent there is a most powerful or dominant personality. If there is not, the therapist, who usually attempts a "reintegration" around such a personality, is faced with some difficult choices. Cases of multiple personality disorder can be completely incapacitating if the switches are too frequent or the infighting or the recrimination too bitter. Many of them, however, seem to be classical cases of neurosis—and the incidence of childhood sexual abuse is apparently very high.

Perhaps multiple personality disorder is a form of schizophrenia—or perhaps some cases are. But I want to make another suggestion. It is not, I think, an incompatible suggestion—although it does put at risk the generally atheoretical, the determinedly fair-minded, attitude of this book. Perhaps many or most cases of multiple personality disorder are Freudian cases.

Part of what is at issue here is the question of how similar, on symptomatic grounds, multiple personality disorder is to the classical neuroses. But this is a no-brainer. The neuroses exhibit a wide variety of symptomatic patterns so there is no problem at all about fitting multiple personality disorder in. There are, though, two further questions. Freud was fond of splitting people up into two or three systems or agencies. How many cases of multiple personality disorder involve two or three personalities? Or how many can be thought of as involving two or three broad types? Quite a few, surely. Some of the personalities in a majority of cases are, after all, less prominent or more attenuated than others. And the reports of very large numbers of personalities in a single case can be safely ignored. You would be hard pressed to find more than a dozen or so in your average small town. Still, none of this is really critical. For there might well be various clusters of mental items in someone's unconscious without much relationship to one another. So we can be fairly orthodox Freudians and go beyond three. And more than one personality can, as I've said, be coconscious—which leads to the other question. There are difficulties about the notion of full coconsciousness where two or more personalities have equal control. Perhaps, though, they are only the difficulties of envisaging the outlandishly chaotic behaviour—Dr. Strangelove's warring hands writ as large as the body, including the mouth—and of wondering, phenomenologically, what it could possibly be like—a nightmare of strange tugs and pulls, glimmers and flashes, pressures, scents and flavours. Well, perhaps; that's all I said. I don't see my way very clearly here. But perhaps there could be voices of equal authority in one mind or, at any rate, one head, so to speak—and closer to one another than any two telepaths could ever be. But whatever we make of this, in other cases—much easier to comprehend—a second voice might be nagging or calling from the back of the mind or commenting occasionally from off to one side. In how many Freudian cases is the unconscious experienced as just such a voice? Or, to ask the other half of the question, in how many cases of multiple personality disorder is a second personality experienced in some nonvocal way and in how many Freudian cases does the Ucs make its presence felt nonvocally? Some sort of less than full coconsciousness, it should be noted, is quite consistent with Freudian theory. Freud's own version of this in *The Ego and the Id* is that "the ego merges into the id" and in other places he talks, once again, of a grey or an indeterminate area between the Cs (or Pcs) and the Ucs. So I think that many

cases, at least, of multiple personality disorder might well be phenomenologically very similar to certain Freudian cases. The stories of
childhood sexual abuse are obviously significant. And Freudian cases
seem to be declining while multiple personality disorder is very much
on the rise. Are a lot of cases of the former being diagnosed as the
latter?[34]

Neither is there a worry here about thinking of some or even all
cases of multiple personality disorder as schizophrenic. I see nothing
wrong with the view that Freudian therapy might sometimes be
appropriate for schizophrenia. A diagnosis in terms of the effects of the
Ucs is, of course, implausible for schizophrenia in general—as it is for
autism, say, or mania. Nevertheless, these effects can be of an
absolutely devastating kind. Maybe Freud failed to notice or to
emphasize the pronounced cycling nature of some of his cases. Or
maybe diagnosis influences symptoms. For there is, again, an element
of wilfulness in Freudian cases and we would do well to remember
Freud's "choice of neurosis" here. Besides, the suggestion was only
that a lot of cases of multiple personality disorder might be Freudian
cases. And while the splitting, in multiple personality disorder and
schizophrenia or other kinds of schizophrenia, is rather different, there
is, again, nothing to prevent us from thinking here in terms of mosaics
or types and, perhaps, of fineness of grain.

And now for the obvious philosophical question: Is there more than
one self or person in multiple personality disorder? The correct
response, it seems to me, is also obvious—although it might be
disappointing. All that could prevent one from accepting it is the
misguided but fairly common philosophical view that came up in
connection with Freud, the view that there must be a clear-cut and
unequivocal answer to all questions about identity and to all questions
about the identity of people, in particular. Let me repeat what I said
earlier. We cannot hope to find a method of counting—for trees, rivers,
governments, proofs, people or anything else—that gives such an
answer in all cases. Some real or imaginary cases will always be
unprovided for. Once we have realized this, we can cheerfully admit to
the straightforward truth that while multiple personality disorder does
challenge our ordinary unthinking confidence that we can count no
more than one self or person for one body, there are no easy answers to
be had here. And as for why this disorder is sometimes felt to be the
key to personal identity in general, that is another question entirely.[35]

A second example that deserves special attention is depersonalization or derealization, a disorder, or a pair of disorders, of more than
usual philosophical interest. In mild forms, the self or the rest of the

universe is unstable, without substance, not important or to be given serious consideration—or there might be doubts, sometimes, about its existence. In extreme forms, the self or the world it inhabits does not exist, it has been destroyed or it was never more than a passing fancy.

Derealization of the extreme and psychotic variety—for there can be genuine delusions here—is a concrete and highly committed version of a philosophical position even more bizarre and uncommon than solipsism. Solipsism is the belief that one is alone, that there are no other people, minds or consciousnesses. What reasons could one have for believing that? And what reasons could one have for believing the physical world as well to be nonexistent? Perhaps, we will be told, there are no reasons, this goes beyond reasons—and perhaps, we might agree, it does. Then we should be asking, not "Why?", but "How can you, how can you possibly believe that only you exist?" Extreme and psychotic derealization implies solipsism and also scepticism about other people and the external world—and less than extreme cases sometimes express themselves precisely as a kind of doubt. Scepticism too is bizarre and uncommon. In this case, however, there are powerful arguments for the view—which brings up a point of methodology. Many philosophers assume that if a philosophical view is mistaken, this can only be because it is contradictory. Derealization, surely, does not consist of anything as crass or banal as a flat contradiction; the mad are typically much more clever, much subtler, than that. But a judicious assessment of—I can't think of a better word than this—a judicious assessment of the sense of derealization would throw considerable light on the proper assessment of the above philosophical views. And, I can't help adding, for scepticism, that assessment should include a kind of failure of courage, a sort of intellectual or academic cowardice. But then again, there are, as I've said, formidable arguments in favour of scepticism. The moral, clearly, is that there are other things—things other than argument—that are important in philosophy.[36]

Extreme psychotic depersonalization is stranger still. Isn't there something deeply unintelligible about the belief that one does not exist? Not just about the content of the belief but about the very having of it?

I don't think so. Those who are afflicted with this condition do have what we can only regard as beliefs. Their use of language is admittedly queer but they don't believe that I don't exist or that you don't—and neither do they believe that they don't exclaim, say, or don't expect or explain. The queerness does mean, though, that we can't understand their beliefs fully or exactly or without a residual degree of murkiness. As though our sane concepts couldn't quite do justice to the mad ones. But this, of course, is a more general truth or concern about the mad mind—and it must make the blood run cold to have someone look straight at you and say "I don't exist". The best they can do and the best we can do in trying to describe their view of their awful predicament is to say that this one, this one here, does not exist, is not real or actual, is not and cannot be a genuine item in anyone's considerations.

Depersonalization can, as I've said, amount to a living disproof of certain familiar glosses on Descartes's Cogito, including his own. It is not that the Cogito is "self-evident" or must be believed by anyone to whom it applies. For it applies, quite simply, to everyone. And some people with depersonalization, as a matter of fact, believe precisely the opposite. It is not that it is "indubitable" or somehow logically immune from doubt. Some people with depersonalization, as a matter of brute inescapable fact, insist on this doubt. And extreme cases, once more, are committed to scepticism. If there is no self to know about, there can be no knowledge and no way of knowing. So it is not that scepticism is impossible with regard to the Cogito or the self. But however perplexing and irrational it might be, the judicious assessment of such a scepticism is available in the terms and concepts of abnormal psychology. Part of it is cowardice, again, if it's a philosopher we're talking about, but a crazy cowardice. For depersonalization, especially of the extreme and psychotic kind, has to be the most arcane, the most fundamentally incomprehensible, of all the disorders. Unless that prize should go, instead, to the double delusion, the belief that nothing exists, neither the self nor the world, just nothing, nothing at all. How could someone possibly believe that? The only answer, and a not very informative one, is that he or she would have to be extremely mad. And why not, once again, why not schizophrenic, in particular? Kant's left-handed glove, Spinoza's substance, Thales's everything, Occam's razor, the universe as a single giant black hole—all these are downright profligate ideas by comparison. Nothing, nothing at all. But what could that mean?[37]

Which brings me to autism. The autistic does not doubt or deny the existence of the self; he—for the statistics are about four to one, male to female, even though girls are often more seriously disabled than boys—he withdraws into it, rather, and thus diminishes it. There are three main areas of concern: interpersonal relationships, linguistic competence and a discomfort with differences, a fear of the new. Other people as well are impoverished, reduced to mere props—or they are, instead, treated in an inappropriately personal fashion with their boundaries ignored. And the autistic too has a hard time with language, ranging from a profound difficulty with personal pronouns so that "he" and "you" might be substituted for "I" and vice-versa to upwards of 50% of autistics never developing spoken language at all. Finally—and perhaps most puzzling or most striking—things have to be orderly, the agenda clear and undemanding, the toys or the possessions and the pointless activities always the same. Connected with all this is that "most" autistics, according to *DSM-IV*, are retarded with the figure in some studies going as high as 80%. Some of them, to be sure, have unusual abilities in circumscribed areas and the chances of an idiot savant being autistic are, apparently, about even—but retardation hangs like a blight over this disorder. There are two obvious questions about autism. Should it really be distinguished from schizophrenia and childhood schizophrenia, in particular? The distinction is tenuous, to say the least. Autism, remember, has often been regarded as a symptom of schizophrenia. And while many childhood schizophrenics do exhibit other symptoms, the view that we have a connected range of cases here—maybe, who knows? with autism at its centre—is not even considered. The reason for this, I believe, is another prejudice. The signs of autism have been reported at no more than a few months and must be present before the age of three whereas the threshold for the onset of childhood schizophrenia is usually pegged at five or six years. They're treading a pretty fine line here. But the point is that one can't be born mad, surely. Why not? *DSM-IV* tries to be consistent on this issue by distinguishing between autistics and schizophrenics—and, one supposes, old autistics and old schizophrenics, in particular—on the basis of the latter's "prominent delusions or hallucinations". But this is not, for *DSM-IV*, a requirement for schizophrenia in general. So why the distinction? I will return to this first question, this question about a prejudice, in a moment and then, at greater length, later on. The second question is: Is autism a kind or a consequence of retardation? I ask because *DSM-IV* assures us, once again, that most autistics are retarded, often severely, and because there is, it seems to me, a conceptual link between autism and retardation. The claim about most autistics could be explained in any one of several ways. But as for the conceptual link: autism is one style or mask in or through which one might very well expect retardation to manifest itself. It is not the only one; there are a small though indefinite number of others—like an overall vacancy or a stubborn refusal to cooperate, a marked garrulousness or a promiscuous amiability. Some cases of retardation might not match, or match at all closely, any of the styles or masks we can think of. Nevertheless and as I say, there is this conceptual link, this overwhelming need for repetition and familiarity, this nearly complete lack of interest in or curiosity about others and the world. It is loose enough to allow for autistics who are not—or should it be not otherwise?—retarded. And it might explain *DSM-IV*'s "most". Or it might explain most of it or some of it. One also gets a lot of jumping up and down and rocking and grimacing in autism. There is, however, the same sort of behaviour, not infrequently, in schizophrenia. All of these disorders are brain-based, of course, so this won't distinguish either. Not much is known, by the way, of the details with autism although some autistics have high serotonin levels. Is autism, then, where madness and retardation overlap? Is it, indeed, a mostly low I.Q. and solipsistic form of schizophrenia? You know that the right research is not being done, the right questions are not being asked. The official view that there is a distinction between autism and schizophrenia discourages such research.[38]

Tourette's disorder is also more common in males though not, perhaps, by quite the same margin. The tics come in various kinds—eye-blinking, tongue-protrusion, sniffing, throat-clearing, squatting, twirling and so on—but the most fascinating symptom is one of the vocal tics, coprolalia or the uttering of obscenities. And while all of these symptoms, it is claimed, are involuntary, they can, again, often be controlled or completely resisted for extended periods even though this might take considerable effort. A fair amount of shame and depression exists and disturbances in sleep are sometimes reported or observed. There are strong ties with obsessive-compulsive disorder and attention-deficit/hyperactivity disorder and Tourette's is, in spite of the few cases in which it disappears entirely by early adulthood, usually life-long. And it is, of course, a brain disorder with antipsychotics suppressing although not eliminating symptoms in many cases. But why is it—or autism, for that matter—a typically male disorder? And why the filth in Tourette's? Is it anything more than slugs and snails and puppy-dogs' tails? And whether or not it is, what are we to make of these puppy-dogs' tails? They must be embedded in the brain—we surely know that. But are they produced by training? Are they there by nature? Are they somehow both?—for haven't most of us let the assumptions of genetics pass largely unnoticed and undiscussed? And just how involuntary, one has to wonder again, wholly caught up in this by now, can the uttering of sometimes complex obscenities be? As involuntary as the disconcerting facial tics that children often develop and that usually go away in weeks or months? As involuntary as nose-picking?—which can, God knows, be hard to eradicate. As inten-tional—difficult as it can be again to do anything about—as the chronic retention of faeces? More slugs and more snails. And what other signs of social or sexual deviance are exhibited by Touretters? They can't just be normal folks in these areas, not solid bourgeois citizens, at any rate—and there is the general profile of being poor, more or less uneducated, isolated or kept mostly within the immediate family, ridiculed often, even reviled, by other people.[39]

And now for the organic disorders—for there is a large question here that is not being asked or not, anyway, with the right options available. I gather together certain things that came up in Chapters 2 and 3 and the last section of this chapter. *DSM-III-R*'s organic disorders were those in which an organic etiology is "known or presumed", whatever that was supposed to mean; *DSM-IV*, more cautiously, picks out its nonprimary disorders only by enumeration and insists that no difference in principle is intended by its distinction between the nonprimary and the primary. Psychiatry catching up with philosophy on this point for all of the Isms popular in the philosophy of mind for more than fifty years now—Behaviourism, Identity Theory, Functionalism, Eliminativism, Supervenience—all of them agree about the importance of the brain across most, anyway, of the psychological board. But so too does Interactive Dualism, whether in its classical Cartesian guise or reincarnated as Mutual Mapping Theory. So too, in a way, do Epiphenomenalism and Reverse Epiphenomenalism. The only Ism that leaves the brain out of the picture entirely is Parallelism. What is seldom noticed, however, is that even Parallelism might still be true as long as it is presented in no more than a partial form. For many disorders have a known specific image in the brain—so no one is going to buy a completely general two-clocks-running-in-tandem story. But still, as I say, Parallelism might be true over some perhaps small part of the territory—as might Epiphenomenalism or Reverse Epiphenomenalism—for there is no reason to think we must take our Isms just one at a time. Magical views, perhaps, or near-magical—but whoever supposed that the truth about the mind would turn out to be utterly pedestrian? *DSM-IV*'s list of organic or nonprimary disorders is, besides, oddly and obviously incomplete. Many of the disorders familiar from books on clinical neurology or in hospital neurology wards are not even mentioned. Then there are the very different ways in which various functional or primary disorders are said to be preempted by organic disorders and the fact that some of them, it seems, are not so preempted.

It should be noticed, in this connection, that we know that the brain can sometimes be altered by the use of the mind just as the mind can be altered by tampering with the brain. If you are nervous over an upcoming interview or angry at a friend, you might be able to dissipate the nervousness or the anger and thus interfere with your bodily

chemistry by arguing to yourself that the nervousness is quite unjusti-
fied, the anger, really, no more than simple resentment on your part.
But if you are nervous from having drunk half a dozen cups of coffee
within the first two hours after waking up, you had best wait for the
level of caffeine in your blood to subside—and anger, like resentment,
can be remarkably impervious to the claims of rationality. So there is
sometimes empirical evidence as to which of the two related or locked-
in items, the mental or the physical, is directly manipulable—although
some of the results of biofeedback and, maybe, of prolonged or intense
meditation suggest that we ought to be extremely careful about this.
What is the question, exactly? One version of it is: Is psychoanalysis
appropriate if the drugs work?   Another is: Will the province of
clinical psychology shrink as we discover more and more about the
deranged or demented brain—and is there any limit to such discoveries
and what lies beyond? We have come across this question before as
well. But it is, I think, important that we see it arising against a more
sketched-in philosophical background. Indeed, it should now be clear,
given that background, that we might have two or three questions here
and not one. I will, again, return to it—or to them—in a later section.

I should say a word or two about memory disorders at this point
although *DSM-IV* seems loath to. In many cases of amnesia, whether
retrograde or anterograde, we are pretty sure of a physical cause and
sometimes, as in Korsakov's syndrome, we can actually point to the
damage.   But in two of the memory disorders that *DSM-IV* does
discuss—the only two apart from those, including Alzheimer's and
multi-infarct or vascular dementia along with Korsakov's in the odd
grouping, "Delirium, Dementia, and Amnestic and Other Cognitive
Disorders"—in dissociative amnesia and dissociative fugue, the cause
is psychological. As well or instead? For *DSM-IV*, these disorders
usually follow "traumatic" or "stressful" events. There is, however, no
mention of Freud. It is, notoriously, difficult in many cases to assess
the soundness of a Freudian diagnosis or measure the success of
Freudian therapy.   But aren't these paradigmatic Freudian cases—
doesn't their official description subscribe to Freudianism—even
though a Ucs is typically here acquired in adolescence or adulthood? If
they are, does this make it more plausible to think of all or some cases
of dissociative or multiple personality disorder, whether schizophrenic
or not, as Freudian?   And shouldn't dissociative or psychogenic
amnesia and fugue be more closely tied to multiple personality
disorder—leaving depersonalization and/or derealization rather off to
one side? As for the cases where the cause of amnesia is simply or
straightforwardly physical, the effects can be totally devastating. There
are reports of people who go through life on a knife-edge with this vast

people who go through life on a knife-edge with this vast forgotten abyss trailing behind. Think of what that would do to reason, emotion or purpose or to any integrated sense of self. And yet we don't regard these people as mad. Why not? Is that another prejudice—or is it part of one that was mentioned earlier?[40]

And now for something different, something newer, a couple of disorders that are currently receiving at least as much attention in some quarters as multiple personality disorder. Codependence, which came up briefly in Chapter 1, is a sort of folie à deux of mutual needs on the neurotic or disordered personality part of the spectrum, usually at the very mild or low-level end. It is a matter of an undue concern or preoccupation with another's perceived vices or shortcomings. But it must be reciprocated, inviting exactly what it offers. It's all over the place, allegedly, and there is a great deal of emphasis on addiction, enabling and denial. All sins, no doubt—with vague Freudian undertones. Denial, after all, is merely a poor man's version of repression. Genuine cases of codependence do exist, of course, although they are, it should go without saying, much less common as well as less serious than most of the literature suggests. There are no drugs for the condition. Neither is the appropriate therapy Freudian, or not particularly. It is, rather—in most of the alleged cases—of the firm and no-nonsense "Get a life" variety or it should be. Easy to say, of course, and often hard to do. We are in Kurt Vonnegut territory once more. Freudian bits and pieces might help in some cases as might mood-improving drugs. But these things, God help us, might always help. Sex addiction, by contrast, is somewhat trickier. Satyriasis and nymphomania have been with us forever—though you wouldn't know it from *DSM-IV* any more than you would know about codependence. But *DSM-IV* does list, primly, hypoactive sexual desire disorder under "Sexual Dysfunctions". Mustn't there, then, be the hyperactive type too? And mightn't this lead to sin? Still, sex has never been thought of as an addiction before. Or has it? Isn't it just the plain obvious truth that most of us are extremely, even inordinately, interested in sex? And don't some of us go off the deep end? Sometimes anyway. And isn't this sin if anything is? All right, how many times? Three or four times a night for five or six nights a week is a tremendous, an awful lot. Double or triple that and the result is positively kinky. But we have to ask: Is there any physical or emotional toll on others?—and what sort of sexual equipment do these people have or are they into self-mutilation? It would be nice, I suppose, if the desire were of the right or the healthy kind. I'm not a believer in the alleged instinct to propagate the species. But you get too far away from impregnation or conception, too far, anyway, from some sort of clear impact or statement, you know you're in trouble. And sometimes the frequency is of partners—but how many is too much? Two? Is there secrecy, infidelity, danger? Three? A dozen? Frequency, mere numbers—it's hard to be judgemental about that although someone might, again, go over the top. An addiction? Perhaps. And then, on the other hand, God could have made sex a thousand or ten or two or three times better. Maybe He did for Martians or for dragonflies; maybe He did for us or, instead, for some of us. The therapy? Bromide has traditionally been the treatment of choice in the military and a number of other possibilities come quickly to mind. The treatment is easy; it's the diagnosis that's the problem.[41]

I have not meant to give the impression that we should be reluctant to countenance new or reemerging or redefined mental illnesses or disabilities. On the contrary, the existence or the incidence of a disorder might well depend on, not only the whim of invention, but time, place or circumstance.

I mentioned a few such cases in Chapter 3. There are all sorts of others. The Ojibwa of the subArctic of North America sometimes suffer from windigo, a usually male paranoid state of spirit possession that can be either melancholy or violent and that occurs in the long winter after hunting has been bad. The Eskimos, farther north, more sociable and less competitive, don't get windigo. They get pibloktoq, affecting mostly women but men too apparently, a dissociative and often berserker state of sometimes as little as two hours' duration. It is more common, again, as one would imagine, in the winter. Then there is the full-on amok of Malaysia that is, most of the time, exhausted in a single assaultive paroxysm or frenzy. A "Crazy-dog-wishing-to-die" syndrome is reported among the Plains Indians where behaviour precisely opposite to what is normal or expected produces an eerie disorienting effect. And South-East Asian men, particularly Southern Chinese, are, it seems, susceptible to shook yang, a delusional panic state in which the penis is thought to be shrinking or retracting into the stomach wall with death as a possibility if it should disappear completely, an eventuality that is often warded off by primitive mechanical means. It can occur in epidemics—a form of hysteria, one wants to say, in spite of the outrage to etymology—and its explanation surely has something to do with the fairly common belief that Asian men have small penises. Pretty common too, it seems, or in particular among those who ought to know. And then there are the cargo cults of Melanesia and New Guinea where a frequently psychotic leader persuades his followers that an ancestor or a benefactor is about to bless them with great material wealth or spiritual powers. Closer to home, we have Jim Jones, the Solar Temple and Hale-Bopp.[42]

And then, of course, there are the French. None of the above cases begins to establish, although the question did come up in Chapter 3, that the taxonomy of mental disorders is somehow relative. Most of them map straight on to a disorder or type or mixed diagnosis in *DSM-IV* and are triggered or informed by local conditions and sometimes by myths and legends, as in windigo. The disorder is becoming rarer as belief in spirits among the Ojibwa recedes—but shorn of spirits, windigo is a sort of dissociative environmentally-induced manic-depression or a fancy form of posttraumatic stress disorder. The only halfway difficult case is "Crazy-dog-wishing-to-die" syndrome. Quite genuine sexual identity disorders are sometimes involved here but there are all sorts of other cases. Children sometimes play this game or with this myth or this ideal of contraries. And it does fascinate. I suspect that its prevalence among the Plains Indians and its elevation to the status of a disorder says as much about their sense of humour as it does about their pathology. The French, however, do things very differently.

The Capgras syndrome has at its core a delusion of doubles or impostors in people who are usually closely related to the victim. So one's lover, wife, husband, daughter, father might be both a stranger and not—and the possibility of erotic thrills is right on the surface. In the Fregoli syndrome—also French in everything but name and perhaps only a variant of Capgras—a particular person, usually close again, "takes over" the bodies of other people, not always but often strangers. At least as intriguing. And then there's De Clerambault's syndrome, the delusion that some person, typically famous, is in love with one. Why should love or anyway titillation be at the basis of so many disorders? Well, something rather like this but on a much grander scale was tried in Vienna around the turn of the century. Many of the profession still have a fair amount of faith in it and some are wholly committed. Besides, De Clerambault's syndrome is pretty much *DSM-IV*'s erotomania—and it is the French we are discussing.

But the French have Cotard's syndrome as well, delusions of negation. What is negated or denied can be anything of importance. So someone might believe that the world is completely silent or devoid of opportunity or interest or that others have no thoughts or no feelings. And depersonalization and derealization are extreme forms, paradigms in a way, of the syndrome. Psychoses that are central to the taxonomy, great Gallic shrugs of disorders, full of nausea and nihilism, anguish and nonbeing. The French also recognize some of the more old-fashioned disorders that are still diagnosed in certain parts of Europe—

degenerative psychosis, psychogenic psychosis and so on. Are these eccentricities simply la foie revisited but this time on the psychological level?

I don't think they are. I think the French raise legitimate questions about a taxonomy like *DSM-IV*'s. These questions coincide with mine over depersonalization and derealization but they are comparatively limited in number. Nevertheless, the precedent for such questions is there among the French—and the French are, after all, Westernized, intelligent and more or less civilized. But again, the questions I have brought up are not motivated by any sort of generalized scepticism or relativism. They are quite specific questions about a quite particular concept or family of concepts.[43]

I have, however, left until last what is in some respects the most puzzling and the worst example—hysteria, one of the examples that Szasz fastens on so shrewdly. *DSM-IV*, as I've said, has dropped hysteria although with no fanfare. Whether or not it was right to do so can wait for a little while. But in *DSM-III-R*—only a short time ago in the mind of the profession—all of the following were described as "hysterical": conversion neurosis, somatoform pain disorder, multiple personality disorder, psychogenic amnesia, psychogenic fugue, depersonalization and derealization, histrionic personality disorder, brief reactive psychosis and factitious disorder with psychological symptoms. A strange collection. What sort of thread runs through these cases?

Conversion disorder is much more common in females than males. Certain forms of pain disorder are observed more frequently in females. Multiple personality disorder is anywhere from three to nine times more common in females. Both psychogenic amnesia and histrionic personality disorder are, according to *DSM-III-R*, most often seen in females—although *DSM-IV*, in both cases, is much more circumspect. There are no relevant figures, for either *DSM-III-R* or *DSM-IV*, on psychogenic fugue, depersonalization and derealization or brief psychosis, reactive or otherwise. They both agree, on the other hand, that factitious disorder with psychological symptoms is more common in males. Finally, somatization disorder—which, as *DSM-III-R* acknowledges, is sometimes referred to, simply, as "hysteria"—is rarely diagnosed in males—at any rate, as *DSM-IV* adds cautiously or is it smugly?, not in the United States. How did it happen? How could it happen?

Take conversion disorder and somatization disorder; these two constitute the classical core of the notion of hysteria and they have, historically, a distinctly female air about them. Throw in somatoform

pain disorder with its predominantly female belly-aching. Throw in
multiple personality disorder and psychogenic amnesia—Freudian
cases perhaps but more common in females—and then let's include the
allegedly similar psychogenic fugue and depersonalization and
derealization. Add histrionic personality disorder, of course; there's
women for you. What on earth are we going to do about brief psychotic disorder, cross-sectionally identical to any psychosis but oddly—
or should it be suspiciously?—a brief and one-time or rarely recurrent
thing? Throw that in too. And to finish up? Let's invent a disorder.
Let's invent factitious disorder and with psychological symptoms, in
particular, and include it too. Isn't there something intrinsically female
about lying even though the statistics don't bear this out? Besides,
putting it in will show we're not biased and not driven, merely, by
etymology. Even if we're Freudians and therefore wedded in some
ways to the past, we're not driven just or only or exclusively by it,
however suggestive and exploitable it might be. It's as though *DSM-
III-R* wanted a scandal.

   DSM-IV, once again, has abandoned hysteria. Those who were
brought up on *DSM-IV*, however, are mostly still doing their residen-
cies. The vast majority of the practising profession were trained and
educated on the basis of something earlier, whether *DSM-III-R*, *ICD-9*
or whatever. Hysteria, this many-headed and blatantly sexist disorder
in *DSM-III-R*, is fixed deep within the psychiatric consciousness. The
American Psychiatric Association has, again, tried to get its act
together here. It might be a worthwhile exercise in mental hygiene to
say so—loudly and publicly.

   Should we just junk hysteria? Perhaps. Or we could, instead, retain
it in a much narrower form covering no more than conversion neurosis,
somatization disorder and, maybe, some of the other somatoform
disorders and some of the dissociative disorders. While its history—
and its recent history, in particular—might have been unfortunate, there
are plausible arguments for the theoretical integrity of such a notion.
But perhaps the American Psychiatric Association was right on this
one; truly radical surgery might, indeed, have been in order.

   And why, finally, don't we do the right studies on the relative
incidence of all these disorders in males and females? *DSM-IV*, as
should be evident, sometimes offers softened or more careful estimates
than did *DSM-III-R*. So there is, again, no hint of an imbalance
towards either sex for dissociative amnesia or histrionic personality
disorder, there is the hemming and hawing over whether men might
succumb to the latter and only some versions of pain disorder, not all,
are said to be more common in females. But then again and by

contrast, it is not merely that one symptom of conversion disorder is more common in females as it is in *DSM-III-R*; the disorder itself is more common in *DSM-IV* by a factor of between two and ten. How can the studies provide such different results over so short a period? And who, exactly, is doing the studies? The situation out there in the field, as I say, is anyone's guess in general—and it has got to be, at times, pretty frightening.[44]

There are other disorders that give rise to doubts and questions: the gender identity disorders and kleptomania, some of the eating disorders and phobias of bizarre sorts and panic attacks over, it seems, the very act of breathing, the more exotic or revolting sexual disorders, perhaps, like klismaphalia or necrophilia and, of course, borderline personality disorder. But these doubts and questions are, I think, mostly of a less basic or serious nature. And we have, anyway, done enough of this. So I am going to stop here to sum up.

Our concepts of madness, neurosis and personality disorder, both in general and with regard to more particular examples, are a mess. They are not all as much of a mess as is the concept or subconcept of schizophrenia. For there the landscape can be redrawn very differently and in various ways whereas some of the questions I have raised in connection with this or that other example have not been of an undermining sort. But it is also true that large parts of the rest of the taxonomy can be rethought and to a significant extent or on a significant scale. There is something right about the grouping of the so-called "mood" disorders—although their separation from the panic and anxiety disorders and, for that matter, intermittent explosive disorder is surely arbitrary. The sexual disorders, if disorders or mental disorders they are, constitute another obvious group and there is something right again about the somatoform or body disorders as there is about some of the personality disorders. Still and all, these concepts of madness, schizophrenia, depression, obsessive-compulsive disorder, multiple personality disorder and, say, histrionic or narcissistic personality disorder are in pretty deplorable shape. Then there is the concept of organic or nonprimary or nonfunctional mental disorders, the brain cases. As concepts go, they are crude, ill-defined, ad hoc, fundamentally problematic, sometimes wildly conjectural.

This makes life difficult for everyone—for the patients, for the members of the profession and also for philosophers. These concepts have, again, a relatively short history as concepts go. They are likely to have—on, as it were, a priori grounds—a peculiar characteristic. They are likely to contain prejudices, misguided assumptions whose truth we seem to have learned when we were young. Not only are they likely to;

they sometimes do. This can, let me repeat, be a difficult business. We are all able to distinguish, in principle, between a conceptual fact and some mistaken view about a concept. But here we have to be close enough to the view to insist that it is part of our concept, distant enough to see it as a prejudice. Then a conceptual fact turns into a mistaken view about the concept we ought to have. So we get a tight-rope sort of problem. Close enough to feel, and reasonably, that it is in our conceptual blood but far enough away to argue, and reasonably, that we ought to reject it. None of this, though, makes the problem insuperable. For these concepts, these snapshots from a hundred years ago and from the forties and fifties and sixties have become outdated. In some ways, they always were.

The Self—and Related Matters

Before we get to the self or as a preamble, some comments about the faculties or the compartments of the mind and a few remarks about strategy. So—the faculties or basic building blocks of the mind. What are they?

Well, there's memory, of course. And there's the will and the emotions—and thought or reason or understanding. There's perception. And there's introspection—in addition or as one kind of example. There's the self. And there's...what? What have I left out? For the chief danger here is a sin of omission.

I mentioned, earlier on, Descartes's lists. If we add the imagination, we have taken care of Descartes. Hume's preferred list when doing epistemology is the senses, reason and the imagination. He does, however, oppose reason to the emotions—and he takes both the memory and the will to be of considerable significance. But we have taken care of all that. Hume on the self?—or a sin of commission? We will get to Hume's doubts in a little while.

Should we add desire, interest, intention? We could list them—but let's subsume them under the will. Beliefs? They can be included with thought or reason. The stream of consciousness? It does have close ties with introspection and also with thought—so it could be included under each of them. But things are starting to get very murky. The preconscious?—and the unconscious? I don't know. They cut across memory, the will, the emotions and so on. They can also be explained—in part at least and in different ways—in introspective terms. But doesn't the stream of consciousness cut across thoughts and feelings?—and isn't it closely connected to memory? So I really don't know. I don't know if any of this second group of items should be on our list of basic components or elements of the mind.

Sensation? There's introspection again and there's perception—but perhaps sensation should be given a place. Imagery? Perhaps—though there is a great deal of overlap with imagination. Intelligence? Well, yes—but doesn't that come under reason? Language-learning or processing? Language is not thought and neither is thought language—but they are, again, closely related. Habits? Maybe again. Instinct or appetite? All right.

Anything else? Thought or reason is getting to be a pretty big bag but maybe we can't do much better with this not very precise notion of the basic areas or components of the mind. We have, though, enough for what we need. Look at the list: memory, the will, the emotions, thought, perception, introspection, the imagination, sensation, habit, instinct, the self. *DSM-IV* chooses from this list emotions and thought as the foundation of its taxonomy—with an occasional aside to perception, say, or volition. There is no argument for this way of doing things, no evidence that this perspective and no other is correct—in *DSM-IV* or anywhere else. Hume did, again, contrast reason and emotion in one of his views. But there are other contrasts, other views, other basic aspects or elements of the mind. They are simply ignored by *DSM-IV*.

We also have enough to raise a critical philosophical problem: How, exactly, are all these faculties related to the self? So out of these simple questions comes this most profound of concepts. For isn't the self what the faculties somehow compose?—or is it that the relation between the self and some, at least, of its faculties is less intimate? And we mustn't forget to ask the standard questions for all faculty talk: Isn't such talk explanatorily useless?—and doesn't it involve a paradox in making each of us many? I will return to these questions towards the end of the discussion.[45]

And now for strategy. One of the claims I am arguing for is that there is no reason for choosing *DSM-IV*'s taxonomy over certain alternatives. I am not in the business of defending *DSM-IV* and the view that the concepts of thought and emotion are legitimate and that the distinction between them is important; I'll leave that to others. But I do feel the need to defend the two major alternatives I am suggest-ing—partly, of course, because I am suggesting them but partly because both of the concepts at issue—that of the self and that of the will—have been looked on with suspicion by philosophers. Both of them—but especially the first.

So what of the self, the self itself? In Chapter 1, I referred briefly to reflexivity, to the "Self/Not-self" distinction and to unity or indivisibil-ity. Two points should be made. Reflexive concerns have to do with self-reference, for example, or self-apprehension and the question of whether the self can introspect itself. And it ought to be clear by now that some sort of unity or indivisibility can be demanded of only the sane or the normal.

We have to recognize, going in, that the concept of the self might well turn out to be a bit of a collage. There might be no clean and tidy way of mapping the above concerns on to one another and there might be other concerns. But I am going to start with James's "Self/Not-self" distinction. If we could get straight about the right-hand side, about all the things you own or possess, all the things you're related to, all the millions of things you don't possess and are not even related to except, perhaps, in some refined philosophical sense of that word—if we could get straight about all that, we would know what the self is by simple subtraction. So this is, as James realizes, the distinction that is crucial. There are, however, problems here. Your parts, taken collectively of course, are you. But what are we to do with your properties—your height, your weight, your wit? Are they possessions though of a rather special sort? And, James warns us, we are dealing with a "fluctuating material". Indeed, he suggests, in a moment of exuberance, that one might include, in one's self, one's "wife" and "children", one's "reputation" and "works", one's "yacht" and "bank-account". But this does raise the familiar question of whether your body is merely yours and mine merely mine—or whether our bodies are parts of us or, maybe, even us.[46]

We have, as is noted by Ryle among a number of others, two ways of talking here. We say "I burned my leg" or "I burned myself", "He bumped into me" or "He stuck his great fat chest into my shoulder". We say "I'm getting creaky" or "My body is beginning to betray me", "I'm feeling better" or "My body is finally recovering from the physical effects". Our language, then, is quite noncommittal.

But, as is less often noted, we do exactly the same with the mind—or most, at least, of the mind. We say "I'm becoming more forgetful" or "My memory's going on the blink", "I'm far too emotional" or "I can't control my feelings", "I'm sober" or "My mind is behaving, thank you, precisely as it ought to". Our language seems to think that just as the body belongs to James's fluctuating material, so too does the mind—or, as I say, most of it anyway. For don't we need something to hold on to? Still and all, though, and even if we do, we can, it seems, say what we like over most of the territory.

And speaking of language, we seldom use the word "self" in ordinary conversation. There are the personal pronouns, of course, where "self" is encapsulated. But they apply to everyone. And then there are all those double-barrelled expressions in which "self" is merely hyphenated: "self-service", "self-aggrandisement", "self-denial", "self-deception", "self-confidence". They seem to have little in common but reflexivity—a theme emphasized by the pronouns. And then, sometimes, "self" will occur by itself in an arch or a pretentious remark. There's someone playing with a theory, we think, so the remark is not ordinary in the required sense. Back in the sixties, one couldn't say anything philosophically if it wasn't positively endorsed by what we ordinarily nonphilosophically say. Those days, thankfully, are gone. But here is an ordinary concept that is pretty crude and pretty minimal. So if you have a concept of the self that is at all complex, at all structured or elaborate, it will be, to a considerable extent, a technical concept. We already knew that this must be so. The concept of the self employed in philosophy and psychology is of something animate and psychological in spite of the impersonal pronoun. But a partly technical concept is partly made-up. So if you have a theory about the self, it will be a theory about something partly made-up. It must also be said that philosophers who discuss the self typically have more than one self, more than one concept. Descartes, for example, has at least two, Locke three, Kant two, Husserl two, James four or five. Freud has two—or is it three? Nagel has two and even Dennett, in a way, has two. A bad case of the ambiguities, apparently—for all these writers agree that a number of accounts of the self can be given. We are back with James's fluctuating territory. James did, after all, help himself to a rather injudiciously large number.[47]

But there is a question about this fluctuating territory that we have not yet asked. For any one of us, many many things go on the right-hand "Not-self" side of the above distinction. Suppose there are some things—the body, for example—that lie in an area where we can say what we like. Is there anything that must, if it is true of me at all, go on the left-hand side? Not: Must anything be true of me? This question is raised by philosophers but it is not the one I have in mind. Rather: Is anything true of me, necessarily, contingently or whatever, such that it must, if and when it is true of me, be explained in terms of the left-hand side of James's distinction? Is there anything I can't distance myself from, can't see as off or out or over there?[48]

I have, it will be noticed, put the question in the first-person. It is by no means the clearest of questions. I think, though, that I have enough of a grasp of it to be able to sketch an answer. The distance is in many cases spatial. Just think of the external senses and how they distance what is beyond the skin. Think of the proprioceptive sense or the stomach growling or the toes feeling numb. The introspection of sensations this time—and yet still spatial. And then, with thoughts, space suddenly drops out. A thought of dinner offers itself—but why bother about it just yet? A feeling, of humiliation or loss, but an old one I've pretty much learned to live with. A desire that I've fought against a hundred times and know I will fight a hundred times more. But these thoughts and feelings and desires are not spatial. Neither, on the other hand, are they me. In fact, I am composed of no such elements. Thoughts and feelings are what I have had or experienced, acquired or developed. I am the one who has them. I am—whatever I can't set over or against myself. Me, the inner core.

I go back to James. His official version of the "self of selves" or the "sanctuary within the citadel" is oddly humbling—even or perhaps especially when his contrived and only momentarily held title is tacked on. I am, James says, my present thought. I am, then, extremely circumscribed, very small. This search for a centre or for smallness often lurks behind talk of unity or indivisibility. But this is to say that many other philosophers have had very small or focused concepts of the self, almost always understandably mental. Hume, for example. What he rejects is just such a concept. And trying to withdraw into oneself, certainly, into one's bare psychic essence, has to be about as reflexive an exercise as one could ever undertake.[49]

Any question that is good enough for Hume and for James, however, is good enough for me. So for me—allowing for the possible difficulties of introspection that can, James says, be "desperately hard" in this instance—it is a matter of a vague central presence. This presence portrays itself as a "this" or a "here" or a "this here". As opposed to—everything. Everything out there with which it is nevertheless connected because it can sense them and sometimes push them around. Just as it is introspectively acquainted with and can in some ways control its thoughts. It presents itself as a source for there is a "from this" or a "from here" about it. Part of this is spatial again. But I also have this sense, especially if I close my eyes, of me some-how nonspatially behind my thoughts, crouching further in, the source of all this attention and control. And then, sometimes, I am aware of myself by myself. As a faint glow, on occasion, when day-dreaming, for example, or a mere receiver, during an exam, waiting for that next thought to form or a centre, alert and attentive, at that sudden noise in the dark. But even in these cases, I might be persuaded, there is this surrounding sense of from-this-or-here-to-that-or-there.

For James, it "consists mainly of the collection of ... peculiar motions in the head or between the head and throat." Although James includes in these motions "acts of assenting or negating" and "feelings of welcoming and rejecting", I think this is just his tough-minded positivistic side leading him to make too concrete this familiar sense of a presence. But James also maintains, under the heading of "how all men, up to a certain point, would describe it", that the self is the "source of effort and attention." And the results of his introspective experiment have to do, he emphasizes, only with what is felt—and by him, James.

For me? For James? There is another disclaimer in the *Treatise*. "For my part, when I enter most intimately into what I call *myself*, I always stumble on some particular perception or other, of heat or cold, light or shade, love or hatred, pain or pleasure. I never can catch *myself* at any time without a perception, and, never can observe anything but the perception." Hume has been influential on this question. How are we to understand his introspective blindness? And how far have we got with the self?

Hume came to this experiment crippled by a crude empiricist theory of meaning and with the sometimes clear recognition that the key concept of identity has already been fatally compromised in earlier discussions of existence, time and the senses, half-exhausted and half-feverish in these closing nihilistic sections of Book I and insisting that his own strict sort of simplicity and complete and absolute invariability are among the criteria, a little anxious more generally or metaphysically anxious, like Descartes, that he might face extinction if he were to cease to think—and, on top of all this, Hume was a lousy introspector with very little notion of what he was looking for. He thought of the mental as being composed of images, usually visual, or, sometimes, sensations—these predominantly stream of consciousness phenomena. So introspection was: "You know; what you do with images or sensations." Hume would have missed anything subtle or complicated, anything involving patterns or connections or rhythms. He would, in a way and like Descartes, have been baffled about the entire area of the mind that is not, at any given moment, part of the stream of conscious-ness. And as for what he was looking for in the present case, he thought, again, that it ought to be like an image or a sensation. That, not surprisingly, is all he found.[50]

The self as one more source of attention and control in the universe is obviously of enormous importance. It is what marks us off—or helps to, at any rate, and along with birds and monkeys and perhaps even bees—from what merely responds or doesn't do that and it links us with angels and aliens. It is essential to our concepts of perception, thought and action. And we can now fill the hole in Hume's "bundle".

For isn't it precisely the self that is not there in Hume's sea of "impressions" and "ideas"?

I confess to two reservations here and a qualification should be added to what I have said. I have tried to separate my philosophical views from my views about what is available to introspection. But have I, like Hume, allowed the former to affect the latter? Not, I think, as to the existence of the self in introspection but to its existence as a source? All I can say is that I have done what I could and tried to keep things clean. That is all one can say. And there are, besides, nonintrospective philosophical arguments for this concept of a source of attention and control.

But I am also philosophically uneasy about this notion of a source, a notion I have described, in part, no more than metaphorically. Much more could be done in an attempt to spell out the sorts of control and sensory or near-sensory acquaintance we have over and with our minds and bodies and through them, of course, various parts, some mental, some physical, of the rest of the world. I suspect, however, that this notion of a source, a brute "This" or "This here" or "This and not that" contains unspeakable mysteries. It is analogous to this equally obscure and unnerving notion we all have of an inner mental voice. And for us, for grown-up sophisticated speaking selves, the link is even more direct. But what is it to speak, to have and use a voice at all? What sort of picture or inner image could I have of my own public speech? What of the hermit and of talking to oneself and of privacy or growing up alone? And what, exactly, is wrong and what is right about Plato's view of thinking as a conversation with oneself?

Which brings me to the qualification. It is that this concept of the self as a source of attention and control is offered as a candidate for only a minimal or very small concept of the self. There is a question we have been postponing. What else is important? We can, not unreasonably, add other accretions or requirements. A rather higher level of intelligence than is already presupposed and some modest sort of memory. Maybe, even, some fundamental beliefs and instincts. The emotions, though, and imagination seem strangely irrelevant. Aren't they more in the way of refinements or the results of particular directions of evolution? Indeed, don't we all know people with only the most blunted emotional lives or examples of little or no imagination? The former, for Hume, would be paralyzed but Hume did smuggle desires, pains and pleasures and even instincts into emotions; the latter might be the result of having no intellectual individuality, of being a Borg, say. We should be reminded of the unconscious here— once again, not every human being has an unconscious—and perhaps,

even, of the preconscious—the mind of a hamster can't have much of
the preconscious about it either. Nevertheless, more robust or elaborate
concepts of the self can be constructed and I have not meant to rule
them out. But even here, I would want to emphasize the central and
important position that should, in any larger concept, be given to the
self as this attentive controlling being. We have, then, answered one of
our questions about faculties, if only very roughly. The will, perception, introspection—together, again, with some level of intelligence—
these are most critical. They cannot be separated from the self. Other
faculties or compartments, by contrast, play less of a role or seem more
subject to individual variation.[51]

But now for the body in all of this. Or, to put things rather differently, now for the entire crew—or the more respectable members of it,
at any rate—and then the decision. I am not going to consider disembodied existence. The notion is a dubious one and I will simply set it
aside. Which leaves us, basically, with two sorts of selves. Both
involve a body. But for exclusively mental selves, the self is merely
associated or linked, perhaps necessarily, with a body; for "public"
selves, the body is part of or even identical to the self. We can,
however, surely reject the self as being entirely constituted by the body.
This is, at best, a degenerate throwaway concept with little application.
We can also reject the obviously implausible self as substance—and the
equally implausible self as a Kantian kind of abstract entity. The self
must, it seems, have something to do with the mind and/or the body.
So the only real contenders are the purely mental selves, of different
sizes but all associated with a body, and those that include some part of
the mind, at least, along with the body.

The arguments? It will be said that there is a problem about
location for purely mental selves. Where, exactly, are they? The
problem is of no consequence; it can easily be resolved by reference to
the associated body. A purely mental self is, approximately, where the
associated body is. For neither can "public" selves be given an exact
location, not even as exact as the body. It will also be said that there is
a problem about counting or individuation for purely mental selves.
Couldn't two minds be qualitatively indistinguishable?—so on what
grounds could we then count two? But again, the problem can easily
be handled in terms of the associated body. We can just stipulate that,
in normal cases anyway, one mind or one self goes with one body. We
do, after all, identify people at times by the most incidental or trifling
features. "The one you were talking to earlier on" or "The one in the
long grey coat", "The one whose aunt died of fright" or "The one we
have agreed not to discuss". And this, of course, is one reason for the

enormous variability as well as the enormous tenacity of reference. Isn't there, though, a causal problem about purely mental selves? There is; we talked about it a while ago. According to Mutual Mapping Theory, it will be solved by the future of science. According to Identity Theory and Supervenience, it will be replaced by another about identity or supervenience that will be solved by the future of science. And "public" selves give rise to the same dilemma. They too sanction these allegedly illicit causal relations between very different sorts of properties. Everyone has some version of this problem. And while our dismissal of the notion of substance is based, in part at least, on its having no properties, even the very small and exclusively mental selves have some properties. And how many properties does an entity need in order to able to exist? The arguments, then, are quite indecisive.[52]

Our language? It is, as I say, noncommittal. This is not, however, just a matter of the way we talk. It permeates our thinking. We think or conceptualize of ourselves as separate, standing back from, opposed to our bodies and most at least of our minds. We are deeply divided on this.

We have reached a conclusion. We reached it quite a while ago. Our concept of the self provides no answer to the question of whether the body and how much of the mind belong to the self. It leaves it up to us, to be settled by what we take to be important—and here we have another source of the enormous variability of reference.

Us—or our faculties? I have already suggested a kind of answer to that question. Some faculties, that is, are more closely related to the self than others. But aren't faculty explanations useless? Three strands of criticism should be separated out: As many faculties have to be postulated as we possess abilities; the faculties must have the same properties as the self and thus reproduce the original problem; what sort of answer to "How is it that one can do that and that kind of thing" is "One has the faculty, the wherewithal or the wit, to make it possible"? The proper responses, respectively, are: Of course they don't, the point of faculty talk being precisely to get lots of explanations out of a few faculties; of course they need not though they might in some inept versions of faculty talk; not much of an answer, not much of one at all. Faculties don't explain much. It depends on what you do with them but simply listing them doesn't explain much, any more than listing the main themes or headings on any topic explains much. I didn't intend it to.[53]

I do want to repeat, however, that what is considered by us to be important is crucial in any very specific concept of the self. This can, to be sure, attract the opportunistic or the woolly-minded. But it can, instead, be treated reasonably and responsibly, with self-consciousness and common sense. I have tried, in the above, to be on my guard about this.

Existentialists of the Sartrean persuasion, it occurs to me to add, proclaim that existence—for us for-itselfs—precedes essence. Nothing is fixed. Everything, always, is possible and equally. Eliminate the obvious falsehoods, make the doctrine less extreme, round off the rough edges. Isn't this just an exaggerated as well as a highly dramatized version of a plain fact, of what I have called "the enormous variability of reference"? But isn't this, in turn, a fact about, not merely self-reference, but reference in general?[54]

I have, in this discussion of the self, highlighted the attention and the will. Some often neglected questions about the latter will take up much of the next section but I should say a little more at this point about this notion of ours of attention, of sensory or near-sensory attention. This is Locke's way of putting the alternatives. He says of introspection, his "reflection", that it is not vision, in particular, but "very like" it. Earlier on in this chapter, I discussed introspection at some length. So first, a few more words about introspection—and then some more about sight and touch and so on. I will finish up by coming back to the question of how useful the self is in taxonomy—and thus we begin to move sideways out of this section just as we drifted into it.[55]

Is introspection, we have to ask, a sense? Well, is there an introspective sense-organ? Perhaps—but is a sense-organ necessary? And what is the sense-organ for touch? The tips of the fingers, the entire skin?—and how deep inside? What for the proprioceptive sense? For telepathy? And what sense do we employ when we feel the shifting of liquids or gases in the stomach or a gurgling or a rumbling? Is there a medium for introspection? Perhaps again—but what is the medium for taste or telepathy or that sense sometimes that one is being watched? In any case, if introspecting is not sensing, what is it? It would have to be a form of thinking—this easy distinction we make between the two—but even then, it would have to be thinking of a very special information-gathering or information-obtaining kind. An analogue, at least, for the mind of sight, say, or hearing for the external world. Can it break down or malfunction? It can indeed—but let's set that aside for a moment.

The external senses acquaint us with certain familiar features of our environment. They each have a hallucinatory mode or a hallucinatory companion—and they each have, or are usually regarded as having, a corresponding sort of imagery. They can be heavily influenced by our most basic beliefs. And they differ, as should already be evident, among themselves. Touch seems to be several senses ranging from playing the piano to feeling the sun on one's back to—why not?—the stomach growling again—and maybe introspection is several senses too. We cannot adjust, but only cock our ears or sniff with our noses. Taste is like touch and unlike smell, vision and hearing in requiring gross physical contact with its object. Smell is nondirectional, like taste—though what about touch? And while we can have a taste of coffee or experience the smell of a rose, what do we have or experience of what's in front of our eyes? A look? A glimpse? And do we have a hear of a noise? Echoes of sense-data. These days, they're usually called "sensations"—and as soon as one says it, one knows, still, that more than terminology is at stake. For how many visual sensations do you have right now? By all accounts, quite a large number. But less than you would have if you were looking at a bicycle race or out over the city at night? And do all accounts come close to agreeing on the number in these various situations? Let's go with the received wisdom, though, this seemingly inevitable reification or too inflexible reification in the realm of the senses. Are auditory hallucinations, for example, similar blips in the stream of consciousness to those involved in hearing the real thing? Of course they are—although one might or might not be gulled, Austin was right about that. Images are similar too. But are images always involved in hallucinations? It's not so clear. And of course causality has a lot to do with it in one way or another—as does representation and even imagery on some sufficiently wide or casual reading of these enormously vague terms. There are defects in seeing that won't show up at the optometrist, in smell that only a "nose" would recognize, in touch that simply boggle the mind. But a question that is not often discussed is that of whether we have privileged and direct or introspective access to our visual, auditory or tactile sensations. Not infallible, by any means—but privileged and direct. Of course we do. The common acquaintance we have with the external senses and introspection, the similarity? It is acquaintance with a living, a constantly changing reality. The acquaintance? It too is of the living variety.[56]

We can now state a broader conclusion. The concept of the self is, indeed, something of a patchwork. Central to it are James's distinction between "Self" and "Not-self" and some not very clearly related questions, to the distinction or among themselves, about reflexivity. Arising from a consideration of the distinction and the reflexive question of the self's introspectibility is this notion of the self as a source of attention and control. Unity or indivisibility? There are all sorts of ways in which the mind can split or fragment. Cases of multiple personality disorder, for example, or psychogenic fugue. Freudian cases more generally and cases where the emotions are alarmingly at odds with reason or where belief doesn't fit with desire. Schizophrenics of some kinds and obsessive-compulsives—and, what is one of the least fathomable splits of all, a division in this source of attention and control in cases like Janet's and James's Lucie who could carry on one conversation with her mouth and another, completely insulated from it, with notes written by her left hand in response to questions from over her shoulder. A form of coconsciousness, it should be noted. And here in particular—though in some of these other cases as well—we feel a strong temptation to speak of two selves. For the notion of unity or indivisibility—this requirement of normality—is built into this notion of a single individual source. And this notion also provides us with one sort of halfway palatable answer to another question not infrequently asked under the heading of the "Self": What is unique about each of us? Any answer, by contrast, in terms of our generosity, say, or our originality would be hard to defend. But it must, once again, be acknowledged that other, larger, selves can be con-structed—and then the relations among the various strands become even more questionable, even more strained. And, given the quasitech-nical nature of the concept of the self, is it so surprising that some writers go on at great length about self-image or self-esteem?

So what are we left with for the mad and taxonomy? I have argued for a view of the self. And the cases I listed earlier of psychotic breakdowns in or of the self were depersonalization, catatonic stupor and hebephrenia. I mentioned paranoia and paranoid schizophrenia as perhaps borderline examples—and I raised questions about multiple personality disorder and autism. A little later, I referred to induced psychotic disorder and some cases of mania. The extent to which these cases involve marked breakdowns in the self or in attention and control should be obvious. But the concept of the self, it must be admitted, is a fluid one.   It is therefore potentially dangerous for taxonomical purposes unless it is handled with great care. Not an impossible thing to do but perhaps it is all too easy in the end to explain this or that disorder in terms of some maybe plausible though usually vaguely described view of the self, too easy to try in terms of some totally garbled account.

There can be no question of dispensing with the self. But if, because of its slipperiness, we prefer the categories of the attention and the will themselves for taxonomy, we should think, along or overlap-ping with the above list and starting with the attention, of Freudian cases again with their introspective barriers or failures and those schizophrenics again with their voices and hallucinations. For don't hallucinations, again, excite the sensory parts of the brain? And aren't they, once more, indistinguishable sometimes from the real thing? Visual hallucinations, of course, interfere with vision, auditory ones with hearing and so on—and vision can be completely disfigured by delusions. It is, on the other hand, hard to know what to make of the studies suggesting that the senses of schizophrenics are otherwise impaired. And then there are different kinds of confusional states where the external senses are clouded or distorted and there's oneiroform schizophrenia, in particular. Then the cases of schizophrenia, say, or mania where introspection, quite generally, can't do justice or keep up. And as for the will, the obsessive-compulsives again and the kleptomaniacs, the catatonically excited and those with abulia or many of the depressed—and we will, once again, discuss this in greater detail and with more background in the next section. But it is, we should remember, a discussion of the self that has thrown these notions—of the attention and the will—into prominence. And then again, it must be asked: How different would this section have been had it been written by Marilyn Monroe or Annie Lennox, Arnold Schwarznegger or Jack Nicholson?

There are some other unanswered questions. Is there anything I can't distance myself from? The best candidate seems to be this, this source of attention and control. I can't, for myself, put it away from myself. You can—for you can see me asleep or in a coma. James's distinction, it turns out, has a reflexive aspect to it. Is there something we need to hold on to? Only when we're awake—although then we have no say in the matter. Is it the same thing, the same source, when we wake up the next morning? Only by courtesy of that large part of the mind that does not belong to the stream of consciousness—or perhaps again of the body. Or by Einstein, instead, or Jonathan Winters, Bobby Fischer or Garcia Marquez?[57]

The Will—and Free Will

I approach this topic of the will through a consideration of a number of problems, the last of which is that of freedom. They are linked to one another in various ways—as should, as we proceed, become clear.

The will is obviously related to desire. But to put the problem more generally, is the will exhausted by, can its operations be explained solely in terms of, desire, interest, emotion and so on or what Hume called its "influencing motives"? No. Strength of will or resolve is possessed to different degrees by different people or by one person on different occasions. It is what enables us to fight sometimes against urgent or persistent desires, to resist what can be almost overwhelming temptation. There is, perhaps, the possibility of different thresholds for desire or pleasure but this cannot account for the huge range of cases or the diversity of their descriptions. And it is surely a truism that some people are strong-willed and some weak. But isn't the possession of resolve itself subject to the will? One can resolve to have more resolve in the future and be successful in one's resolution. This is difficult to do but those who are weak of will can, we might feel, be despised on this score. And then again, courage, like dignity or a sense of self-worth, is so often something one is born with or acquires, anyway, before the age of five or ten. And things are harder, besides, for the weak of will than they are for the strong. That's just what it means to be weak.[58]

But if the will does exist over and above its desires and motives, mustn't there be acts or exercises of the will? Mustn't there be volitions? Even those who have reservations about some of his other attempts to dismantle the mind are often persuaded by Ryle's attack on volitions. How many did you have or effect before breakfast?, Ryle asked—and the resulting silence, first puzzled, then gleeful, was supposed to amount to an argument. But for what? How many thoughts did you have before breakfast? How many feelings? How many decisions did you make in writing that memo or mowing the lawn? Does the impossibility of giving any very sensible reply mean the right answer is "None—and neither could there be any"? Of course there are volitions. Think of resisting an after-dinner drink or cigarette or of forcing yourself to open that letter, of beginning to concentrate again on the knot in your plans or of firing the starting pistol exactly, right, now. Or think of the last time you tried to thread a needle or of a paraplegic breaking into a sweat with the effort to move his or her limbs. And think, in long drawn out activities like walking, of pulling yourself away from the river you've stopped to look at for a while, of reminding yourself as you turn left to the store that you have butter to buy, of bearing down on that last little steep bit. Do volitions occur in any clear-cut way in all cases of intentional or voluntary action? Of course not. Much of our behaviour is more unthinking, automatic or second-nature—though an awful lot of volitions as we grew up went into making it so. And some of it, perhaps, is too arbitrary or random. But then again, something that is more, or more or less, unthinking or practised or quite unexpected might also be, arguably or to some extent, a matter of volition. A more subtle or nuanced one or one that is no more than a momentary flicker at the edge of the mind. And neither is there a continuous volition in walking or a succession with no gaps—although there are all sorts of willings and tryings, avoidings and though there are all sorts of willings and tryings, avoidings and committings and little decisions. This fact, that there are not always volitions, means that a definition of voluntariness in terms of volitions and nothing else can't be given, that volitions had better not figure in any simple one-dimensional explanation of why we do what we do. Still and all, they have to play a substantial part in any definition or comprehensive explanation. Are we always aware of our volitions? No again—any more than we are always aware of our thoughts or our thoughts in general. But we do, as we do with the latter and as Descartes believed, have privileged access to our volitions. We often know, and directly, that we are exercising our will to do this, that or the other. Isn't there, though, a regress hovering over this notion of a volition? Yes. Just as one can resolve to be more resolute, so one can and sometimes must, if it's going to get done, will oneself to will. Again, this is difficult. And that one doesn't always have to is essential to the operation of the will. The question, however, is whether the regress, in the cases where it comes up, is at all worrying. It isn't. The threat fades in the light of the thought that many of our volitions are at least half-automatic or semi-routine. It disappears completely with the recognition that the difference between one level of willing and the next one up in the relatively noncomplex human mind very quickly dissipates, simply ceases to have application. The experience or contemplation of this regress, whether phenomenological or philosophical, is felt as a vacillation or a flip-flopping in the problem of the strength and weakness of the will.[59]

Is someone with no desire—and no interests and no needs—capable of exercising his or her will or of volitions? I am inclined to say so. I see little wrong with the Existentialist notion of wholly spontaneous action—although it won't help, of course, to try to bring one off in order to prove the theory. But why couldn't someone be as it were possessed and cry out in the most inappropriate of circumstances and uncharacteristic of ways, "They'll all pay for it, they'll pay for all of it"? As it were possessed but possessed by nothing—except himself. For the possibility is undeniable if it is expressed in terms of this Lockean notion of a man as opposed to a person. The value of such an action would be highly questionable but the only conceptual worry is whether we can say it's the person's as well as the man's. And it is worth emphasizing here that people sometimes do things just to do them, just to get them done, because they have to be done. It will be said that they must have some desire, some metainterest or other. I won't quibble. But the strength of any metamotive—in many cases, at least—is not enough to provide us with a complete explanation. So if

something is done just to be done with or out of the way, it takes, or it
often does, a sort of clenching of the will's teeth. I don't see why this
ability of the will to engage is not such that someone with complete
abulia and anhedonia—or as near as we can imagine that bleak and
awful state—could, nevertheless, exercise his or her will. It might
require an enormous effort or upheaval. But the will, then, as much as
the person taking over.[60]

Can someone have no will? The will is much more fragile in some
than in others and it is, it must be admitted, sometimes destroyed by an
absence of desire. Or by great fear, say, or consuming grief. And there
are other cases. The man who is prey to his every impulse, every
attraction, every whim. The woman who can't decide or make up her
mind about anything even though she wants to or wants to be able to.
The adolescent who can't get out of the house or out of bed. Whatever
we say and however they try or go anyway through the motions, they
can't help it or they can't seem to. And if the will does rise up in
someone after having lain dormant, perhaps, for years, it is not easy to
decide who should get the credit.[61]

Is the will blind? Of course—by and large, at least, or in the main.
We have divided the mind or the self into faculties and, in doing so,
contrasted the will with reason. There might be connections—just as
many philosophers remind us of the rational aspects of emotions. And
perhaps there might have to be if faculty talk is going to work. But if
we start out by assuming that the will is blind or more or less so, it
ought not to surprise us if it can't be relied on in judgement. We have,
however, not only the will to consider but its "influencing motives" as
well. These are reasons of one sort or another. So they are not causes?
Well, what's the difference? Go back to being nervous over an
upcoming interview and being nervous from having drunk too much
coffee. One thinks that the interview justifies nervousness or makes
sense of it, makes it intelligible—but the coffee will have its effect
whatever one thinks. The interview, the interview that is so scary, is a
reason, the coffee a mere cause. A reason functions, as we might put it,
only with the consent of the agent—even if that consent is unconscious.
And the fact that the will can be influenced by reasons seems to mean
that it must, to some extent, be enlightened. But reasons come in a
number of kinds. There are those that merely make sense of—and then
there are those that justify or help to contribute to what ought to be so.
And these latter too operate differently in different cases. Briefly,
reasons for believing guarantee, provided one sees clearly what one is
doing, the appropriate state of belief. So belief is not, in this important
respect, subject to the will. Descartes and James were quite wrong

about this—and Hume was quite right. But reasons for desires and intentions are never that compelling. One might decide that it would be worth having or that one did ought to do it and nevertheless not really desire or intend. For there is a tiny spark of lust in every want, of brute resolution in every intention. The same sort of thing is true of emotions and motives—and, indeed, of action, of physical action. One's reasons for acting might be overwhelmingly in favour and yet still one might fail to do whatever they are reasons for doing; one might, indeed— Plato was notoriously wrong about this—know what one ought to do and yet not do it. And this gap—for desires or intentions or emotions or actions—is where the will can insert itself. Sometimes in covert or subtle ways, as in a particularly wilful desire or an emotion that is, perhaps, a bit forced. Sometimes unmistakably, as in many examples of physical action. Then what gets in is the blind will, what is left over after all the reasons have had their say. But desires too, of course, are more or less blind. We have separated them off from reason as well. For some desires, moreover—although maybe they are only instincts or whims—there are no reasons. And take, again, physical or bodily action. Reasons—or a lot of reasons, at any rate—are not causes of actions because they cannot, without the will, give rise to actions. And even if they could, approving of them and their influence is a lot different, a lot less uncomfortable, than being pushed around by causes or mere causes.[62]

So what causes actions? This is, in a way, or it is often the wrong question to ask. For while acts of willing or volitions in many cases lead to or bring about actions, that's where the story ends. A volition itself has no further antecedents—unless there does happen to be a second-order volition. We have to make use here of Chisholm's notion of a "prime mover unmoved". It is the person in the end who executes and freely or from out of the blue. Compare O'Shaughnessy's notion of action as a "gift to the universe". And then sometimes, by contrast, actions are the result of habit or routine. But neither is this a straight-forward causal matter. Habits too usually require the complicity of the will because actions of this sort can typically be halted or held back from by its exercise. Are these actions uncaused then? No, one thinks immediately; they are caused by certain states of the brain—just as the other, willed kind seem to be. They don't, rather, have a cause outside of the brain. Desires, intentions and emotions are like habits here for they too can, in some cases at least, be resisted by the will. And beliefs, again, are certainly not caused by reasons. As though one were to say that four-sidedness is caused by being a square. Reasons, to repeat the point, are what we consent to or approve of—or what, anyway and minimally, make sense of and give meaning to who we are and the world we live in.[63]

Do we, then—as the above remarks suggest—have control over our minds? In some ways and to some extent—just as, in some ways and to some extent, we have control over our bodies. Desires and intentions can, again, be influenced by the will. Obviously with intention, a mental state that has resolution at its core. But lust too can sometimes be ignored or fought against or it can, instead, be given free rein. Anger and fear can, if we're blessed, be affected by reason; in other cases, they can be brought to heel, if at all, only by the sheer power of the will. Beliefs, on the other hand, along with memories and most sensations, these are mental phenomena we have very little control over or very little direct control. Even here, though—for beliefs and for those emotions, say, that can be changed by reason—we might be prepared to talk of a kind of control. For one can't acquire physical things just by thinking that they're worth having; neither can one get rid of them merely by deciding that one didn't ought to have them. There is, however, an area or aspect of the mind—the stream of consciousness and, in particular, the stream of thought—where the control we can exercise is of a familiar though special sort. The crude picture here is that of a stream of thought, governed perhaps by laws of association or of rationality but anyway with a mind of its own, while the owner of the stream makes minor adjustments on the fly, causing it to shift slightly in direction or slow down a little maybe. It is crude— but it does, as a very rough generalization, point to certain features of large stretches of our thinking. And then again, it ignores some of the important features and all of the detail. The stream drifting, for example—or coming to a complete stop for a moment. James's gaps or absences of one kind or another. The start-up of thinking again and the difficulty, always, of who is responsible for it. The questions one asks oneself along the way, questions that might include "Do I really believe?" or "What is it I want?" or "How do I feel?" and so might lead one to examine more static and deeper structures in the mind. The retrackings and reaffirmings and the sense of purpose or relative indifference, the digressions and missteps, the nudges and hesitations and skips and jumps. James's welcomings and rejectings, not always but often of some idea, some thought one has just had. The feelings of satisfaction or amusement—and the intrusion, sometimes, of a feeling of tiredness, boredom or dejection, a knock at the door, a glance out of the window, one of those small cerebral accidents and—where was I? The problem about taxes—that's what it was—it can wait until tomorrow. But he has been misbehaving lately. I should talk to his father about it. Maybe I will. Then a pause—and then a thought of my aunt, the delinquent's grandmother—such a miserable woman. The taxes can't wait; they're due tomorrow. There's also the doctor's appointment in the morning. My aunt would love it. So who said life should be happy anyway?—or even comfortable, for that matter? You know how it goes. And all shot through, as should be obvious, with the lets and plays and hindrances of the will, much more subtle, usually, than simply doing or not doing, executing or otherwise. These more subtle phenomena have received a fair amount of attention in the philosophy of action recently but mostly in connection with bodily actions. And the operations of the will within the stream are, once again, introspectible. We have, that is, direct and privileged access to them.[64]

Are volitions themselves actions? Yes, of course—although there are actions and actions. We do, sometimes, manage to resist reaching for a cigarette or we try our best to thread a needle. Of course these are things we do. Only a misguided and wholly general requirement for what constitutes an action could prevent us from saying so.

Basic actions? We do some things by or through doing others. Or, to reverse directions, we do some things in order to do others. But either way, mustn't there be things we just do—not as results or upshots and not as ends to means? This notion of a basic action is, then, defined in terms of those of by, through, in order to. Rough and shifting as they are, they give it its only content. So what is it that we just, simply, do? Sometimes we just will. Occasionally, in rather special cases, we will ourselves to will. Sometimes we just keep on walking or steer automatically to the right. And sometimes we just rub our noses as we speak or shuffle our feet as we wait for the next teller. We just do it—and no explanation is possible that relies on other things we have done. But basic actions are clearly of various kinds, some mental and some physical. There is, again, no legitimate generalization here, no single kind of thing we just do in all cases.[65]

The self and the will? To repeat: Nothing lurks behind the will in action for there is nothing any further back. We can, of course, always blame the self but the will and the self are fused in action—just as the attention and the self are fused in perception. So an act of will is not usually made to happen by anything. It simply happens or occurs in a vacuum. The vacuum of ourselves as this source of will and control. This surd behind or beneath or beyond its belongings, this point of origin or departure that lies at our centre.

So what, finally, of pathology? First, some reminders though with a few more details. Earlier on, I listed, as disorders of the will, catatonic stupor and catatonic excitement, a lot of cases of disorganized schizo-phrenia, many cases of paranoid schizophrenia and paranoia and perhaps some cases of obsessive-compulsive disorder, phobia and panic. Then there are the impulse control disorders, some of the eating disorders, major depression—and so on. The will and desire, I have argued, can be separated from one another. They are, nevertheless, intimately connected. Much of the time they wax and wane together—for it is, again, that much easier to do something if one wants to. And depression, for example, can bring with it a total or near-total absence of desire and so, typically, of will. Catatonic stupor is similar, it seems, at least with regard to the body. Disorganized schizophrenics, by contrast, often have a blunted will and diminished or fragmented desires—and the catatonically excited, like the extreme obsessive-compulsives, have very little or no control over their thoughts and actions. The paranoid schizophrenics and paranoiacs I mentioned are involved in a struggle in the mind but so too are those with panic and phobias—although fighting against a fear, say, is not the same as fighting against a half-recognition that one might be wrong, perhaps mostly or terribly wrong. And the idea that the will is implicated in less extreme cases of obsessive-compulsive disorder, the impulse control disorders and, indeed, some of the eating disorders needs no defending. There are also other cases. For someone might will or desire only what is impossible or self-destructive or be engaged in a chronic battle for power with the mind of God. But if we do take the notion of the will—along with that of desire and its other influencing motives—at face value, we can accommodate a great deal of the official taxonomy. There are—we should be clear about this—certain problems with this notion of the will, of which I have discussed a fair selection. I don't, of course, expect that my brief and sometimes dogmatic responses to these problems will satisfy everyone. I do want to emphasize, however, that these are philosophical problems. None of them even begins to threaten the legitimacy of the notion of the will, none of them comes close to justifying the neglect or opprobrium that is more or less routinely accorded it by most philosophers and most scientists. There are, after all, comparable philosophical problems about thought and emotion and, for that matter, about any part or aspect of the mind. It is not that these problems are insoluble. That is a large question about the nature of philosophy. But the mere existence of such problems, by itself, proves nothing about the legitimacy of a notion. And we rely, critically and quite happily, on the notion of the will every day of our lives. So a taxonomy that gives a prominent place to the will or is even done pretty much entirely in terms of it seems to be an eminently viable option. A note of caution, though, is needed here—for we have not yet discussed the largest problem of all. We should turn now to that problem, the problem of freedom.[66]

Without freedom, the notion of the will is empty, meaningless—in spite of the fact that some writers on this topic have tried to make sense of a wholly determined will. But for the problem of freedom, much of the above about the intricacies of the will drops out. Even if something is done or wanted or felt for reasons, there must, one can't help thinking, be an underlying cause in the brain. And even if we do approve of our reasons, there must, one thinks, be a cause of this approval in the brain. It is the brain and its relation to the mind that is the source of the problem. The problem takes two forms, one linguistic, the other about the interface between the brain and the mind. Interface? Is this the pineal gland all over again? Given that the brain affects the mind, there has to be some sort of interface—or, perhaps better, millions and millions of them. I will put the problem in terms of arguments in favour of Determinism. The arguments are very good— as good as philosophical arguments ever get.

The linguistic form of the problem starts by assuming that the brain is a regular common or garden physical object. Enormously complex, of course, but regular nonetheless. Then the language in which the brain should be described and discussed is that of physics and chemistry. Causes, at the macroscopic level of the brain, are pervasive, freedom does not exist. The language we use to describe the mind is sometimes that of causes. But it is, as well or instead, the language of freedom and reasons. These languages are not merely incommensurate, however; they straightforwardly conflict with each other. They can't both correspond to a single reality. They can't even correspond to two different realities that are inextricably linked. The links would be rendered questionable by the conflict—for how can Determinism lie side-by-side with freedom? The language of physics and chemistry has proven itself time and again. It is clearly the one to prefer. So freedom does not exist.

The interface form also starts by assuming that the brain is a regular physical object. Then a complete explanation of its behaviour can be given on the basis of its internal make-up and its relations to other physical objects. But it is a brute and an indisputable fact that the brain is tied to the mind and vice-versa. The net energy exchange, let us allow, must be zero. The brain, after all, belongs to what many people claim to be a closed physical system. Still, causal energy goes into the mind—it must be causal, it originates in the brain—and causal energy comes out—it must be causal, it affects the brain. So there must be laws in the mind, on the other side of the interface, that regulate what happens there to ensure that the balance is kept. Either they are ordinary causal laws or they are not. If they are, Determinism is true. If they are not, the relation of the mind to the brain is fundamentally unlike the relation of some extra added-on physical system to the brain however tight the hook-up between these latter because one sort of explanation of the brain's behaviour will be in noncausal terms. But that can't be right. Determinism is true then—and freedom does not exist.[67]

Perhaps there is only one argument here, in a shorter and more long-winded version, rather than two. But why is this a problem? What are the possible solutions—and what, in particular, of Determinism? For isn't that a possible solution?

I don't think it is. I think we know that we're free. Indeed, I have claimed that we are introspectively aware of our freedom with regard to both our bodies and our minds. It will be objected, however, that we can't know by introspection that Determinism is false.

I am inclined to say we can—just as we can know that scepticism with regard to the external world is false through perception. I know that this is a pad of paper and that a book and, beside it, a lamp through or by means of vision. But there is no point in disagreeing about this. Simply saying that we know such things won't satisfy us philosophically. That claim itself has to be defended against the arguments for scepticism. And the claim that we know we're free must be similarly defended against the arguments for Determinism. The comparison with scepticism, it will turn out, is instructive. Determinism maintains that we can't know we're free. This is one half of the sceptical thesis in this area; the sceptic also maintains that we can't know we're not. So Determinism denies exactly what scepticism calls into question, something that we would all, ordinarily, insist we know to be true, something that conditions and informs our lives and our relationships with others at any and every moment. Determinism is correct, then— like scepticism—only if we and our lives, what we feel in our very sinews, is or might be wrong and massively wrong. Is this a good argument against Determinism? Not really—any more than it is against scepticism. In fact, it is hardly an argument at all. The most that it could be thought to show is that there is something amiss with the philosophical arguments to the contrary; it doesn't begin to tell us what. Still, don't we know, however philosophers might argue, that Determinism is mistaken—just as we know that scepticism is? We can watch someone walk up to the counter and freely, deliberately, raise a gun, cock it and then shoot the cashier between the eyes or park quite intentionally in a tow-away zone—and we are, as I've said, introspectively aware sometimes of our freedom. But if we know, Determinism is false.

If Determinism is false, if it has to be, must be, by every canon of common sense and by all of our actions and reactions and decisions and choices, what of the alternatives? Pretty bleak, as far as the tradition goes. Classical Indeterminism is the view that our actions and thoughts are uncaused, random. So much for responsibility and blame and most of what we hold dear about freedom. For the suggestion is not merely that an act of the will or a determination of the self has no nonneurological antecedents. It is, rather, that an act of will, a self-determination, can have no cause, not even in the brain. And this—for the great majority of us, at any rate—is an enormously implausible view. Soft Determinism, the other alternative, is typically expressed by specifying a subset of what are conceded to be causes—the subset of desires and beliefs and motives of the agent as opposed to a knife in the ribs or a forcibly administered dose of drugs—and then claiming that we're free if our actions and thoughts are determined by members of the subset but not otherwise. There is an obvious worry about reasons being construed as causes. How can an action, for example, be free and caused at the same time? There is another, not unconnected, about the mere enumeration of the members of the subset. Isn't this arbitrary? Why not some other subset of causes or alleged causes? That would, of course, make the view false or so we want to say—but it wouldn't be any more arbitrary. And, most importantly, the arguments in favour of Determinism are left completely untouched. For don't our desires and beliefs have causes in the brain? It is, after all, these causes and, more generally, our robustly physical constitution and our equally physical environment that make the case for Determinism so persuasive. We do, certainly, feel different or we do often when we are motivated by reasons as opposed to causes or mere causes. But the Determinist will portray this as the difference between having a gun at your head and having a gun at your head and your arm twisted half-off as well. Besides, someone with a brain tumour might still feel free, as free, indeed, as you and me.[68]

So what progress have we made? The arguments for Determinism are extremely good. I think they are, in a sense, irrefutable. They do, to be sure, exhibit a bias. The first, or the shorter, version picks the language of physics and chemistry given a choice—but this is surely understandable if we do have to choose. The second, or the longer, version looks at the interface between the brain and the mind from the side of the brain—but this is one perspective from which it can and should be looked at. The alternatives traditionally offered to Determinism are, moreover, quite unacceptable. And yet the conclusion of the arguments for Determinism is also unacceptable. It is false and obviously so, arcane theoretical nonsense. But how can all of this be true?[69]

We should think, again, of scepticism. For the arguments in favour of scepticism are extremely good. Indeed, they are among the handful in philosophy on any topic that are as good as the arguments for Determinism. And yet their conclusions are simply bizarre. The lesson to be learned here is that we must set the sceptic's arguments aside, beg the sceptic's question. And so too for those of the Determinist. That we are free is a datum, something we cannot give up if we are to count ourselves as reasonable and sensible, whatever the arguments that might seem to threaten it. That we know is also a datum. But it is at this point that Determinism and scepticism part company. In the latter case, we can, once we have begged the question, see what has gone wrong. We have to tailor-make our standards for knowledge to the human condition, to recognize, as Wittgenstein has it, that a doubt is not necessary just because it is possible. This does not provide us with a different sort of defence against scepticism, one that avoids begging questions. An account that insists on an anthropomorphic cast to the standards for knowledge is, simply, a question-begging account. But in the case of Determinism, we are, when we have begged the question, left high and dry. We cannot see how to reinterpret the notion of causality, in particular, to lay the Determinist's argument to rest.[70]

So what to do? The future of science has come up before. I suggested earlier on that only the future of science can decide between Identity Theory or Supervenience and Mutual Mapping Theory. That issue too, on one side of the fence, has to do with causality, with the problem of how the mind and the brain can, being so different, causally interact. I argued that while we cannot solve it, the future of science, together with philosophy presumably, might very well—although its solution need not be in causal terms. The problem of freedom is that of whether causes can tolerate reasons, of what sorts of causes in the brain are compatible with the operations of the will in the mind—although it too can be put in terms of identity and the fundamental maxim of Supervenience, that of an asymmetrical fixing relation between the brain and the mind, is, by itself, an easy route to Determinism. This second problem, rightly understood, is one aspect of the above, broader problem about Materialism and Dualism. And it too will be solved, I think—in one way or another—by the future of science. Only then will the flaws in the arguments for Determinism be detectable; at present, those arguments are, as I've said, irrefutable. For we have no real idea of the concept of causality that will be needed to show where they go wrong. There are two sorts of parallels I can think of here. The first, once again, is the problem of the causal powers of light and of gravity. How can a massless photon carry any causal clout? And how can a graviton or something as abstract or attenuated as the curvature of space push around a molecule let alone the earth or the sun? Only the future of science, with a new and more sophisticated concept of causality, will be able to tell us. The second is what remains of the above, broader, problem if we subtract the problem of freedom—its other aspects. Functionalism has made a great deal of fuss over the problem of qualia or raw feels in the mind. How can these things be explained in causal or neurological terms? It has also made a fuss over the problem of intentionality or meaning. How can meaning be found in the brain any more than it can in the spleen—or in a pebble or boulder? These problems too, it seems to me, can be solved only by the future. So I offer this as the solution to the problem of free will and Determinism: Its solution lies, if it lies anywhere, in the future and it will require, among other things, a more highly developed concept of causality than we now possess.[71]

I have made a fuss over the power of what can be said in favour of Determinism. And on reflection, something important though vague does come out of this. The main assumption of both arguments or both versions of the argument for Determinism is that the brain is a regular physical object. This assumption must go. The brain is, rather, a magical physical object. For it has characteristics that defy our present philosophy and science and in the most fundamental of ways. And that, in a strict sense, is what magic is. A physical object that can give rise to and sustain the mental—and one that often and not accidentally moves to the dictates of rationality. And if Identity Theory turns out to be true, one that is, besides, introspectible. After God created the other, regular, kind of physical object, it would have taken a miracle, one finds oneself thinking, to invent or even imagine the brain. Still, this distinction between magic and miracles, between what defies our philosophy and science and what violates them or shoves them unceremoniously aside, is itself not very clear—and who knows which kind He created first? So I don't want to press the point. I'll settle for magic.[72]

This can be put a little differently. We begin to oppose Determinism if we insist that just as the brain affects the mind, so too the mind affects the brain. We oppose it more unequivocally if we say that mental language needs no defending or that it might as well be mental energy that mediates between the mind and the brain—it either begins or ends up as mental—and that the net exchange need not be pegged at zero since the physical universe is manifestly not closed. But we also oppose the Determinist if we insist—what is the same thing—that we're free. So we don't have an argument here either. All we have is the thought that whenever a limb of yours moves as a result of a decision you make, this is one more proof of a sort of telekinesis as a banal, an everyday, an utterly familiar fact. This is not, of course, an argument in the other direction or in favour of Determinism. Introspection, a sort of telepathy, is also an utterly familiar as well as a magical fact. But the brain as magical? What, exactly, is one supposed to do with that?

It is, let me concede, a rough thought and, surely, a rather negative or sobering one. It is also, someone might think, clearly overblown and the vagueness, moreover, must be due to some defect inherent in Dualism. But while the Interactionist is still very much in the dark about the concept of causality contained in mature Mapping Theory, the Identity Theorist is equally in the dark about the details of identity as is the Supervenience Theorist about supervenience. No one is any better off than anyone else here. And while Eliminativism would get rid of the problem by rejecting freedom, why should we have any faith in a doctrine that denies the existence of anything we can't at present understand? And why, especially, when the object of denial is something as basic and as indisputable as freedom?

One thing, though—and this should be highlighted—one thing that follows from all this is that Freudian therapy with its search for reasons and drug therapy where the immediate effects are uncompromisingly physical are perfectly compatible—case by case and not merely the one for some cases and the other for others. We don't know how but they are. The profession can therefore relax and concentrate on the question of which methods are appropriate to which disorders. This is largely an empirical matter but the Freudians are right, it also includes much more difficult issues about the patient's autonomy and the virtues of self-knowledge. Still, we can tweak whatever end of the equation or the causal link or whatever it is that is tweakable—and it might, of course, be either end in some cases. And as for the profession shrinking, the Freudian again is or ought to be safe. But so too is the clinician whose theoretical commitments, whatever they are, are fairly reasonable or not, anyway, entirely unreasonable, who is thoroughly familiar with the day-to-day speech and behaviour of the schizophrenic, for example, and who is knowledgeable about drugs and aware of their dangers. The profession is not in that sort of trouble.

The profession does, however, have another problem. It too brings up concerns about freedom. It is the problem of the brain cases. Schizophrenia or obsessive-compulsive disorder, defined symptomatically, can be caused by a car wreck or brain tumour. Then why don't we say that all of the neurologically impaired victims of car wrecks and brain tumours are mad or neurotic or have personality disorders? Many of them don't fit into the categories of *DSM-IV*—but isn't that the fault of *DSM-IV*? This problem, as I will try to make clear in the final section of this chapter, is of an absolutely fundamental kind for it calls into question the very concepts of madness, neurosis and personality disorder.

One last note. I have proceeded, in the above, as though there is a physical side or counterpart to every mental fact. What I have referred to as "Partial Parallelism", in particular, denies this. I will get around to this problem, an oddly disturbing one, in the next section. But that view doesn't shed any light on freedom. It simply rejects the causal tie, giving us nothing in return—and there is, besides, no reason whatever for thinking that the territory it might pick out is just the territory where the notion of freedom is applicable. Neither, it should be said, does talk of quantum mechanics help in this connection. For here we have mere chance and probability again. The indeterminacy that rules at the quantum level does not, in any case, mean that dropping a pane of glass on to the sidewalk from two stories up won't cause it to break or that the various parts of the brain don't have considerable causal powers—and without special provisions that are quite independent of indeterminacy, this would make the most stolid rock or clod of dirt as free as a bird. As free, that is, as you or me.

But as for our worries about alternative taxonomies, we have uncovered nothing that might pose a threat to a taxonomy based on the will. The problem of freedom is, once again or so I have argued, a problem we cannot at present resolve. There are other such problems, however. Some have to do with certain basic issues in physics; others have to do with the mind, like those of qualia and meaning. So the presently intractable problem of freedom does not jeopardize the notion of the will. On the contrary, we have the problem we do only because of the manifest necessity of that notion, only because we are sometimes free.[73]

Some Further Problems

Some Further Problems

I discuss, in this section and much more briefly, a number of problems of very different kinds. They all have to do, in one way or another, with madness.

I have treated introspection rather shabbily as far as taxonomy is concerned. And yet I have placed it at the centre of the mind. I did list Freudian cases as failures of introspection earlier on. I also mentioned some cases of schizophrenia and mania—and multiple personality disorder, it can be argued, typically involves introspective breakdowns. But for introspection, as opposed to the will, the taxonomical pay-offs seem fairly limited. Introspection, of course, requires that the attention be focused on or caught by the contents of one's own mind. So the right comparison here is control over one's own mind—and then the balance is more even. There are, besides, other cases. Given that the self is introspectible, depersonalization can, when it is extreme, be seen as an introspective disorder. And the objects of introspection are as elusive in catatonic excitement as they are, often, in schizophrenia and mania. We should, though, be wary of alleged introspective defects if they are too extravagant. No sense can be made of the idea of complete introspective blindness, or not for a mind whose contents are at all complex or elaborate. In this respect, introspection is quite unlike vision. Nevertheless, the view that the mad must have the same peculiar and impressive epistemological relationship to their minds as we have to ours is absurd. The difficulty is that we can know very little of the details. Failures in introspection can't, trivially, be apparent to the person involved—or they can't at the time they occur. Neither is it easy to keep track of them in others. And for the mad, in particular, we have to rely, largely, on mad descriptions and try, by whatever means we can, to figure out how they misdescribe a reality that is itself mad. So the reasons for the comparative soft-pedalling of introspection are boring. Still, this is surely why the frequent introspective deficiencies of the mad—and, on partly similar grounds, many of their equally frequent inabilities to control their thoughts—are not very useful for taxonomical purposes. Perhaps more could be done here. But none of this should be taken to suggest that introspection and control over one's own mind are not important—either for the mad or for the rest of us.[74]

Self-awareness and self-control, however, can bring in the body as well or as a consequence. So what of the body in madness?

Assume, as I've suggested, that Logical Behaviourism is true or, at any rate, one strand of the truth. Then the body will continually make possible and express madness as it does for us the sanity we lay claim to. But even if Logical Behaviourism is true, it can be true in the standard formulations for only the sane and the normal. Ryle's skater, for example, who believes that the ice has a thin patch with his propensity to warn off others if they should get too close. It makes such sense. But a madman who is thinking might think that the poppies are especially pretty this year. He might then have a sudden desire, he might feel an urge to pick them. Then he might think: So she has to die. A madman who acts might kill his mother because the flowers were pretty and he wanted to pick them. Because—naturally, as it were. The idea of life without the body is, of course, as problematic for the mad as it is for us. It's just that we should be more than usually cautious and will be less than usually successful in interpreting the body in madness.[75]

Those meaningless postures again in waxy catatonia, imposed from outside by others moving the limbs and maintained sometimes for hours: what do they mean, what is their content? Or a man might stand with his arms akimbo as though anticipating an explanation or a violent confrontation—but all of the time. Or an intelligent well-mannered girl of seventeen will act like a whore or launch herself from the top of a ten-story building. Or someone will respond to a greeting with a knowing chuckle or a long drawn out sigh or by curling up into a frightened ball in the corner. The behaviour sometimes resembling a foreign language, each movement or gesture completely indecipherable. And in mania and catatonic excitement, the body can be a buzz-saw—or that of a famous ballerina or of enormous dimensions or just somehow stuck or in the way. The body, in schizophrenia, might lie for days in its own vomit and faeces while the mind waits for the panic to subside or for the awful impending darkness. Behaviour in some of the sexual disorders can be downright bizarre, in body dysmorphic disorder and the eating disorders extremely hard to credit let alone comprehend. Then there are the pathetic driven rituals of the obsessive-compulsives, the bewildering switches of the multiples, the near-paralysis at times of a depression that might be the manifestation of guilt for having destroyed all joy, all interest in the world, or simply of incredible unutterable tiredness. The silliness again or the shallowness and the imitating, the ticcing, the rocking, the crying—and the sadness or horror or the grinning complacency like a smell in the air.

So sometimes we know what's behind the behaviour or we know something; often we don't or not much. There are, however, some other, more theoretical, worries that might give rise to or underlie epistemological difficulties here. I am not, let me emphasize, a believer in Descartes's pineal gland. But we must, as I've said, make sense of the notion of an interface between the mind and the brain. This is, after all, what Mutual Mapping Theory, Identity Theory and Supervenience all promise to do. The interface is not in one place or, in any straightforward way, in many places. We are all aware of the dangers of simplistic localization theses in this context. But could there be cases where the body is experienced as too large or heavy or too far away to move or where proprioceptive acquaintance is hysterically cut off? Could someone's actions be interrupted in mid-stream every few seconds or very much speeded up? Could they be delayed—for seconds or hours or days? Could they be scrambled in time as compared with the corresponding volitions, if and insofar as these latter occur? Could volitions produce actions that are inappropriate to them even in the eyes of the agent—or could the body have a mind of its own? At least some of these things could happen—more trouble for Logical Behaviourism—although I'm not at all sure how or when they do. I don't think anyone is. But more attention to these sorts of questions might throw considerable light on the mind and behaviour—and on madness as well.[76]

And now for the problem of whether Partial Parallelism, for example, is or might be true. The problem, however, is much broader than that. Suppose one is inclined to believe in Interactive Dualism or Mutual Mapping Theory. Then the problem is most naturally expressed by asking if any of Partial Parallelism, Partial Epiphenomenalism or Partial Reverse Epiphenomenalism is true. These are all, traditionally, dualistic doctrines but they differ from Interactive Dualism in insisting on a causal insulation or a causal asymmetry between the mind and the brain. And for an Interactive Dualist, they can be true in only a partial form, at best. For the question is simply that of whether the preferred view—in this case, Interactive Dualism or Mutual Mapping Theory—is true wholly generally. But a precisely similar problem arises for Identity Theory and Supervenience. It has to do with their scope. Is either Identity Theory or Supervenience true across the board—or might there be, in the light of one's theory, rogue mental phenomena that have to be handled differently? And this could, of course, involve the idea that some sort of Partial Dualism is or might be true.

The problem is made more acute when we remember the following. Thoughts need not have causal relations or relations of reason, indeed any relations at all, to other thoughts. Thoughts sometimes come out of the blue. Could there be a thought completely independent of everything else in the universe, one that had no explanation or occurred by itself and didn't make a bit of difference, the ultimate in ontological isolation? And could such a thought escape the introspective attention so that no one would or could ever know, the ultimate in epistemological black holes?

I should emphasize that none of this is motivated by scepticism. Not really of the "Anything is possible" variety and certainly not of the inductive kind. I am not complaining that while the evidence we have for Mutual Mapping Theory, Identity Theory or Supervenience is impressive, it is inconclusive because merely inductive. I am complaining, if you like, about the sometimes perplexing nature of the mind, about the mystery that is the human brain with its seemingly unfathomable secrets.

Partial Parallelism, for example? One thinks, here, of inconsequential or especially fleeting thoughts or mild enthusiasms, perhaps, that don't last too long. One thinks of day-dreaming—provided it doesn't give too much pleasure, anyway, or create too much excitement. One thinks of pure or abstract reflection, relatively uncluttered or not cluttered at all with gross mental imagery, visual, auditory or whatever. And then one gets bolder and thinks that maybe—let's get this question out into the open, at any rate—maybe Freudian cases are just not treatable by physical methods. Such cases do exist, or so I have argued—but maybe there couldn't be a pill. Still, it's hard to make this persuasive, hard to prevent it from slipping back into the too easy "How do you know?" or "Do you really know?" of scepticism. But what is going on? The unconscious is—whatever else—an epistemological category. Introspection too has to do with epistemology. And if we could come up with a satisfactory or even a promising neurological story about introspection, we would have gone some way towards constructing—by subtraction, as it were—an analogous story about the preconscious and then, in turn, the unconscious. But what do we know of the brain in introspection? Precious little, if anything—and nothing at all, as far as I'm aware, about what happens in the brain when a desire or belief that was preconscious becomes part of the stream of consciousness. It is also true that we have done very little thinking about the introspective sense-organ or sense-organs—and, more generally, that the right questions about introspection are seldom even raised. Things are complicated here by a consideration I have mentioned before, that complete introspective blindness is impossible with any more or less sophisticated mind. Some sort of story about introspection should, nevertheless, be tellable. And neither do we know anything of a neurological kind about what it is to be preconscious. It is, however, an indisputable fact that most of the mind is, at any given moment, preconscious. And while there have been a few attempts to find the Freudian unconscious in the brain, they have not been at all convincing. This is a strangely neglected area in neurology—partly, of course, because of the historical divisions between neurologists and Freudians. So do I believe—as a matter, at least, of what we philosophers think of as logical possibility—that introspection and the unconscious might not show up in the brain? That certain desires, say, might not? That complex theoretical beliefs might not? That passing thoughts or those that merely hover, briefly, at the edge of the mind might not? Or do I believe that they might show up but only and always from a single perspective? As causes of the mental that are not effects?—or as effects of the mental that can't be causes? And what, in this instance, is the connection between epistemology and ontology?[77]

I don't know what to believe—and the links between epistemology and ontology are sometimes pretty murky. I am by no means sure that Antipodeans, aliens who seem to have no minds but who are fluent in neurologicalese, could not exist. Logical Behaviourism, as I've said, has to be bracketed "For the normal". Why not "For the normal—and adult and competent—human being"? But while what does duty for a brain in an Antipodean produces behaviour, it doesn't, apparently, give rise to a mind. Only some forms of hardware, only some types of chemical make-up, might be capable of that. Of course, a pretty fancy concept of causality would be needed by Mutual Mapping Theory to accommodate Antipodeans. And what Identity Theory would need instead is an equally fancy concept of identity—with Supervenience, again, requiring a mixture of both. Still, why not?—who knows? Something we do know is that reasons operate within the mind. And reasons, again, are not causes or not in general. Rather, because of their dependence on the will, they are or they are often, to use a phrase of Hume's, "more gently prevailing forces". We also know that the mind is tied to the brain although in ways we can hardly begin to understand. Might "more gently prevailing forces" operate between the mind and the brain? Indeed, might they operate within the brain itself? For we already have strong grounds for thinking that the brain is no ordinary physical object. Or might it be that, for some parts of the mind, there are no ties or ties of a kind we can't yet imagine? Searle, however, is surely right—whatever the details and however they are to be described—in claiming that the ontology of the stream of consciousness differs from that of the unconscious and, at least implicitly, that the brain's differs from the spleen's. But I have, I must confess, an uneasy feeling about all this. I am not sure I am discussing the problem in the correct terms or what would count in the end as settling it. Some of our most basic assumptions about the mind and the brain are at stake here. And yet I don't know what to make of this business of the mind and causal insulation or asymmetry or partial Isms. I have more questions about it than answers.[78]

The next two problems both have to do with ontology and antiRealism and, in the second case, with the subject-matter of philosophy.

Nagel's bat shows, it seems to me, that we have to be antiRealists about the mind. Nagel says, though, that he is a Realist. The clearest way I know of to formulate this verbal issue is to allow for two kinds of Realists and antiRealists. The village kind disagree about whether some putative reality actually exists, the Realist claiming that it does, the antiRealist that it does not. So Eliminative Materialists are village antiRealists about the mind and the rather less popular Eliminate Everything or No Reality Party counsels widespread or global village antiRealism. But two options are available to the village Realist. If an objective description of the reality in question is completely independent of human abilities and conceptual equipment, philosophical Realism is in order. If, by contrast, the reality carries, within itself, the mark of humanity, philosophical antiRealism should be endorsed. And there are, of course, other versions of the philosophical Realist/antiRealist distinction for other species although they are, for obvious reasons, usually of less interest to us than the human version. Nagel, then, is a village Realist about the mind, a philosophical antiRealist of the bat persuasion about the bat's mind and a more familiar sort of philosophical antiRealist about the human mind. For isn't he right in maintaining that we have a very limited sense of what it would be like to be a bat precisely because the bat's mind is permeated by the bat's general intellectual and conceptual point of view—just as ours is by ours?[79]

And this introduces the possibility of philosophical antiRealism squared or cubed. One might not, so to speak, merely be a bat; one might be a mad bat. Or a mad Martian bat—or is a bat already a kind of Martian? Or a mad Martian and horribly disfigured bat—although my concern here is not with disfigurement of any and every kind. It is with a state of mind that might well be produced by gross disfigurement, the state of mind of John Merrick, for example—perhaps only fictional—when he realizes that a couple of town toughs along with their girl-friends are watching through an open window as he combs his hair in front of a mirror. Try as we might, we can't understand, not that sort of—what?—how does one express it? Or a mad Martian and horribly disfigured bat who is profoundly retarded besides. And maybe a giant or a dwarf—although the degree of antiRealism here might well be less pronounced. But the point is that there are orders or magnitudes of philosophical antiRealism with regard to the mind. The more we add, the further Nagel's bat recedes.

Madness, however, tops the list—together, it should be said, with severe retardation and certain cases of organic disorder. For the minds of the mad, the truly mad, are unintelligible. In principle. They cannot be understood by anyone—not even by God. I don't offer this as some new theological riddle; I offer it, rather, as the sober truth about the mad. We were all taught that if a description is unintelligible, it must be a misdescription. It couldn't match reality for reality itself can't be unintelligible. But this philosophical maxim is false. The mind of someone mad constitutes a part or an aspect of reality that is unintelligible, incoherent, incomprehensible. In itself, in the very nature of things.

The second problem about ontology and antiRealism is one about concepts. Given that we have to be philosophical antiRealists, species by species, about the mind, we have to be philosophical antiRealists about our concepts. They exist, of course—as an enormously complicated network of pictures or fundamental beliefs that most of us share—but they are, inevitably, constructed out of human experience, human perception and human ways of thinking. So the solution to the traditional philosophical problem of universals is that we should be village Realists and philosophical antiRealists about our concepts. Physical reality, it turns out—where the only plausible view is philosophical Realism—is of a rather special kind. But might our concepts fail to correspond to reality? And does their closeness to us make them the easiest things in the world to understand—or does it make it more difficult to see them for what they are?

The above form of Kantian scepticism about concepts is, like scepticism with regard to rationality, global scepticism in another guise. Its rejection, like that of all forms of philosophical scepticism, will involve us in begging the sceptic's question. Should we beg it? We have been through this before. Is this a pen and a pad of lined paper? Am I feeling rather light-headed at this early hour and half-thinking of stopping for another cup of coffee? You have to take my word for that—but if the positions were reversed, I'd have to take yours. Of course we should beg it. The closeness of our concepts, however, can be disquieting. We know them, as we know our children, through and through and yet we sometimes want so much to be able to accept or take seriously what they say. What can we do, though, but look again and listen some more and try to figure it all out? And sometimes we succeed, more or less, at this business of sketching and clarifying concepts. A peculiarity of the concept of madness is that it is itself tinged with madness. It is affected and partly structured in accordance with what the mad can manage to tell us about their state. But this distancing too, surreal as it can be, has its advantages as well as its disadvantages. It certainly doesn't make it any more difficult to criticize the concept. For since we can know about reality and know about our concepts, we can, one by one or in a piece-meal fashion, evaluate our concepts. Doesn't this require that we somehow get outside language, outside thought? Nothing so grand. It is not, again, as though we have to try to evaluate all of our concepts at once. And sometimes a case that is not covered by our concepts can be directly observed—and sometimes one can show that there is a hitherto unnoticed gap between two basic beliefs or that one causes trouble for the other. So a deconstruction, even, of this, that or the other concept is entirely conceivable.

A not unrelated problem is that of the proper categories of philosophical assessment. I will have more to say about this in the final section but philosophy has something to learn here from psychiatry. In spite of the work of Wittgenstein, there is still a fairly widespread myth in philosophy to the effect that only two kinds of truth are possible, the necessary—a.k.a. the analytic or a priori—and the contingent—a.k.a. the synthetic or a posteriori. Not much wrong with this as long as at least one of these categories is enormously broad and therefore not very useful. But philosophers, perversely, tend to favour extremely narrow definitions for each half of this allegedly exhaustive distinction and, even more worrying because more influential, equally narrow sets of paradigms. So "Squares have four sides", for example, "Bachelors are unmarried" and "If A is larger than B and B than C, then A is larger than C" constitute one set of paradigms, "It's overcast this morning", for example, "There's no cheese left in the cupboard" and "Lima is the capital of Peru" the other. Two, just two, kinds of truth. And the flipside of this myth is that only two kinds of falsity are possible, the necessarily false or contradictory and the contingently or empirically false. A third kind of intellectual sin, however, can be committed, that of coming out with blatant meaningless nonsense. Preferred examples of this can be found in the best—or the worst—of Lewis Carroll or in the babbling of a child. But aiming for contingent truth is not the job of philosophers. So they seldom, if ever, fail in that enterprise and utter contingent falsehoods by mistake. And only the most cynical would claim that philosophers are guilty, with much greater frequency, of manifest and indisputable gibberish. We do, most of the time, make at least a minimal kind of sense. The single philosophical sin, then, of any importance is that of contradiction. You try not to think of how many times you've heard that earnestly insistent or irritatingly complacent voice from the back of the room in one more philosophy colloquium intoning "It is not a contradiction to suppose..."—as though, if that were so, everything would be right with the world, as right as it could ever be. Avoid contradiction—and achieve philosophical glory.

I gather together some cases. The madman who kills his mother because he wanted to pick some flowers does not utter or act out a contradiction, something of the form "A and not-A". But neither does he say or express what is merely contingently false or complete unadulterated nonsense. And so too for the one who claims that everything is frozen in time and space and isolated from everything else and for the one who questions you closely to make sure you're not a Russian spy or an emissary from the Queen sent to check on his manners. The categories of contradiction, contingent falsehood and mindless gibberish are not even contenders here. Then there are the philosophically loaded cases, the cases that are much closer to home. For some mental disorders mimic or are anyway significantly like mistaken positions in philosophy. The baffling condition of depersonalization, for example, exhibits, in extreme versions, not only the strength of Descartes's Cogito, but also its weakness. Extreme derealization and those cases of obsessive-compulsive disorder in which the iron is never unplugged or the stove safely off have clear and unmistakable connections with scepticism about the external world. Religious paranoia and the delusion that one is God, in particular, should remind us of solipsism; some cases of hebephrenia are living embodiments of Hume's view of personal identity; antisocial personality disorder is a pathological endorsement of some of Nietzsche's views on morality—as well as Ayn Rand's. On those philosophical accounts of the will in terms, solely, of desire, we would all have impulse control disorders. Certain wholly general accounts of the self positively trade on the kind of fragmentation seen in multiple personality disorder. And, we might hazard though perhaps a little more frivolously, depression and persecutory paranoia are or ought to be, given some of the darker strands of Existentialism, our normal everyday lot. But what is wrong in these cases, what makes them disorders, is not contradiction, in words or in actions. And what is wrong with the corresponding philosophical positions is not contradiction either. It should go without saying that contingent falsehood and simple nonsense are also inappropriate categories for these cases and positions. Psychiatrists—one doesn't like to admit it but there you are—are much more sensible, much more realistic, in their assessments here than many philosophers. It is not that they are constitutionally smarter or more insightful. It is just that they don't have the same history, the same weight of tradition, to get in their way. For this reliance on a two-fold distinction between the necessary and contingent—or the analytic and synthetic or a priori and a posteriori—where each side of the distinction, moreover, is construed extremely narrowly, this has haunted philosophy for more than two thousand years.[80]

And now we come crashing back to earth. A great deal of what I have said in this chapter has been about problems, not so much for philosophy, as for psychiatry. There is, of course, the large problem of taxonomical alternatives but there are all sorts of others. In the previous section, for example, I argued for the compatibility between Freudian therapy and physical methods of treatment, something that is openly and clearly acknowledged by no more than a handful of psychiatrists. I also mentioned, once again, the problem, still unresolved, of the brain cases—and I discussed, in the present section, only to give up on, the mirror-image problem of whether Partial Parallelism, say, might be true, a problem that is at least as pressing for psychiatry as it is for philosophy. But while the last two problems I want to draw attention to are, yet again, problems for psychiatry, they are, in part at least, problems about psychiatry as a profession in a somewhat narrower or more backroom sense of that word, problems about public relations.

The first of these problems has to do with the divisions within psychiatry. There is, to be sure, fairly widespread agreement over the efficacy of drugs. But what of other therapies? At the end of Chapter 3, I suggested that Freudianism—suitably qualified and cleaned up—is the only halfway serious alternative to drugs or to physical methods more generally. Take cognitive theory and therapy, for example, This is simply an attempt to downplay the significance of noncognitive elements of the mind—like emotions, say, or the will. It employs an eclectic range of therapeutic tools, some of them Freudian, but what unites them, again, is the overall programme of devaluing or denaturing the noncognitive. Does this give us an adequate account of the mind? Of course it doesn't; the question answers itself. By contrast, a Freudian account of the mind, as I argued in Chapter 1 and the second section of this chapter, is, in spite of some important questions, right on some large points and sometimes downright insightful. An existential account of the mind or a humanist account? Versions of such an account, if and when they exist, are all over the map. An integrative or a supportive account? Look... There are, as cognitivists make clear, various tricks and techniques that might sometimes help—and behaviour modification is, as a matter of empirical fact, useful in a handful of disorders. The single comprehensive—as far as epistemology goes anyway—the only comprehensive, often correct and highly fertile account of the mind in all this is the Freudian account. I say this well aware of the excesses and abuses, including those for which Freud himself is responsible. And I'm all for good healthy competition. But the above fragmentation, this proliferation of acceptable or not unacceptable shingles, is one thing that gives the profession a bad name in some quarters. There is, after all, nothing comparable to this quarrelling over methodological fundamentals in physical medicine.[81]

The second problem, and the final one of the section, has to do, more specifically, with drugs. I pointed out in Chapter 1 that positive results have been obtained with antipsychotics for, not only schizophrenia and paranoia, but also organic disorders, schizophreniform disorder, schizoaffective disorder, brief reactive psychosis, mania and psychotic depression as well as other types of depression, anxiety and eating disorders and borderline personality disorder. Similar, although not quite as spectacular, claims are made for antidepressants and anxiolytics. These results can be due to a drug's sedative powers, for example, but there can be no doubt that the drugs have appreciable and sometimes desirable effects. Still, if you had a drug that seemed to help with tuberculosis, kidney stones, indigestion, diabetes and measles, you would know something had gone badly wrong. I am not talking of dishonesty or rigging results—or not exactly. But it must be tempting to take a drug with a proven track record in one area and see if it works in another. And these drugs always have relatives or near-relatives that might be worth a try. There are papers to be written and careers to be made and all one needs, after all, is a positive finding. And then there are the variables—which can be daunting or easily forgotten—and the difficulty of judging success—although this is also the difficulty, sometimes even more formidable, of judging failure instead. There are the drug companies—and there is all that money. But the profession has a choice here. It can either do more careful, more thorough and more closely scrutinized studies on the effects of drugs in the hope of making the profiles of success and failure sharper and more specific. Or it can concede that the drugs we now have available really are chemical bludgeons, no more or not much more legitimate as a means of treating mental illness than insulin or camphor—or a few c.c.s of sulphur, say, or dish detergent injected intravenously. For what might that do? To put all this more prosaically: Drug therapy for the mad is, in some ways, more primitive than chemotherapy for cancer with a fair amount of hitting and an awful lot of missing—and the profession, as should be clear, has its own peculiar problems with diagnosis and decisions about cure or improvement. Things should be cleaned up.[82]

The Place of Madness—and Some Definitions and Conclusions

I try, in this final section, to locate madness in our common intellectual consciousness, in our very general scheme of things. And I try to say, not just what its place is, but what it ought to be. One way of achieving these objectives—although not the only one—is to indulge in the complicated art of definition. So I do my fair share of that—with regard to "neurosis" and "personality disorder" as well as "madness". There is, however, a fundamental prejudice in our attitudes towards the mad that, properly understood, gives rise to a constraint on all such definitions. It has to do with the brain cases—and thus we do, in the end, get around to that issue.

We don't think of brain cases as mad—however psychotic, so to speak, they might be. And some of them certainly are. The man who, because of the virus eating away at his brain, can remember no more than the events of the last ten or fifteen seconds, who has, almost, no concept of the past. The woman whose inoperable brain tumour has left her blind and completely demented. The victims of car wrecks who are nearly comatose or given, instead, to destructive rages or periods of sheer terror or endless directionless confabulation. We don't think of these people as mad however irrational or bizarre their speech and behaviour, however disfigured their minds. But we do—and here is the prejudice—think of the mad as mad. We think of them as possessed of defective minds and brains, or we do in most cases, and mad besides or in particular. What, though, is the subclass of brain cases that constitutes the mad?—or the mad, the neurotic and those with disordered personalities? For these mental disorders do seem, by and large at least, to be brain cases. So what is the subclass?

Assume that "schizophrenia", "obsessive-compulsive disorder" and so on are defined symptomatically. In enumerating cases of madness, neurosis and personality disorder from among all brain cases, we will then have two kinds of schizophrenia, for example—the known brain cases and the brain cases where we still know few of the details or the as it were real schizophrenics. But the question is: Can we do anything more than enumerate?

Assume that "schizophrenia", "obsessive-compulsive disorder" and so on are defined partly in terms of symptoms but partly in terms of the still mostly unknown neurological cause. In enumerating cases from among all brain cases, we can, if we want to, hang on to the idea of one kind of schizophrenia—and then why not the as it were real kind? For the cause of what we now call "schizophrenia" is, presumably, different from that of symptomatically similar known brain cases. But the question is: Can we do anything more than enumerate?

To put the question in another way: Is there any principled difference between schizophrenia and brain cases or known brain cases? No. Let's suppose, for the moment, that schizophrenia is a disorder of thought; it won't affect the argument. If "schizophrenia" is defined symptomatically, the only difference between the two kinds, the "organic" and the "functional" or "primary", is a different cause in the brain—and there are, besides, other thought disorders among known brain cases. In neither sort of example do we have a principled difference.   If "schizophrenia" is defined with some reference to its neurological side, there are schizophrenia-like disorders, as well as other thought disorders, among known brain cases. In neither sort of example do we have a principled difference. However we define the words we use to identify mental disorders, these disorders are not clearly separable from brain cases—except in the way that stomach flu differs from mild food poisoning. Exactly the same point can be made if schizophrenia is construed as a disorder of the will, say—and exactly the same point can be made for all mental disorders that have a neurological etiology, known or unknown. For what I mean, in the above, by a "principled difference" is one that is over and above, different in kind from, the difference that exists between mania and paranoia or between aphasia and agnosia.

So there is no principled difference. We can only enumerate. History has picked out the mad from all brain cases by enumeration. But to say this is to say it has done so arbitrarily, for no good reason. Other enumerations, other prejudices, have an equal claim.   What claim? The claim to the title of "madness". For there is, in that title, not one thing, but two: a mere enumeration and a mystique or an aura that sets madness off from brain disorder in general. This latter is no more than a hoax perpetrated by history, the history of the last hundred years when the hoax crystallized and became much clearer together with the history of centuries before when it began to slowly take shape, centuries when witches and demons were everywhere and science was still in its infancy. We might want to trace it back to the Greeks, even, if not to early Biblical times. The mystique or the aura, whose only reason for existence is an arbitrary enumeration, had its initial stir-rings—at least, to put it modestly—many hundreds of years ago. It is a groundless prejudice; if you like, a kind of near-universal superstition we have inherited from the past. It can be described, as can all superstitions. We treat madness as somehow and importantly different, as containing some special element or feature not present in other brain cases. But beyond that, as with all superstitions, it has no real content—or none over and above the mystery and the uneasiness, the fascination or distaste or the awe. This applies to, not only madness, but also neurosis and personality disorder for they too are subject to this superstition; they too are the business of psychiatrists. The shrinks or the mind doctors as opposed to the physical people, particularly the neurologists. What follows from all this, however, is that there is no principled difference between clinical psychology and clinical neurology—unless, once again, something like Partial Parallelism is true and functional or primary disorders, disorders that have no neurological etiology or counterpart, do actually exist. As far as we know and in spite of my bringing up this difficult question a while back, there are no such disorders. It is this fact that constitutes a constraint on all definitions. I will return to it in the final few pages.[83]

The above is not our usual view of madness. Most people have a very different view—and on a number of fronts. One aspect of it—and here philosophers are as guilty as anyone—is that we continue to place the Aristotelian notion of intellect or rationality at the centre of madness. To go mad, it is so easy to tell ourselves, is to lose one's reason, one's grip on reality. And if human beings are rational animals, those disorders that afflict us but not pigs or kangaroos must be disorders of rationality, irrationalities, nonrationalities, arationalities.

It is not that this view is false—and I have not, in this book, tried to show that it is. Reason or thought—to give this notion a more stream of consciousness cast—is, of course, important. So too is the distinction between it, on the one hand, and mood or emotion or feeling on the other. And madness can be seen as depending, critically, on these notions. But certain large qualifications need to be entered at this point. We are, by now, familiar with them.

The first—and one or two minor detours will be in order here—is that the notion of rationality has to be understood extremely broadly, a message that is of particular significance for philosophers. Some philosophers, those of us who remain unreconstructed or undeconstructed, continue to place rationality and reality at the centre of philosophy. A substantial part of epistemology is the study of what it is reasonable or rational to accept and on what grounds, if any. Ontology has to do with existence or reality—as does epistemology when it comes to knowledge and to truth. The philosophy of mind deals with both reason and reality. And ethics, while about a set of practices or norms that are not purely or strictly rational, emphasizes those elements of morality that are rational—just as the philosophy of law tries to make sense of the oddities of legal argument with its reliance on precedent and convention and aesthetics does what it can with the notion of aesthetic argument or reason in art. But let me quit while I'm ahead and say, simply, that rationality means a lot to us philosophers.

In the last section, I discussed, briefly, the philosophical tradition to the effect that only two kinds of truth are possible—the necessary or analytic or a priori and the contingent or synthetic or a posteriori. I also pointed out that this tradition has a negative face. It is that our utterances, and indeed our thoughts, are subject to only three kinds of defect—contradiction, contingent falsehood and mindless undifferentiated gibberish. But to say or think what is contingently false—that there is cheese in the cupboard when it's all gone or that Lima is the capital of Brazil—is, according to the tradition, not to be irrational. It is just to be wrong about the empirical facts. What the tradition amounts to, then—although I didn't put it in these terms earlier on—is that we are capable of only two kinds of irrationality: contradiction or affirming and denying one and the same thing in a single breath and nonsense or babble with, essentially, no content.

It should be said—to keep the record straight—that there have been occasional protests against this position. Kant claimed that we have more than one basic distinction here, thus generating the hybrid category of synthetic a priori truths, Quine that nothing is analytic so everything is synthetic and Kripke, more recently still, that the necessary/contingent distinction differs from the a priori/a posteriori distinction, the one being metaphysical, the other epistemological. And over the last twenty or thirty years, philosophers, and especially philosophers of mind, have become fascinated again by science with the result that the line between philosophy and science, at least, has thankfully been blurred—although the members of this new breed of philosophical-cum-scientific cat are often prepared, quite cheerfully and without hesitation, to identify the nonempirical and empirical strands of their accounts or theories or models. But the protest that, for some of us, undermined the tradition completely came with the work of Wittgenstein. There was the talk of "games" and "criteria" and "family resemblances", of "natural history" and the idea that a satisfactory philosophical assessment might consist, simply, of "This is what we do", of the need for and the inevitability of "roughness" in philosophy and the inadequacies and evils of formalism, of new and almost unimaginable "logics", of "language going on holiday" and of "wheels that turned though nothing moved with them", of certain mistaken philosophical views as "dreams" and "image-mongery"—and, in the epistemological writings, of what might seem to be straightforward empirical truths like "Here is a hand" and "The Earth has existed for longer than five minutes" and their "peculiar logical role". Straightforward but as fundamental as you can get. Heady stuff—and, sometimes, tantalizingly difficult. But whatever else it meant, it meant that there are all sorts of rationality and all sorts of ways in which reason can fail.[84]

I won't rehearse again the philosophically loaded cases from abnormal psychology I listed in the last section. Many of them, certainly, can be regarded as disorders of reason or thought and yet there are not—or not usually or significantly—infringements or violations in them of the laws of formal systems of logic. There is not, again, that much contradiction going on. And neither, again, are they cases of nonsense, or not of the kind where, on the basis of content, one case can't, or can't clearly, be distinguished from another. Wittgenstein, however, is often ignored in contemporary philosophy—as though this most original of thinkers had never existed. So what was, by and large, the received wisdom in philosophy until the time of Wittgenstein and what still is for a lot of philosophers abdicates to psychiatry the job of carving out the categories of assessment within the broad domain of rationality and its possible defects that are appropriate to these cases. For the received wisdom, this is uncharted if not mythical territory.

A further moral can now be drawn. A lot of philosophers—the same lot—believe that the only way in which a philosophical view can be right is by being necessary. If they happen to be philosophers of mind, they think of what they do as issuing or endorsing necessary and therefore universal truths about the mind. About any mind—human, alien or divine? Yes. About the normal mind and the abnormal? Yes. About the mad mind? What truths are there about the operations and contents of the mind, about the self, knowledge or thought or emotion or desire or the will, that can't be falsified in the loss or the destruction of madness? There aren't any such truths—or there are hardly any. And madness, once again, is special. I spoke earlier of levels or orders of abnormality and the possibility of antiRealism being squared. Madness—or so we like to assume—offends against reason, that faculty we take such particular pride in. And true madness, as I've said, is unintelligible to everyone, including God. I sometimes think that madness is already squared, all by itself.

The first qualification to the view that the notions of reason and emotion are crucial to madness is, then, that reason has to be under-

stood broadly.   A second—and this is of special significance to
psychiatrists—is that emotion should be similarly understood.   It
should, anyway, not be understood absurdly narrowly and arbitrarily so
as it is by *DSM-IV* and the profession in general. Earlier philosophers,
like Descartes and Hume, did tend to have a small number of emotional
elements out of which all other moods and feelings were somehow
built.   Wonder, for Descartes, was the most important but Hume was
less daring or less imaginative.   More recent philosophers of mind,
however—or the relative few who have much to say about emotions—
are usually much more willing to let the facts speak for themselves
without trying to impose some artificial structure on this admittedly
untidy area. Depression and mania, feeling up and feeling down? How
breathtakingly simplistic.   And how much more sophisticated, how
much richer and more plastic, could *DSM-IV*'s sort of taxonomy be
with even a halfway adequate take on emotion? But I won't pursue this
matter.   My concern here is not, after all, not at this point in the
proceedings, to try to bail out *DSM-IV*.

The third and final qualification I am going to mention—and here
too psychiatry is particularly responsible and especially vulnerable
although there are some difficult questions for philosophy as well—this
last qualification can be expressed with economy since a great deal of
this chapter has been devoted to it.   It is that there are competing
taxonomies, other ways of seeing madness—in terms of the self, say, or
the will. The way that gives prominence to reason and the distinction
between it and emotion is just one option among several.   Only the
weight of prejudice and the past confers on it its official status and
makes it so widely accepted within psychiatry and, from there and by
extension, more generally.[85]

But whatever taxonomical system we employ, not much can be
done about the distance—between the system and what it is supposed
to represent, between sanity and what we conceive of as madness. And
it is the difficulty of conceptualizing that adds to the distance just as the
distance adds to the difficulty. The mad might not be "the hierophants
of the sacred".   But they inhabit two worlds—just as we do.   The
shared physical world with its inanimate objects and other human
beings and the inner world of the mind. For the mad, however, this
second world, this second sort of reality, is itself mad—a reality that is
not merely very different from those we are familiar with but strictly
unintelligible. And they experience the public world through this filter,
through this madness. There is, for us, with our distant perspective, an
uneasiness about this, a sort of fear even, a fear of the unknown and the
unknowable. Madness inspires fear as death does or profound disloca-

tion. The fear of intermittent or conscious death or the fear of being out of your mind without having the slightest suspicion that you are. The fear of being dead while you're alive or of being right, judicious and right for an awful lucid moment, in your firm conviction that you are mad. I talked, at the beginning of this chapter, of the mad as freaks. But that doesn't seem to me to quite do them justice. They're human, of course—or the ones we run across are. And most of them can provoke the laughter or scorn that is the other, less uncomfortable, side of terror or awe. There is, though, another myth, another shadow, that has grown up in our midst. It is that of the alien. The alien has captured our imagination—in the tabloids and in novels, on television and in film and even within science itself. So what is it, exactly, about that really very odd neighbour—down the block or the next galaxy over? I once overheard, in the courtyard of a motel in Arizona, one biker say to another of some mutual acquaintance that he was "a hog worse than a pig". An alien, I can't help thinking in the same search for precision, an alien worse than a freak. For the mad, despite their human shape and language, can be at least as unreadable to us, as masked and essentially unapproachable, as the most unlikely or outlandish alien. The phenomenology incomprehensible and one's mind a reality or a hell that can't be coherently described. One's mind? Sometimes there is no evidence of an owner, of a watcher and controller, and the mind itself might, again, be a mere Humean bundle or it might be conscious and yet completely still and silent. I realize I have barely scratched the surface on some questions and that there are others I haven't asked. Madness, like death and like scepticism, is hard to get close to. Like the flame of a candle, it's hard to get close to without going too far.

I want to turn now to the question of definition. There will, inevitably, be certain difficulties here. I have said that the concept of madness is relatively new, still fairly primitive and changing rapidly. It stands at the crossroads of a future none of us can know very much about. But if the human race stays around and more or less healthy, there will be major and radical shifts over the next, let's say, fifty or one hundred years in our understanding of the mind and the mad mind, in particular. So the concept of madness is an object-lesson in humility for us philosophers, a sobering corrective to the Platonic ideal of not only transparent but eternal philosophical truth. The following is a report in progress.

Before trying to give explicit definitions of "madness", "neurosis" and "personality disorder", I want to go over some preliminary definitional material. I also want to make some comments about the relationships between and among various bits and pieces of the territory covered by psychiatry. We have, in earlier sections, discussed parts of this as well.

It should be clear that one path along which we can move from psychosis to neurosis is that marked by intensity of emotion. Whatever *DSM-IV*'s views, bipolar disorder can fluctuate between deep depression and hypomania or mania and a milder depression. Major depression of the as it were nonpsychotic kind is, nevertheless, symptomatically indistinguishable from the depressed side of many bipolar cases. Melancholia is especially debilitating—and good old-fashioned neurotic depression is, of course, mild or minor depression. Are there any other such paths?

We might differentiate between depression, panic and the fear associated with phobias on this score although not in the way that *DSM-IV* does. Panic can be mild or infrequent but it need not be. And while a fear of snakes is one-dimensional and at least half-reasonable, there are irrational terrors or dreads over the most pervasive or common features of our environment. Birds will do it sometimes or other people, sudden movement will or darkness or change, the phobia of autism. And these terrors can, again, be disabling. So there surely ought to be psychotic and neurotic kinds here too. What are the opposites of panic and fear? Calmness, I suppose, and equanimity or even smugness. Abulia and anhedonia can be regarded as more or less pathological examples. Do these emotional states—for example, panic and a morbid calmness—go in cycles? I don't know. What does it say about the brain and emotions if they don't? And even if cases of unipolar mania and hypomania exist, far fewer of them are observed than the corresponding depressions. What does that say about the brain? And speaking of abulia and anhedonia, there is also the will to consider. We ought, I think, to allow for a psychotic form of obsessive-compulsive disorder with less severe cases as neurotic and kleptomania and pathological gambling as sociopathic or self-destructive personality disorders and trichotillomania as an oddly specific neurosis or perhaps, even, a sort of body dysmorphic disorder. But I'll stop here and say, simply, that there are other paths from psychosis to neurosis and other criteria for making the distinction.

Are there always these paths? Is there a mild or neurotic form of schizophrenia?

DSM-IV lists schizoid, schizotypal and paranoid as personality disorders. But it also lists borderline personality disorder—"a pattern of instability in interpersonal relationships, self-image, and affects, and marked impulsivity"—and it tells us that this disorder is sometimes conceptualized at the "level of personality organization". What this means is that borderline disorder is sometimes thought of as a neurosis, and a Freudian one besides. This is an issue with a long and tangled history in the profession. Still and all, borderline disorder is the only neurotic counterpart to schizophrenia if there is one. By contrast, we have lots of noncontroversial neurotic cases among the mood disorders—and with obsessive-compulsive disorder, panic and phobia, the neurotic cases do, it seems to me, represent the core of the condition. But underlying all this, of course, is the question of what, exactly, is the difference between neurosis and personality disorder.

Then there is the question of whether there is always a path from neurosis to psychosis. I won't go into detail. But it's difficult to see psychogenic fugue or hypochondria as full-blown psychoses—although the latter might, I suppose, be the neurotic analogue of a kind of paranoia. And the difference between somatization disorder and conversion disorder seems to have no psychotic counterpart. Then there are the personality disorders. Four of *DSM-IV*'s ten are, once again, related to schizophrenia and/or paranoia, one is to obsessive-compulsive disorder and perhaps two of them are to certain somatoform disorders. None are related to the mood disorders—although *ICD 10* differs on this point—and none are to the panic, anxiety or dissociative disorders—unless borderline disorder really is a personality disorder and has clear connections with the latter. These disorders, remember, have all these pigeon-holes for neuroses instead. But what, again, is the difference? And while much more thinking needs to be done about all of this, there are empirical facts that might help to resolve some of these questions. Again, I don't think anyone knows or knows very much of the empirical facts about this background material, about these mostly little discussed and sometimes barely inhabited annexes and byways off or within the main structure of the concept of madness.

And now, very briefly, for some of the closer relatives, the adjacent areas. The mildly retarded don't so much transgress against reason as impoverish it. But in severe or profound retardation, reason is often abused and it becomes, for some and like everything else, incomprehensible in even the vaguest or most simplistic terms. And some cases of hebephrenic schizophrenia, for example, are symptomatically indistinguishable from some cases of retardation although the former can also be marked by a volubility and richness of speech typically absent in the latter—just as catatonic stupor or excitement can pass as the most vacant or giggling idiocy although often with significant fluctuations over time. And then there's autism. Retardation, again, is common—and those autistics who are intelligent by some standard still exhibit the stereotypy and repetitiveness characteristic of the disorder so that the possibility of any genuinely creative intelligence is, in the great majority of cases at least, nonexistent. A complete failure, we might think, of the imagination. Or, we might think, the ultimate phobia, of other people and the world and everything interesting with the fear encircling, eating away at the self.[86]

Certain cases of emotional deficiency—vastly overrepresented in the prison population and, it is often suggested, at the highest levels of business and government—pose moral and legal problems. Emotions are restricted to anger, lust, resentment and envy or they are always superficial, perfunctory, little more than routine. Just built differently, it sometimes seems; that's all. We could say that such people have a personality disorder—antisocial, sociopathic, psychopathic—but we have to recognize that this is a personality disorder whose content is closely linked to moral concerns and possible legal minefields. Its status as a disorder is therefore especially, not questionable, as much as sensitive. And violence marks some of these cases. The mad or the mad in general are more likely to be violent than the rest of us—by a factor of three to five, according to some studies. And some cases of the so-called "sexual disorders" and "addictions" belong here. Are there, or can there be said to be, impairments of reason in these cases? Often—and this should be emphasized. But even a pervert or fetishist can be thoroughly charming and the smooth-talking or expansive psychopath enormously difficult to resist. They just have very easily brought on or ignored, paper-thin, readily negotiable or spine-chillingly unimportant feelings.

And then there are the memory disorders. Someone with a memory defect is not thereby irrational—or, for that matter, without a will. He or she has, however, lost a more or less fundamental and wide-ranging source of information or expertise for reason—or the will—to work with. And conversation can be strange with someone who believes it's still 1958 or who is trapped in the confusion, in the sheer voids and gaps and emptinesses, of Korsakov's. Then there are the children who are brought up or survive among animals, the pathetic wretch of a middle-aged man found in some basement in Italy where he has been imprisoned since adolescence, the adult who has somehow overcome full-on schizophrenic parents or repeated and systematic abuse. There are tribes from New Guinea or the high Andes, there are whole pockets or villages, sometimes, of marginally functioning incestuously related people. There are…there is no end. And we are, anyway, back where we started.

A large, then, an uneven and a not always clearly demarcated territory. I mentioned, in Chapter 3, *DSM-IV*'s not very helpful attempt to define "psychosis". *DSM-IV* doesn't try to define "neurosis"—it doesn't recognize it—or "personality disorder"—it most certainly does—but, mindful of this larger territory, it tries its hand in the Introduction at the very general "mental disorder": "Whatever its original cause, it must currently be considered a manifestation of a behavioural, psychological or biological dysfunction...." *DSM-IV* is not, as I have said—and I will return to this for one last time in a little while—unaware of the problem created by the brain cases. But its solution to the problem here, in this critical exercise in definition, is, with the inclusion of "biological" as one of its disjuncts, to allow measles and arthritis, skin fungus and diabetes in as mental disorders along with the most labrynthine and exquisite paranoia. Ah well, it's a tough business, this constructing of definitions . Everyone wants to take a pot-shot. But here goes, finally, with suggested definitions for key terms.

Madness/psychosis/insanity: A breakdown in the structure and capacities of the mind. Usually or always accompanied by and perhaps explicable on the basis of pathology of the brain. Any one of an arbitrarily chosen list of disorders. [The arbitrariness—this is not really part of the definition—is by comparison with all brain cases, known or otherwise, as well as all non-brain cases, so to speak, if there are any.] So we have the various types of schizophrenia with paranoia, if you like, as a separate entry and then the cross-sectionally indiscriminate brief psychotic disorder, the odd or overlapping schizo-varieties and folie à deux—and we have mania and major depression. [Psychiatry has—a queer circumstance—recently dropped the last two from its list of psychoses with no explanation. But the connection between madness and mania, in particular, seems strong enough to withstand such attacks from within. Doesn't one piece of arbitrariness deserve another though? In a way it does; in others it doesn't. Historically sanctioned arbitrariness, besides, is much less raw, much easier to live with, than a sudden whim—and arbitrariness that sees itself for what it is always has that much more to be said for it than the other kind.] Officially conceptualized as disorders of thought or reason, on the one hand, or mood on the other. These notions of reason and mood are fairly complex and can be misunderstood but alternative taxonomies—relying on the self or the will or even the emotions construed more sensibly than is typically the case in psychiatry—are at least as plausible. And madness, psychosis or insanity must be severe. I make no apologies for the word. While it constitutes no more than a rough gesture towards one crucial feature of madness, some such word or expression, some synonym or near-synonym, is needed here. Compare severe v. mild angina or a severe v. a mild cold. [*DSM-IV* will have none of this with its chronic need for more precision than the subject-matter will admit. And—a note on insanity. Sometimes thought to be more of a legal notion; see below.] But given the present state of our knowledge, madness is just this—or this together with what I have called "preliminary definitional material" and more detail on various points a presupposition or possible elaboration, available, as it were, on demand.

Neurosis: Another disturbance or disability of the mind. It appears to have the same sorts of connections with brain pathology as does madness—although what is known about neurosis and the brain is much more scattered and uneven. A hundred years ago, any one of all of the rest of the disorders studied and treated by psychiatry. But the personality disorders have since been carved out so now most easily definable by just listing the relevant twenty-odd disorders that range from panic through hypochondria to depersonalization. The list, again, is arbitrary and for the same reasons as with madness but this time it's much longer and all sorts of threads run through it. A few of these disorders, like conversion hysteria and dissociative fugue, are, by definition, broadly Freudian or psychodynamic anyway. Most of them are not even though Freudian therapy might, as a matter of fact, be helpful or lead to a cure. [Since *DSM-IV* suggests that being primary is incompatible with being organic, it commits itself, not only for the above special cases but for all its alleged primary disorders, to Partial Parallelism, for example, or Partial Reverse Epiphenomenalism. There might, I have argued, be something to this.] And some of the neuroses, once more, have corresponding psychoses. Neurotic depression and hypomania are obvious examples—but think also of the neuroses of the will and certain psychoses construed in the same terms. Then there are the others with no particular or striking link with psychoses: some of the somatoform disorders, dissociative fugue, again, and amnesia, perhaps simple agoraphobia. The differences, moreover, are different in different cases. [I have *DSM-IV*'s classification primarily in mind here but the point I want to make is independent of that classification.] Dissociative amnesia and fugue are more like one another than either is to depersonalization or multiple personality disorder; body dysmorphic disorder, however profound, stands out from what surrounds it as a more or less aesthetic predicament; and what, exactly, is the place of that marked disorder of the will and sometimes near-psychosis at least, obsessive-compulsive disorder? More arbitrariness—and more absence of fit. And neuroses are, in general, milder or less severe than psychoses. Maybe a handful of levels or degrees instead of two are possible but, beyond that, this crucial notion of mildness and its opposite or complement can be made no clearer.

Personality disorder: Another mental disorder, usually or always tied to the brain again, sometimes arbitrary again. But essentially a background disorder so less arbitrary in one respect for this does give the notion more content. "Background" means "deep"—two uninterestingly different metaphors in the present context—though not, or not necessarily, in the Freudian sense. "Background" therefore means "relatively recalcitrant to change" or "other things being equal and without therapy, long-term". So it sorts with—I hesitate to say it implies—"typically mild". "Long-term" is incompatible with "acute", that not infrequent indicator of severity. And "background" makes an upfront psychotic episode unlikely. It also make an upfront neurotic episode unlikely. No useful judgement can be made, on the other hand and in spite of my raising the question, as to whether personality disorder is, in general, less severe than neurosis or vice-versa. And to say that a disorder is a background disorder is to say that it need not preoccupy whereas the stream of consciousness of a neurotic or a psychotic must, as I've claimed, be riddled with the signs of the disorder. [It is not that a neurotic or a psychotic must know, by introspection, that he or she is neurotic or psychotic; he with his obsessions and she with her delusions will be peculiarly ill-equipped to do so. And it is not that someone with a personality disorder can't know that this is so. But a neurotic, say, in the midst or in the grip of neurosis, has the most blatantly neurotic thoughts, sensations and feelings. By contrast, few of us pay much attention to our basic psychological style, our motivations and desires, our most general beliefs and emotional tendencies. And while that style is, for many of us, fairly unified as well as broad-ranging and must and does show up in the stream of consciousness, one's personality might shape or guide one's thoughts but it is seldom part, even, of their content.] The list of personality disorders is, again, sometimes arbitrary although there are, I think, some fairly solid groupings of symptoms. It also contains disorders of various kinds—but what, again, of the question of personality disorders that have to do with mood? Sometimes, again, a personality disorder raises legal concerns—and sometimes the diagnosis, anyway, has to do with age or sex. And here too, of course, there are the neurological counterparts and the same constraint. [*DSM-IV* has such a counterpart for each of its types along with organic personality change; the single entry in *DSM-III-R*, under "Organic Mental Disorders", reads "Organic Personality Disorder".]

Mental disorder: Any of the above. In a broader sense: Any disorder that directly affects or involves the mind.

Sanity: Strictly speaking, not insanity. But if insanity = madness = psychosis, not madness or psychosis either. If, however, one were to talk of a life-long neurotic or someone with a disordered personality as sane, it would, in many circumstances, be tasteless or potentially embarrassing. "Insanity" as a legal term. This might mean nothing more than that lawyers use it a lot. Then lawyers are talking about what we talk about when we talk of madness or psychosis. It might mean that lawyers have a technical notion of madness. Then, one wonders, why not architects, barbers or at least pharmacologists? And what is this notion, exactly?—for there are all sorts of suggestions; see immediately below. But it might mean that the inability to tell right from wrong, say, or to properly instruct counsel during a long and difficult trial, the criterion employed in Ezra Pound's case, is a legitimate analysis of our concept of madness. Then it shouldn't. Many schizophrenics and manic-depressives can, much of the time, tell right from wrong—and while Pound, impossibly cantankerous and even contemptible as he then was, was adjudged mad on the above basis, so would a lot of other people be, people who are indisputably sane. Partial analyses? That is another story. Different sorts of definitions? Mostly not even thought of. Other legal criteria? Other issues again. A lack of control over actions, however, crops up fairly frequently and people have escaped the most serious of charges because of multiple personality disorder or some other personality disorder, more properly so-called. Guilty but neurotic? Not guilty by reason of personality disorder? There are, of course, other variables—like diminished responsibility, special pleas and reduced or suspended sentences—and then things get more complicated still. Sanity need not, it should be noted, be in any way admirable or worth having. It might be brutish or narrow, incredibly lonely, entirely negative, more or less dumb or tortured from within.

These are definitions that come with not only preliminary or background material; they also have consequences.

Conclusion 1. I have admitted to being something of a Wittgensteinian about language and about the proper categories of philosophical assessment. I am not referring, with regard to the former, to the social views or the idea that language and thought require agreement. I am referring to the significance given to "ordinary language"—what was, in another day, called "common sense"—as well as the emphasis on "roughness", the view that concepts typically contain gaps or areas of murkiness or uncertainty, that rules do not and cannot cover all cases and they themselves cannot be made exact or even clear sometimes since they too are subject to "friction and air-resistance". But for all my sensible and practical-sounding flexibility about concepts, I have to say that those employed by abnormal or clinical psychology are a scandal. From "schizophrenia" to "anxiety disorder" to "dissociative neurosis" to "histrionic personality disorder", these concepts are often unconvincing about subtypes and their interrelations. Their connections with one another are, where they can be articulated at all, mostly baffling. They can be rethought in quite different ways with sometimes this or that adjustment in their boundaries. They are usually described by *DSM-IV* in terms that are overly elaborate, overly complicated, overly precise parodies. They are like not very bright lights flicking on and off, sometimes farther apart and sometimes closer—but what might that mean? and have they shifted? and how?—against a darker but featureless background. The proper categories of philosophical assessment? Perhaps I should have said, not that, but the standards a concept must meet to be legitimate or acceptable. Wittgenstein's are much more relaxed than the tradition's, much more realistic. Our concepts, after all, are our creations—and yet the tradition often had it that they must be completely without flaw or blemish. But what we have in these concepts from psychiatry is not so much roughness as something of an entirely different order, a structure or set of structures that can barely hold itself together. These concepts have always been and still are surrounded by prejudices. One can't be born mad, for example—what is that and where did it come from?—and one can't die of madness; the mad are all violent or they all do it on purpose because they are evil or immoral; they argue legitimately but from unacceptable premises; Freudian therapy is inappropriate if the drugs work; madness has close ties to genius. Still, these are prejudices and we can try to understand and resist them, to set them aside. The real problem is with the content of these concepts. They are, as concepts go, in really bad shape.[87]

Conclusion 2. This is the more radical conclusion. It goes to the heart of the matter and I will sometimes repeat myself for emphasis as well as remind you, from time to time, of things I have said before.

In spite of a philosophical worry about partial Isms, like Partial Parallelism and Partial Reverse Epiphenomenalism, the great majority at least of cases of madness are brain cases. I have often used this technical term, in accordance with a policy of *DSM-IV*'s, to stand for known brain cases, cases where we know most or many of the details as in botched surgery or a tumour, grand paresis or a gun-shot wound. But if we extend it to cases where we know—or are anyway pretty sure or scientifically sure or as sure as such matters get—that the brain is directly and centrally involved although we're short on a lot of detail, cases of madness too are brain cases. This does not mean that they are genetically determined so that the environment, whether human or otherwise, can play no role. If it does play a role, however, it will do so—given a surely largely correct assumption shared by Interactive Dualism, Identity Theory and Supervenience—only at the expense of altering the brain. So most cases of madness, as I was saying—and, indeed, most cases of neurosis and of personality disorder—most cases at least are brain cases.

There are brain cases and brain cases, of course—and sets of symptoms and sets of symptoms. And you and I are brain cases in our ways. Our sanity is a function of our brain, so are our moods and our level of consciousness, our desires and our memories. But whether we describe "schizophrenia", say, in terms of symptoms or partly or even entirely in terms of the still largely unknown cause, there will also be schizophrenic or schizophrenic-like conditions among known brain cases. There will also, among the same group of cases, be other symptomatically different thought disorders. Or if we think of schizophrenia as a disorder of the will, for example, there will be other disorders of the will. To pick some of these cases out, the functional schizophrenics, so to speak, and label them and no others as "mad" is a kind of witchcraft, an alchemy, an empty unreasoning astrology, the fate of human beings lying, not in their brains, but in their demons or their baseness or somehow in their stars. For madness can be distinguished from its "nonfunctional", "nonprimary" or "organic" counterpart only insofar as there is a different physical cause or side to the story. And other examples or cases make the same point—or a broadly similar one—with regard to neurosis and personality disorder. It is as though we had singled out some forms of physical disorder from the rest and marked them with a special and an essentially indecipherable brand.

It follows from this that there is no such thing as madness—or no such thing as madness as opposed to known brain cases. There is no principled difference between clinical psychiatrists and clinical neurologists any more than there is between dermatologists and ear, nose and throat or bone specialists. The only reason for the distinction, the only difference, lies in the extent of our knowledge.

Does it follow that there is no such thing as schizophrenia? If we can cleanse "schizophrenia" of the taint of "madness"—and the difficulty of doing this should not be underestimated for words will, sometimes tenaciously, sometimes insidiously, cling to their pasts—it does not. "Schizophrenia" will still stand for "functional" schizophrenia or "functional" schizophrenia together with its brain case counterpart. Either or both is/are horrifyingly real major disorders of the mind and/or brain.

So my complaint here is with "madness"—or with "madness", "neurosis", "personality disorder" and "mental disorder" in the narrow sense. Taken together, as a subclass of all brain cases—whether they are known or not and whatever the details—they suggest no pattern that is even halfway reasonable or defensible. "Schizophrenia", by contrast, and "anxiety disorder" and "depression" do suggest such a pattern if they are suitably sanitized—or they do, at any rate, insofar as this is compatible with Conclusion 1. So we have a double whammy—for Conclusion 1 does apply to these terms—only for "madness", "neurosis", "personality" and "mental disorder". Not a particularly Wittgensteinian assessment for Wittgenstein's genius in this field was to emphasize the roughness of what were, he maintained, perfectly serviceable concepts. Still, rejecting certain concepts, arguing that they are illegitimate, is a long-established tradition in philosophy so there is nothing novel or somehow nonphilosophical in this conclusion. Hume, for one, did a fair amount of this sort of thing.

Am I recommending that we just junk these terms? I suppose I am; history, I have argued, means more for them than sense or integrity. But I have few illusions about my influence or, indeed, the influence of philosophy. And if many or most or even the vast majority of us continue to use them as a salute of some kind to the past, we ought to recognize that the concepts at issue have built into them the possibility of enormous expansion or contraction to nothing. Sort of "Take us or leave us" or "Now you see us, now you don't" concepts.

Doesn't *DSM-IV* recognize this with the increased prominence it gives to the "organic" disorders? An uneasiness about the brain cases has been around for quite a while. And "psychosis" isn't exactly *DSM-IV*'s favourite term either—although it is happy enough with "personality disorder". Maybe the uneasiness is growing. But there are, let me repeat, other known brain cases than those listed in *DSM-IV*. And merely putting something in bigger or smaller capitals or in a number of places instead of one is not, by itself, saying much. A let's-face-it, outfront and clearly articulated recognition of the problem? Not on your life, not even close.[88]

Let me try to break all this down a little further and do what I can to prevent misunderstanding.

I am not claiming that there are only "problems in living" or that the mad are sane. The so-called "psychoses", "neuroses" and "personality disorders" are, again, often wholly unintelligible or totally disabling and they are pretty much locked into the brain so that drugs and neurologists are precisely to the point. I insist on these things.

I am not claiming that the profession, narrowly construed or leaving out the specialists in known brain cases, is going to disappear. Specialists in manic-depressive disorder or agoraphobia will still be specialists in these disorders—although they had better keep up with the literature on drugs and they really should talk more to their strictly neurological cousins. But then too, since I'm offering advice, neurologists ought to at least read Freud and give some thought anyway to the mind.

I am claiming that the line between clinical psychiatry and clinical neurology is entirely arbitrary and that no such line should exist.

I am claiming, in that sense, that there is no such thing as madness—or madness, neurosis, personality disorder or mental disorder—as a special subclass of all brain cases. It is a subclass only by enumeration. I am therefore claiming that these concepts have no rational content.

I am claiming, on other and more detailed grounds, that the more specific concepts of abnormal or clinical psychology—those of schizophrenia and kleptomania and narcissistic personality disorder and so on—are, in some cases more than others but fairly generally, in pretty deplorable shape.

A personal note. There are always the personal reasons. Those, for example, of the "Two of my sisters…" or "You should have seen my father…" variety. And those, of course—often connected—having to do with whether you or I could become unbalanced or go berserk. Some of us, besides, just find madness fascinating or profoundly disturbing so it's a matter of temperament. Then one's training comes into it or professional or intellectual perspective. And then, try as one might to be objective about concepts, one will stress this, downplay that and completely overlook the other in a manner that someone else, no less objective, will fail to duplicate. Bias here or simply preference or interest will make itself felt. So there are always these reasons. There are, however, others as well.

The Genaine quadruplets, low I.Q., from the most marginal of families and doomed from the outset.

Daniel Schreber, this sort of judge, impregnated by the divine rays of God and the recipient of various bellowing miracles with Freud, in one of his more embarrassing moments, putting it all down to latent homosexuality.

Lois Vidal with all her wanderings.

The Dinosaur Man or Mr. Sophistication.

John Custance and Clifford Beers.

J. P., all 5'1" of him standing, almost on tip-toe, his hospital gown open at the back, bum white, skin slack, thinning curly hair a colourless brown, shouting, grinding out, "I am trying not to be overbearing."

Miss Holier than Mightest or Miss Amputee, small and not crippled exactly but oddly made so that she looked, in motion, more like a wheel, a tumble-weed, perhaps, or a swirl of leaves. You couldn't see her clearly; she was always something of a blur even when standing still.

Ivan V, incarcerated in a small cell from the time he was an infant and—what else?—stark raving mad by the age of twenty one.

Spider and his thin ones and fat ones.

Nijinsky proposing, on a ship to South America and the minute he got away from Diaghilev, to a star-struck Hungarian dancer without either of them understanding a word the other said. They were married as soon as they landed. And then, later on, he made strange drawings, he became obsessed by money, he endangered their child—and then the awful final retribution.

Mary Lamb, who stabbed her mother.

Virginia, of course.

Patrick Harrison, in his mid-forties, filthy, homeless, who cried in a shop doorway in San Francisco. He cried for the excitement of the crowd and of the night before Christmas and for his homelessness—but most of all he cried for the unbearable wonder of the smoke and flames belching from the top of a hotel two blocks away in the early evening darkness.

Janet's and James's Lucie.

Dr. Strangelove, the body and the will fighting, with each other in a sense, certainly within themselves, the body against itself, the will divided.

Anna O.

Lara Jefferson, mad as a hatter.

George III.

Gerry Maitland, incessantly twirling a lick of his black hair with the rage, at best, bubbling just beneath the surface.

Martha H., her face a gargoyle.

Sally Beauchamp—and Morton Prince.

William Leonard and his Locomotive-God.

Strindberg, the victim of vile conspiracies and bizarre hallucinations, frightened from birth of anything and everything—except, apparently, beautiful women.

The cardboard giants.

The raving crazies of Philip Oldman.

And so on. And so on.

There are, then, all these people, all these reasons, as well. Your list of such people will differ from mine to at least some extent. So there is, here too, room for the personal or the idiosyncratic, the not really justifiable or the mere matter, even, of whim. And yet it is these people who, in the end, constitute the subject, the focus, of any book like the present one. This must be so. There is no other way, no other key to, not only the fact, but also the mystery of madness. There is thus no other method of access to whatever we might, in the future, come to understand of this often bizarre and perplexing state.[89]

Notes

1. Conceptology, so to speak, a topic or concept that is often ignored by philosophers these days. And concepts as pictures—I like the deliberate vagueness, the Wittgensteinian plasticity of the word. Wittgenstein, by the way, makes it overwhelmingly clear that we are not entitled to expect anything like a Platonic sort of perfection from our concepts. He is, however and surely oddly, constitutionally opposed to the idea of mystery in philosophy.

2. Philosophers who have written interestingly about madness include, of course, Karl Jaspers with his *General Psychotherapy* (trs. M. Hamilton and J. Hoenig), Manchester University, 1963, and Michel Foucault in *Madness and Civilization* (tr. R. Howard), Pantheon, 1965. And Dan Dennett and Ian Hacking have written more recently about multiple or dissociative personality disorder, in particular. But one of the better things of this kind, it seems to me,

is T. Champlin's relatively little-known "The Causation of Mental Illness," *Philosophical Investigations*, 1989.

3. While a few of the above relationships have been documented, most of them haven't. One knows of them—however rough this knowledge might be—in the enormously difficulty to describe but completely familiar sort of way in which one knows so many things.

Madness runs through this family of cases. Retardation does too—although to a lesser extent so that the family one chose from this second perspective might well be partly but not entirely overlapping. And so too for what would once have been thought of as circus or side-show material—and so on. I did promise only one way of making the point about kinship more specific. But we have a family of families. So far, it seems, so good. Where, though, in this hierarchy, in these increasing powers, does meaning disintegrate?

4. See the *Treatise*, "Of Scepticism with regard to Reason" and the final long paragraph on pp. 186-87, in particular. Hume is his own worst enemy here. He begins the paragraph with the air of a man about to summarize or tidy up. And yet the paragraph contains a quite new argument for scepticism with regard to reason. It is the argument I have presented and it is much more formidable, much more devastating, than any of the arguments Hume sketches earlier in the section. That commentators fail—typically, at least—to appreciate the significance of the final paragraph is due, however, to more than Hume's tone. There is also the highly peculiar attitude that many philosophers have towards scepticism: "Don't take it seriously or too seriously; it will only lead to trouble." I have heard grown-up philosophers with credentials, colleagues of mine, say this out loud.

5. A much fuller account of scepticism and of the only form that anti-scepticism can take is contained in my "Wittgenstein's Elephant and Closet Tortoise," *Philosophy*, 1995.

6. I argue, in "Truth and Consequences," *The Modern Schoolman*, 1998, that there is something relative about ethics or morality as opposed to reason or rationality. The above justification, it turns out, would have to be—only?—a justification for a human being anyway. What is, on the other hand, undeniably true is that resigned acceptance in the face of the laws of chance or the brute dictates of unfeeling nature sometimes just doesn't satisfy.

And see, by the way, Edwin Wallace, Jennifer Radden and John Sadler, "The Philosophy of Psychiatry: Who Needs It?", *The Journal of Nervous and Mental Disease*, 1997—in which Karl Popper, with his manifestly broken-backed attempt to skirt around Hume's inductive problem, and Thomas Kuhn, with his paradigm shifts and incommensurability, are lauded as being among "this century's most respected philosophers of science"—for an unabashed scepticism/relativism in connection with psychiatry, in particular.

7. See, especially, *The Philosophical Works of Descartes*, Vol. I, pp. 149-53. There are, in fact, at least two versions of the Cogito in Descartes: the classical argumentative version, "I think, therefore I am or exist", and the bare stripped-down affirmation, "I am or I exist." The form of words employed in the *Meditations*—"I am, I exist, is necessarily true each time that I pronounce

200 *The Condition of Madness*

it, or that I mentally conceive it"—can be interpreted either way. It should also be pointed out that Descartes sometimes talks as though God is the ultimate foundation; see, especially, Vol. I, pp. 158-59. And while it is a truism, for some of us, that not even the Cogito is sceptic-proof, the members of a surprisingly large and varied group of philosophers are prepared—grudgingly or in a half-embarrassed way, parenthetically or from out of the blue—to endorse it. Examples include Bernard Williams in *Descartes: The Project of Pure Enquiry*, Harvester, 1978, pp. 78-87 and 95-101—although there are some residual Lichtenbergian doubts here; see note 50—and John Cottingham, *Descartes*, Basil Blackwell, 1986, pp. 38-39. But this is just to say, once again, that the Cogito is a curiosity, a philosophical folly, as it were.

8. Vol. I, p. 325, Vol. II, p. 13, Vol. I, pp. 340, 343, 235, 26, 95, 179 and 352. Margaret Wilson makes the odd claim—see the previous note—that "[Descartes's] commitment to the dependence of the eternal truths on God's will" has no "direct bearing on the status of judgements about thought," *Descartes*, Routledge and Kegan Paul, 1978, p. 152. She does emphasize, however, that the certainty attaching to the Cogito is "casually extended" by Descartes to "particular cogitationes", p. 151. The certainty of the Cogito varies inversely with the specificity of its premise.

9. Vol. I, pp. 44, 137, 92 and 26. Introspection, as will become clear, is often thought of as a kind of sense—and Descartes talks firmly, on a couple of occasions, of one or more "internal senses" and he speaks of "inward vision" and the "eyes of [the] mind"; Vol. I, pp. 290, 369 and 185-86.

10. Vol. I, p. 155. Compare Gareth Matthews, "Descartes and the Problem of Other Minds," *Essays on Descartes' Meditations* (ed. A. Oksenberg Rorty), University of California, 1986, on how little Descartes says about the problem as it is ordinarily understood. But Matthews claims that Descartes has an answer to the problem, a better answer than the traditional argument from analogy. I don't think the answer Matthews gives is better. It is, certainly, an answer to only one very uncommon question about other minds: "If you are going to meet a clod of dirt, a dumb animal or a low-level computer, on the one hand, or what anyway appears to be a person or human being on the other, how do you tell?"

11. Vol. I, pp. 151-52 and 190.

12. Vol. I, pp. 101, 141, 196, 171, 345, 118 and 192. Descartes also suggests, however—see Vol. II, p. 212, and Vol. I, p. 38—that mental phenomena like "pure understanding" float entirely free of the body and/or brain, a fact that Cottingham makes a great deal of fuss over. Still and all, here is Descartes raising the question of whether any Ism in the philosophy of mind ought to be thought of as holding for all mental phenomena. I consider the question in some detail later on in this chapter.

I do not, in this discussion, devote any space to property, as opposed to substance, thing or entity Dualism. While the former is sometimes said to be more acceptable or less unacceptable than the latter—see, for example, Patricia Churchland, "Reduction and the Neurological Basis of Consciousness," *Consciousness in Contemporary Science* (eds. E. Bisiach and A. Marcel),

Oxford, 1988—the reverse is, in fact, the case. Property Dualism solves none of the alleged problems associated with substance Dualism. And its primary motivation is: If we have to be Dualists at all, let's opt for the supposedly less metaphysically important category of properties rather than things. Apart from the implausibility of the supposition, Dualism needs no apology of any sort from anyone. And when I say "Dualism" in this discussion, I usually mean the interactive variety.

13. Vol. I, pp. 27, 232, 160, 174, 358 and 362-63. The doctrine that some of our ideas are innate has, it should be noted, been recently revived by Noam Chomsky and Jerry Fodor—though not always in terms Descartes would have understood.

14. For some of the more significant landmarks in the philosophy of mind over the last hundred years, see the writings of James, Freud, Broad, Watson, Skinner, Ryle, Wittgenstein, Smart, Place, Putnam, Fodor, Paul Churchland, Nagel and Kim—and, over the last twenty years or so, all of the disciples, the teeming throngs of disciples, of Nagel and Kim and still, sometimes, of Churchland or Fodor.

15. Introspection, as I say, has made a bit of a comeback lately. It is, nevertheless, neglected if not repudiated by many and maybe most contemporary philosophers—and for the better part of this century, it has routinely been the object of high academic and so, usually, more or less wretched humour. The reason for this appears to be as follows. Descartes, notoriously, took introspection to be infallible. Then philosophers began to notice its imperfections. Bingo. Not the most edifying example of the philosophical mind at work—and it's just as well that no philosopher ever claimed that vision, say, is infallible. Otherwise, we'd all—all of us philosophers, at any rate, and a lot of scientists too—we'd all believe we were blind.

16. A particularly neglected area, this, introspection and the preconscious. And the views of one of the few philosophers with anything to say about it—Anthony Quinton, "In Defence of Introspection," *Philosophical Exchange*, 1977—are especially revealing. Still under the spell of Wittgenstein and Ryle, Quinton talks, with regard to a belief, for example, of reflecting on how one would or might behave in various circumstances. But this, of course—however effective or ineffective—is not independent of behaviour. Neither—connected point—is it peculiar to the first-person and not just because of the possibility of telepathy. I leave aside here the question of whether telepathy ever is or could be as direct as introspection.

17. Introspection and the unconscious, an almost completely neglected area. But Freud is quite clear on this issue. And given that introspection might well take considerable time and effort when it is directed at the relatively easily accessible preconscious, what we might think of as the "necessity and legitimacy" of this enormously difficult sort of introspection ought to be readily apparent.

Brian O'Shaughnessy, in "Mental Structure and Self-Consciousness," *Inquiry*, 1963, talks of the need to reconcile Freud's views with Cartesianism and G. Myers says in *Self*, Penguin, 1969, that "the relation of Freudianism to

Cartesianism is one of the untold stories of our time", p. 31. "Cartesianism" is, of course—like "Darwinism" or "Marxism"—a term of art. But the link between Freud and Descartes is surely a matter of the introspective or direct access though by no means infallibilist views of the former, views that are crucial to his whole way of thinking about the mind.

18.   Whether the various Isms in the philosophy of mind are actually incompatible with introspection is another question entirely. For a little more on this, see below.

19.   So, it follows that, we have privileged access to the contents of our own minds. A "privilege", after all, is not an absolute right or benefit; it is, merely, a special one. Ryle is responsible for, not only a great deal of the ill-repute in which Descartes's views of the mind are currently held, but also the failure of so many philosophers to understand the English language on this point.

20.   I am not really concerned with what might be regarded as an internal objection to Eliminativism. Eliminativists can, if they wish to be consistent with this nonsense of theirs, maintain that they have no beliefs, not even in Eliminativism. I am concerned, rather, with the manifest absurdity of that claim. It must be said, however, that a much more slippery, a much more insidious, doctrine is often encountered in contemporary philosophy, that of Partial Eliminativism. Indeed, such a doctrine can be found on some of the pages of the flagship of Eliminative Materialism, Paul Churchland's *Matter and Consciousness*, MIT, 1984. Churchland, at any rate, seems not to be unduly worried about consistency. But there is nothing new in the idea that part of the mind or part of "folk psychology" has to go. Hume, for example, had a version of it—and one, moreover, that he argued for. All that is new is the widespread but clearly indefensible attitude to the effect that this doctrine, this idea, can be deployed without giving specific reasons, in a completely ad hoc way.

21.   Supervenience is, typically, opposed to Dualism. It certainly is according to Jaegwon Kim, the leading proponent of Supervenience from the mid-seventies up until very recently, at least. See, in particular, Kim's "Mental Causation in Searle's 'Biological Naturalism'," *Philosophy and Phenomenological Research*, 1995. Occasionally, however, a halfway serious attempt is made to square these two views with each other. See, for example, David Chalmers, *The Conscious Mind*, Oxford, 1996—although Chalmers's Dualism, not surprisingly, is of a very peculiar kind.

The difficulty about qualia for materialistic or reductive theories is, for me as it is for many others, associated with the name of Thomas Nagel; that about meaning or intentionality with that of Jerry Fodor.

The causal problem for interactive theories is thought to be so intractable by Dan Dennett in *Consciousness Explained*, Little, Brown and Co., 1991, that it is presented as though it were, on its own, fatal to such theories. And yet Dennett is as willing as anyone else in the philosophy of mind these days to concede that the various Isms are often speculative and subject to revision or elaboration by the future.

Descartes, interestingly, suggests the gravity analogy himself but with an emphasis on where interaction occurs; *Philosophical Works*, Vol. II, p. 255. See Cottingham, p. 120, and Wilson, pp. 213-15, for less than enthusiastic discussions.

And, finally, Nagel claims, in the Introduction to *The View from Nowhere*, Oxford, 1986, that the brain is no mere or ordinary physical object—and compare John Searle's "Minds, Brains and Programs," *Behavioural and Brain Sciences*, 1980.

22. As should be obvious from the previous note, the above is something of a composite picture. Certain individual differences are to be expected given the very large number of philosophers out there who are prepared to endorse some form or other of Supervenience. For a guided tour, see Terence Horgan's "From Supervenience to Superdupervenience: Meeting the Demands of a Material World," *Mind*, 1993. The notion of supervenience, by the way, had its origins a long time ago in the work of G. E. Moore in ethics. What Moore tried to do with the notion was to capture the relation between natural properties and moral properties, between the world of facts and the world of values.

23. Roger Penrose, in *The Emperor's New Mind*, Oxford, 1989—and compare *Shadows of the Mind: A Search for the Missing Science of Consciousness*, Oxford, 1994—attempts to show that there is, indeed, a difference in scale between the mental and the physical. His attempt fails, it seems to me, as any such attempt must. Physical objects are bigger than atoms, atoms are bigger than quarks,...quarks are much bigger than superstrings,...and so on, infinitely or indefinitely or only until the ultimate, the true atoms are reached. The mind does not sit on top of that hierarchy; it is not a member of that list at all. And yet its allegedly—what?—colossal dimensions and thus its supposed explanatory impotence is what this new mereology, this doctrine of supervenience, is all about. But then again, it must be conceded, Penrose does see the need to argue for a close or a clear analogy between the mind and brain and the macro and micro, an analogy whose power to persuade is almost always simply assumed. Compare the unthinking and nearly ubiquitous "top down" and "bottom up" to characterize possible directions of explanation between the mind and brain.

24. The bat is Nagel's—or B. A. Farrell's. See "What is it Like to be a Bat?", *Philosophical Review*, 1974, and "Experience," *Mind*, 1950, respectively. Nagel says he is a Realist about the mind but, as should become clear later on in this chapter, what he means by that label is not what I mean.

25. The compatibility is quite unproblematic as far as Supervenience is concerned; see below. But Identity Theorists have, typically, not found it easy to endorse introspection. So much so that Searle insists, in *The Rediscovery of the Mind*, that only a radical redrawing of the ideological boundaries in the philosophy of mind can show this to be a possibility. But Herbert Feigl argued for this sort of possibility many years ago—as, indeed, did Richard Rorty a little later on. See Feigl's *The "Mental" and the "Physical": The Essay and a Postscript*, University of Minnesota, 1958, 1967, and "Mind-Body, *Not* a Pseudoproblem," *Dimensions of Mind* (ed. S. Hook), New York University,

1961, and Rorty's "Mind-Body Identity, Privacy and Categories," *The Review of Metaphysics*, 1965.

26. Hume should be given the credit for the above distinction between the intrinsic and the causal or functional. His own account of the distinction—perhaps mistaken—maintains that intrinsic properties are available in a single experience whereas the apprehension of causal properties requires being exposed to constant conjunction. See the *Treatise*, pp. 76-77 and 87. Perhaps mistaken—but only with respect to causal properties. Intrinsic properties certainly are available in a single experience, introspective or otherwise.

27. The above criticism of Wittgenstein comes right on the heels of the acknowledgement of a debt. The need to bracket certain philosophical views so that they apply to only normal and, indeed, human cases is evident in both the *Investigations* and *On Certainty*—although it is, perhaps, more a matter of official doctrine in the latter than the former.

28. The idea that the self is crucial to the taxonomy of mental disorders is by no means new. It can be found in Jaspers, for example, and of course in Laing. The idea can, however, be traced back at least as far as Adler.

29. *Treatise*, p. 417, in particular. The nature of the relationship between the will and desire or, more generally, between the will and its influencing motives is further discussed later in this chapter and in my "Truth and Consequences."

30. Neither is there anything new about the idea that the will is crucial to the taxonomy of mental disorders. Jaspers comes to mind again along with Otto Rank. But see also in this connection the much more recent writings of Leslie Farber.

31. See Michael Taylor, Robyn Reed and Sheri Berenbaum, "Patterns of Speech Disorders in Schizophrenia and Mania," *The Journal of Nervous and Mental Disease*, 1994, and Nancy Docherty, Maddalena DeRosa and Nancy Andreasen, "Communication Disturbances in Schizophrenia and Mania," *Archives of General Psychiatry*, 1996, for recent attempts to come to grips with the issue of schizophrenia and language.

Although the voices of schizophrenia occur in only a minority of cases, they surely play—wrongly?—a disproportionately central role in our picture of the disorder. Compare note 39 on coprolalia and Tourette's.

And *DSM-IV* has, once again, blurred the distinction between schizophrenia and the mood disorders with the invention of schizoaffective disorder and mood disorder with psychotic symptoms; see, by the way, Michael Taylor and Nader Amir, "Are Schizophrenia and Affective Disorder Related? The Problem of Schizoaffective Disorder and the Discrimination of the Psychoses by Signs and Symptoms," *Comprehensive Psychiatry*, 1994, for an interesting discussion of the status of the former. But *DSM-IV*'s motives are quite innocent of any thought of alternative taxonomies. They have to do, rather, with the need to preserve its hierarchies—and, perhaps, the simple need to multiply.

32. It is almost impossible to overestimate the importance of taxonomical considerations in the thinking of the profession. Taxonomy influences, it pushes around, not only psychiatrists themselves—of course—and not only

epidemiologists and neurologists, but pharmacologists too. Of course. And S. Chua's and P. McKenna's "Schizophrenia—a Brain Disease? A Critical Review of Structural and Functional Cerebral Abnormality in the Disorder", can be read, without any distortion, as arguing that there is no real neurological evidence for the official taxonomy—although they themselves do not formulate the issue in these terms.

33. Taxonomy, as I've said, is not an exact or a rigorous undertaking. But to put the problems in psychiatry into perspective, just try to imagine comparable changes in the taxonomy of your favourite flora or fauna—or, indeed, in that of physical diseases.

34. Mikkel Borch-Jacobsen goes much further in "Who's Who? Introducing Multiple Personality," *Supposing the Subject* (ed. Joan Copjec), Verso, 1994, claiming that there is no such thing as multiple personality disorder—although his support for a diagnosis in classical or other classical Freudian terms is, at best, equivocal.

35. Two philosophers with agendas very different from mine—Dan Dennett (with Nicholas Humphrey) in "Speaking for Our Selves: An Assessment of Multiple Personality Disorder," *Raritan*, 1989, and again in "The Reality of Selves" in *Consciousness Explained* and Ian Hacking in *Rewriting the Soul: Multiple Personality and the Sciences of Memory*, Princeton, 1995, agree that there is no clear right answer to the question of how many selves are involved in multiple personality disorder.

36. And perhaps the most important of all is good sound common sense. This might seem to be too down to earth a position, not rarefied or elitist enough, for a philosopher to adopt—and there are, certainly, philosophers who take particular delight in ridiculing the beliefs of common sense. But see, again, my "Wittgenstein's Elephant and Closet Tortoise"—and remember that the Common Sense school used to be a perfectly respectable school of philosophy. For what is contemptible about being sensible, level-headed, balanced in one's judgements? And one might, if this is a worry, have all sorts of other virtues as well.

37. See John Wisdom's "Philosophy and Psychoanalysis" and "Philosophy, Metaphysics and Psychoanalysis," *Philosophy and Psychoanalysis*, Basil Blackwell, 1957, for earlier attempts to bring together the categories of assessment in philosophy and psychiatry. And for more on derealization and depersonalization, see below in connection with psychiatry in France and, later on, the discussion in the penultimate section of this chapter.

38. The distinction between autism and childhood schizophrenia is not made clearer by the separating out of the other pervasive developmental disorders, in most of which, by the way, retardation is at least an associated feature. On the contrary, these other disorders or subdisorders might well be thought to provide bridges of various sorts between the two. Rett's disorder is diagnosed only in females—but this begs an obvious question. Childhood disintegrative disorder involves a regression from a period of normal development—but this begs another. Asperger's disorder is said to have no particular connection with retardation—but around 20% of autistics are not retarded or

otherwise retarded either. And then there's atypical autism where there might be unusual symptoms and/or a relatively late age of onset. What distinction, exactly?

39. Coprolalia, the high point, so to speak, of Tourette's, is, paradoxically it might seem, present in less than 10% of cases. And, it should be noted, Oliver Sacks's "Witty Ticcy Ray," *The Man who Mistook his Wife for a Hat*, Harper and Row, 1970—and compare, in the same volume, "The Possessed"—is an even less responsible, even more glamourized, portrayal of Tourette's than "Rain Man" is of autism. Traces of this "romanticizing" of Tourette's are also present in Sacks's "A Surgeon's Life," *An Anthropologist on Mars*, Vintage Books, 1995. But while the achievements of the surgeon in question are certainly impressive, this is, overall, a more balanced piece than the earlier ones.

40. In a recent criminal case in California, a lawyer tried to get his client's death sentence commuted to life imprisonment on the grounds of insanity. And the reason offered for this, in turn, was that the client had an I.Q. of 60. Progress?—or just one more example of a lawyer willing to say anything that might do the trick?

41. There is, of course, a connection of sorts between sex addiction and codependence. If you're addicted to sex and, for at least much of the time, with a particular and similarly motivated partner, it follows that you're codependent as well.

42. Rather different are those disorders—multiple personality disorder and anorexia nervosa are examples—that are peculiar or largely so to industrialized parts of the world.

43. Part of the reason for the French difference, but only a part, is that the French—rightly?—don't insist on the same divisions between fields or disciplines as the rest of us—between philosophy and literature, say, or philosophy and psychiatry.

44. A measure of the American Psychiatric Association's reluctance to acknowledge its own and as it were official sexist past is that, in a nineteen-page appendix devoted to the differences between *DSM-III-R* and *DSM-IV*, not a single mention is made of the hysteria issue.

45. Jerry Fodor, in *Modularity of Mind: An Essay on Faculty Psychology*, MIT, 1983, is one of the few contemporary philosophers who is prepared to take faculty talk seriously. And he too attempts to defuse some of the grumbling that is usually provoked by talk about faculties; see below again. But while he also suggests that anyone who is at all committed to faculties has a clear obligation to provide a list of them, no such list is to be found in *Modularity of Mind*.

46. Henry Johnstone tries to argue, in *The Problem of Self*, Pennsylvania State University, 1970, that our concept of the self is inherently paradoxical and could, therefore, have no application. This is, I think, too extreme a position—but some of our concepts, certainly, are more elegantly or more robustly constructed.

And, for the above views, see *The Principles of Psychology*, Vol. I, p. 291.

47. "Even Dennett, in a way, has two." A word of explanation is needed in this case. Dennett is one of the great nay-sayers on this topic, invoking Hume's commonwealths and Parfit's clubs and generally likening us, in "Real Selves" in *Consciousness Explained*, to spiders, termites and crabs, organisms where the notion of a self can get no more than a tenuous foothold, at best. He also alludes to what he sees as a mistaken philosophical account of the self, the self as a "soul pearl", a "boss", a "ghost". This is dismissed with no discussion. And then, by contrast, Dennett provides us with a positive account of the self, one according to which, we are reassured, our existence is straightforward and indisputable. We are, he tells us, "centres of narrative gravity". The philosophical technique here that of the judiciously underdeveloped metaphor—but things immediately begin to unravel. For it is in connection with this allegedly positive account that Dennett talks of Hume and Parfit, spiders and crabs—and the narrative in question is, it seems, usually told by ourselves, typically unconsciously and it is usually fictional. So you are not real at all but some made-up character, an invented twist in the plot, a merely imagined happy or unhappy ending. If one did have to choose between these alternatives, I'd take the soul pearl in a flash. And you would think that this view of Dennett's was so manifestly inadequate that no one would find it attractive. But see "The Illusion of the Mind's I" and "Consciousness and the Self" in Flanagan's *Consciousness Reconsidered* where the only differences are that some of the more implausible elements in James's treatment of the self are grafted on to the account—and, to be fair to Flanagan, there is a worry, never resolved, about the genuineness of our existence on this sort of account. A worry? As genuine, once again, as Oliver Twist's existence or that of the scene with the Artful Dodger towards the end where.... You know. And if, as sometimes happens, truth-conditions are reinserted into the discussion at this point with the use of nonfictional examples, we have to acknowledge that we haven't, with all of this talk about narratives, even started to give an account. What is the true story? What is the truth about the self? Isn't this where we came in?

Nagel's way of counting selves is rather different. We are each of us two—an objective self and a subjective self. But apart from the importance of other dualities, isn't it worth reminding ourselves that each of us—or each of us normal nonpathological human beings, at any rate—is one?

48. A question, I am inclined to believe, that Descartes is concerned with in *Meditation II*. For he there speaks—*Philosophical Works*, Vol. I, p. 151—of what cannot be "separated from me"—and, later on in *The Search after Truth*—Vol. I, p. 322—of what "I cannot separate from myself." The other question, the one I don't have in mind, is discussed, not very convincingly, by Saul Kripke in *Naming and Necessity*, Basil Blackwell, 1980. Not very convincingly because Kripke claims that I must be or have been, as a matter of necessity, a twentieth-century individual, a human being moreover, made of flesh and blood, and I must have come from that sperm and that egg, the very ones, that I did in fact come from.

49. *The Principles of Psychology*, Vol. I, pp. 301, 297 and 338-40 and the *Treatise*, pp. 251-52. And perhaps the smallest self ever endorsed is that put

forward by C. O. Evans in *The Subject of Consciousness*, Allen and Unwin, 1970—"the background of consciousness", the faint background noise and glare that Evans thinks is present in any conscious moment.

50.   For the above views of James and Hume, see *The Principles of Psychology*, Vol. I, pp. 301, 300 and 297-99 and the *Treatise*, p. 252. Mostly because of Hume's influence, the self is one of the two areas—the other is that of freedom—where Eliminativism has traditionally been fairly common.

Although Descartes can't quite get his mind around the question, he seems to believe, in a sort of subthreshold way, that the self is introspectible. I leave aside, in mentioning evidence for this, all those occasions when Descartes says he perceives that he thinks but with no particular emphasis on the self— together with those when what is at issue is the purely intellectual perception of basic necessary or near-necessary truths. But for some much more suggestive remarks, see, for example, *Philosophical Works*, Vol. I, 44, 137, 153, 157 and 319 and Vol. II, pp. 33, 59, 217 and 313. Then there is the remark in the *Rules*—Vol. I, p. 7—where Descartes talks of his existence and his thinking as two distinct truths. Reading this view about the self, half-formed and never really or unequivocally asserted, into *Meditation II* does, it seems to me, shed considerable light on what is going on. "Sum", the first primitive cry out of the epistemological wilderness. And the introspectibility of the self is a good reason—although not, in the end, a decisive one—for taking the self to be entirely mental in nature. It also makes extremely quick work of Lichtenberg's famous and often repeated objection to the premise of the argumentative version of the Cogito to the effect that Descartes is entitled to affirm the existence of the thought but not of the self. This is, however, an unorthodox view for Descartes to hold and there are several passages—as is pointed out by Wilson—in which he pays an old debt to his Scholastic training and says that substance is unobservable except through its properties, whatever they happen to be. But the substance introduced in *Meditation II* has a very special and intriguing property, the somehow essential one of thought or consciousness.

51.   There might be alternative accounts of a lowest common denominator concept of the self; of course there might. But the question is a real one—and it does overlap with the question about small selves. At some not very clear point or over some not very clear stage as one goes down the phylogenetic tree, the concept of the self ceases to have application. That point or that stage, as unclear as it might be, is pretty far down.

52.   The relatively modest increase in popularity that Dualism at the property as opposed to the entity level has enjoyed over the last few decades comes from this relatively underdiscussed topic in the philosophy of mind, that of the self. It can, in particular, be traced back to Peter Strawson's *Individuals: An Essay in Descriptive Metaphysics*, Methuen, 1961.

53.   Fodor deals faithfully, in *Modularity of Mind*, with some of these objections to faculty talk. He does, though—or so it seems to me—take faculties to be more important, in their own right, than they in fact are. And his distinction between "vertical" and "horizontal" faculties—those that are and those that are not sensitive to content—is, I think, quite untenable as it stands.

54. This might be a fact, and indeed a plain fact, about reference. For what someone might have been or come to be is virtually limitless. What he or she is, however, is by no means limitless so that a completely open-ended account of the self is much less plausible. Nevertheless and leaving Sartre out of it, Robert Nozick offers just such a boot-strapping account in *Philosophical Explanations*, Harvard, 1981—and Dennett's account too sometimes has this sort of flavour. One's biography, after all, is never finished until one dies—although this is strictly irrelevant if the narrative whose centre of gravity one is identified with really is fictional.

55. For Locke's view of the relationship between introspection and vision, see the *Essay*, Vol. I, p. 123.

56. David Rosenthal's higher order of thought or HOT account of introspection—see, for example, his "Two Concepts of Consciousness"— requires only that there be a causal and thus a possibly dead or inert connection between the introspecting and the introspected thought. The account is criticized on just these grounds by Dennett in *Consciousness Explained*.

57. Although one might, once again, prefer one account to another—and perfectly reasonably besides.

58. Hume's discussion of the influencing motives of the will can be found in the *Treatise*, pp. 413-18.

Ever since the time of Plato, there have been philosophers who have claimed that weakness of the will, as opposed to weakness of the intellect, is essentially and irredeemably paradoxical, a phenomenon that cannot exist. See, for example, Donald Davidson, "How is Weakness of the Will Possible?", *Moral Concepts* (ed. J. Feinberg), Oxford, 1970. But see also Irving Thalberg's "Analytical Action Theory: Breakthroughs and Deadlocks," *Social Action* (eds. G. Seabass and R. Tuomela), Reidel, 1985, for a mostly clear and no-nonsense rejection of Davidson's view. And see Sarah Buss, "Weakness of Will," *Pacific Philosophical Quarterly*, 1997, for an updated and largely unrepentant version of Davidson's sort of view.

59. The stock of volition theories has, as I have indicated, been at an all-time low since the publication of *The Concept of Mind*. Even Brian O'Shaughnessy, sensible man that he is, objects to such theories in *The Will*, Cambridge, 1980. But what O'Shaughnessy objects to carries more baggage than what I here defend—and indeed more than is necessary for a volition theory. It should be emphasized, however, that part of the blame for the unpopularity of volition theories lies with the general methodological doctrine, a doctrine that Wittgenstein is vehemently opposed to, to the effect that the only legitimate business for a philosopher is to discover and articulate necessary truths. Given that doctrine, once it is conceded that there aren't volitions in every case of voluntary action, all is lost.

60. For the notion of a wholly spontaneous action, see any one of numerous passages in Sartre's *Being and Nothingness*. For the notion of a man as opposed to a person, see Locke's *Essay*, Vol. I, pp. 444-45.

61. It should be emphasized—see the previous section—that whether the antecedents of an action include an absence of desire or a lack of will, there can be no separation between the one who acts and his or her will.

62. See, above all, Schopenhauer's *The World as Will and Idea* (trs. R. Haldane and J. Kemp), Routledge and Kegan Paul, 1957, on the blindness of the will. For the views of Descartes, James and Hume on belief and the will, see the *Philosophical Works*, Vol. I, pp. 171-76, "The Will to Believe," *The Will to Believe and Other Essays in Popular Philosophy*, Dover, 1956, and the *Treatise*, p. 624. Hume's not very illuminating because so pithily expressed view poses no threat, by the way, to the notion of self-deception. There is an epistemological failure of some sort in all cases of self-deception—and Hume should be understood as maintaining that one can't, seeing clearly what one is doing, believe what one wants. Finally, Plato's view about the impossibility of acting against what one knows to be so is, of course, connected with if it is not identical to his view about weakness of the will.

63. For Roderick Chisholm's happy thought on the topic of action, see "Freedom and Action," *Freedom and Determinism* (ed. K. Lehrer), Random House, 1966; for O'Shaughnessy's, see "Observation and the Will," *The Journal of Philosophy*, 1963. The idea of a person as a prime mover unmoved, happy as it is, does not, contrary to what Chisholm suggests, solve the free will problem. For that problem—see below—can be put by asking: Given that a person is so firmly rooted in the physical universe—with the brain being of particular importance here—how can he or she be a prime mover unmoved? And the difference between reasons and causes—see towards the end of this section—is just one of a number of fundamental and systematic differences between the mind and the brain.

64. James talks of gaps in the stream of consciousness in *The Principles of Psychology*, Vol. I, pp. 199 ff. and 237-39 and of his welcomings and rejectings, again, on pp. 297 and 301. And see Thalberg again for a discussion of the above more subtle phenomena of the will.

65. The notion of a basic action is primarily associated with the name of Arthur Danto and with his "What We Can Do," *Journal of Philosophy*, 1963, in particular.

66. While the question of whether truth can be attained in philosophy is a large one, the answer to it, I believe, is quite straightforward. Philosophical problems can be solved—and not just, as is sometimes suggested, in the Pickwickian sense whereby the solution to such a problem, once discovered, becomes a fact, not of philosophy, but of science instead. Examples of philosophical truths are: Some mental phenomena lie outside of the stream of consciousness; The standards for knowledge are higher than those for belief; Utilitarianism does not capture all that is important about morality. These are easy cases. Others are harder, often much harder. But the point is a point of principle. So if a philosophical problem can't be solved, this says something more or less specific about the problem, not something about philosophy itself.

67. I have said that the arguments for Determinism are as good as philosophical arguments get. But as I will try to make clear, they are partial,

insisting on no more than half of a truth. The situation is peculiar, however, in that we cannot begin to understand how the other half of this truth can be reconciled with the half that Determinism insists on.

68. Indeterminism is not recommended for the faint of heart because of the near-truistic nature of the claim that responsibility requires nonrandomness. And one would have thought it even more of a truism that responsibility requires freedom. But Elizabeth Wolgast maintains—in "Mental Causes and the Will," *Philosophical Investigations*, 1998—that "The language games of praise and blame and attributing responsibility do not rest on a presupposition about freedom." Rather, she explains helpfully, "They just exist." Such is the power of the arguments for Determinism, such are the lengths that philosophers are sometimes prepared to go in order to circumvent them. And compare John Fischer, *The Metaphysics of Free Will: An Essay on Control*, Basil Blackwell, 1994, who presents a version of Soft Determinism based on the idea that responsibility does not require freedom—or not, at any rate, of the could-have-done-otherwise kind. What other kind is there? A clear corrective to views of this sort is provided by Richard Double in "Misdirection in the Free Will Problem," *American Philosophical Quarterly*, 1997.

69. For the opposite bias to the above—equally one-sided, equally unhelpful—see, for example, Grant Gillett, "Freedom of the Will and Mental Content," *Ratio*, 1993.

70. Supplementary to note 66 and with regard to the issue of data, a comparison is in order between philosophy and science—although the pertinent facts about science are by no means undisputed. Philosophers of science, like other philosophers and like scientists themselves, are so easily seduced by scepticism. But it is a truism that scientific theories are tested against scientific data, observations and experiments. A connected fact is that data are, in general, epistemologically less vulnerable than theories. Some of them, moreover, are completely invulnerable or they are in what Wittgenstein calls "normal circumstances": "The needle on the dial is now pointing between 5 and 6", "The liquid in the test-tube has changed from dark brown to colourless", and so on. Completely invulnerable, that is, to everything but scepticism—and the question of whether scepticism is true should, as I say, be begged against the sceptic. Philosophical theories and data—to put the point in decidedly nonWittgensteinian terms—are different in character from scientific theories and data but the epistemological facts are the same. And yet, for an awful lot of philosophers these days, there are no data, no givens. There are only "intuitions"—as though nothing, however elementary or obvious, could be trusted. So what is it that these philosophers believe in? The collective weight of a number of "intuitions"? But aren't they sure of that in some cases? Or are they never sure of anything? One can't help thinking sometimes that philosophy deserves its reputation of being as effete as it is irrelevant. And—for Wittgenstein's remark about doubt not being necessary wherever it is possible, see *On Certainty*, #392.

71. It is, of course, the fundamental inexplicability of certain mental phenomena that makes Eliminativism with respect to them so attractive to some

philosophers. But all we are entitled to say, in the first instance, is that they are at present inexplicable. Whether we should be Eliminativists—or Determinists in this context—is then a matter of how robust the phenomena are. And the phenomena here, those of freedom, could not be more solid or more stable; they are essential to our understanding of our lives.

72. Perhaps the distinction between magic and miracles has nothing to do with the degree to which they offend against or are impervious to explanation by our present philosophy and science; perhaps the latter is, simply, a theological notion whereas the former isn't. But that this way of expressing things is an improvement is, itself, not very or, indeed, at all clear.

73. And yet—I feel I'm beginning to repeat myself but what we are dealing with here is something of a scandal—the idea of freedom is not a terribly popular one in philosophy these days. This, though, is hardly surprising when one considers the Isms that have been fashionable in the philosophy of mind for much of this century, including the most recent or the most current, Supervenience. They all render freedom paradoxical or nonexistent. An interesting case study is provided by Dan Dennett in *Elbow Room*, MIT, 1984. For there Dennett switches back and forth, from one page to the next, between Soft Determinism, according to which free actions are also caused, and Determinism proper, according to which free actions do not exist. And compare Alan Brunton, "A Definitive Non-Solution of the Free Will Problem," *Philosophical Investigations*, 1993, on Dennett's complete lack of "puzzlement" about his own views and, indeed, about the free will problem itself.

74. John Searle claims, in *The Rediscovery of the Mind*, that there is no such thing as introspection on the grounds that our knowledge of our own minds differs in a certain respect from our visual knowledge. While Searle is extremely unclear about the nature of the difference, the best guess, given what he says, seems to be that complete introspective blindness is impossible for any relatively sophisticated mind—a fact, by the way, that rules out one sort of diagnosis of the Antipodeans who haunt Richard Rorty's *Philosophy and the Mirror of Nature*, Princeton, 1979; see below. But whatever the correct interpretation of Searle on this point, he never explains why introspection has to be exactly like vision. Even the other external senses differ from vision in this or that respect. Neither is it obvious that introspection has to be a sense of any kind. See earlier in this chapter on all of this.

75. Inevitably so. For it is not only that the ties between motive and action might be opaque; the motive itself might be strictly unintelligible.

76. The interface between the mind and the brain has to be in some sense spatial. One side of it, after all, is occupied by a straightforwardly spatial entity. And neither, of course, do the various parts of the brain function entirely uniformly as do those of the liver. Mere stuff, as one might put it, the liver.

A running criticism of the idea of a "Cartesian theatre" can be found in *Consciousness Explained*. Dennett swats at it here, bats at it there. Leaving aside the more complicated and murkier temporal aspect, the idea is that, in the pineal gland or some other single, suitably small and anatomically homogeneous part of the brain, the mind and the brain really do all come together. No one, but no one, has believed that since Descartes. Dennett agrees or half-agrees: "Everybody knows that Descartes was wrong [about the pineal gland]," he says in "Real Consciousness," *Consciousness in Philosophy and Cognitive Science* (eds. A. Revonsuo and M. Kamppinen), Lawrence Erlbaum Associates, 1994. A book needs enemies; they make it flourish, give it life. How could you write a book—or half a book, for that matter—denouncing the idea that Descartes was basically right about the pineal gland? Who, as Dennett says in Finland, cares? What view about time and the mind did Descartes hold that was analogous to his view about the pineal gland? As I said, this is a more complicated and more murky issue.

77. One attempt to locate the unconscious in the brain is Jonathan Winson's *Brain and Psyche*, Random House, 1986. The highly optimistic recipe in this case is: Dreams are somehow involved in Freud's account of the unconscious; memory is somehow involved as well; so tell a neurological story about dreams and memory and—there you have it.

The complex relationship between epistemology and ontology is seldom discussed by philosophers—except to claim, usually without much in the way of reasons, that one of them, quite generally, takes precedence over the other. A concern with this relationships does, however, inform large stretches of *The Rediscovery of the Mind*. I disagree with many of the moves that Searle makes on this issue—but he certainly recognizes its importance. See immediately below for a bit more on this.

78. Hume says, not of reasons, but of principles of association, that they are gently prevailing forces. But he also says of his "influencing motives of the will", a large subclass, at any rate, of reasons, that their operation is peculiar. For it depends, according to him, on the "*general* character or *present* disposition of the person." And he speaks, in the same breath, of our often perplexing and unpredictable "variations of temper." *Treatise*, pp. 10 and 418.

79. I borrow "village", for "Realist", from Dennett's "village verificationist." See "Toward a Cognitive Theory of Consciousness," *Minnesota Studies in the Philosophy of Science*, Vol. IX (ed. C. Wade Savage), University of Minnesota, 1978. And perhaps a more common meaning given to "antiRealism" when strictly philosophical considerations are at issue is: "If a putative reality does not bear the mark of humanity, it does not or cannot exist." The meaning I have given to "philosophical antiRealism" is the denial of the antecedent of this hypothetical. So there is no easy way of getting from my sense to this arguably more common one. But there is, equally, no easy way to move from the latter to the former.

80. I think here, not only of Wittgenstein, but also of Wisdom again.

81. To put this differently, there could not be a philosophy of physical disease in the sense in which this long essay is a philosophy of madness. There could be such a philosophy in the sense that one might say: Don't despise naturopathic remedies—although naturopathy is often a matter of an alternative source for a drug or fewer or less serious side-effects or perhaps a wider range of treatments—but don't use laetrile for cancer or undergo Filipino surgery for anything. What, though, of certain Eastern ways of thinking; should they just

be dismissed? Well, these ways of thinking would, presumably, open up new possibilities in psychiatry too. Still, let's say, not that there is nothing comparable in physical medicine, but that the problem is much larger and more disturbing in psychiatry.

82. The role of money here should not be underestimated. The drug companies, again, are mostly to blame. But then to start at the small end, the books that *DSM-IV* touts on its dust-jacket as "*DSM-IV* related", those you really should buy for all of your "staff members", cost in excess of $500—and then there are all the scholarships and research grants that are available and then the careers, the academic and professional careers, that are so many and so lucrative. Then the fat-cat administrative managing positions. For the furthest that psychiatry can get from pure profit is medicine, that most professional of professions. And the profession in general commands high fees these days. The profession has discovered or rediscovered greed. I have, I must admit, been spending time recently in one of the more affluent parts of California and that sometimes twists a man. But at the risk of sounding priggish, greed can make life awful hard.

83. The idea that a concept might contain prejudices is suggested by Champlin—although Champlin does not claim that isolating madness from brain cases is a prejudice.

And not so much a constraint as a decisive blow to the chin. A definition of "madness"—or anything more than a bare enumerative definition—becomes impossible. See below.

84. *Philosophical Investigations*, #65-66, #182, #415, *On Certainty*, #110, *Investigations*, #107, #68-106, #486, #38, #271, #390, *On Certainty*, #1, #85— and compare *Investigations*, p. 221—*On Certainty*, #136.

85. In a way, one way of putting or thinking of, the biggest prejudice of all.

86. Sacks tries to argue, in "The Autist Artist" in *The Man who Mistook his Wife for a Hat*, that creative intelligence is "by no means rare", "not uncommon", in autistics. I suspect that he and I would differ, and radically, over what creative intelligence is and how common it is in nonautistics. And there are, again, atypical autistics. Indeed, in the case discussed by Sacks, normal development until the age of eight was followed by a very high fever that led to chronic seizures. Still, we ought not to rule out the possibility of quite genuine imaginative powers with autism even though they will usually be minimal or narrowly circumscribed. Sacks's more recent offerings on autism in *An Anthropologist on Mars*—"Prodigies" and the title essay—are, again, that much more sober, a little bleaker, in tone.

87. *Philosophical Investigations*, #120, #107, #130. That our concepts be perfect is, once again, a requirement that goes back to Plato, at least—as Wittgenstein was well aware. The attempt by logicians to take over philosophy came much much later.

Locke's name, not that of Ann Landers, should be associated with the idea that if only they could get their premises right, the mad would have impeccable argumentative manners; that of Lombroso is associated with the idea that madness and genius have a peculiar affinity for each other—although see, for example, Kay Redfield Jamison's *Touched with Fire*, Macmillan, 1994, for a recent attempt to refurbish this thesis.

88. Braver voices are occasionally heard out there.   Thus, R. Kendell says—in "The Nature of Psychiatric Disorders" in *Companion to Psychiatric Studies* (5th edition)—that "it is…reasonable for us to assume that all mental activity…is accompanied by, and could not take place without, [events] in the brain." But this is pointless if it is a prelude to Eliminativism and Kendell goes on to say that "[it] does not imply that…we should abandon psychological forms of treatment." It turns out, however—in "Diagnosis and Classification" in the same volume—that pretty much the only form of psychological treatment that Kendell approves of is "cognitive psychotherapy." And, as John Horgan remarks in "Why Freud Isn't Dead," *Scientific American*, 1996, the goal of what he calls "cognitive-behavioural therapy", anyway, is "to alter unwanted habits of thought and behaviour." These might include procrastination, say, or being negative or too easily depressed.   No wonder this sort of therapy is indicated for many of the mad—as well as for many of the rest of us.   Compare Donald Goodwin and Samuel Guze, leading proponents of the "organic" approach to psychiatry, who, in *Psychiatric Diagnosis* (5th edition), Oxford, 1996, and despite their organic orientation, maintain that "psychotherapy" is sometimes worthwhile. What is positively recommended, though, is not much. "Marital therapy" is mentioned by Goodwin and Guze in connection with somatization disorder (p. 119) and "supportive therapy", even if it doesn't go beyond mere "reassurance", is suggested for panic (p. 98).   And then for depression (pp. 26-27)—not "insight-directed psychotherapy", in fact, that might not be "wise"—but "cognitive therapy" again, then "behavioural therapy" as a separate kind of psychotherapy, then "interpersonal therapy" emphasizing social issues, "group therapy"—as opposed, you know, to individual therapy—and "marital therapy" again—but what is the doctrinal content of that? So be especially reassuring to some of them, pay attention to the social skills of others and don't leave them alone and—yes, if you like—try cognitive therapy on this group. Not much, as I say—and that psychotherapy in this greatly attenuated sense is compatible with drugs is just what we would all have predicted. That sense of the word trivializes the debate.

89. One thing, at any rate, that Freud has in common with Wittgenstein, an obsession with the concrete or with case studies, a fascination with instances or examples.

Index

Note: *Some entries that appear throughout the book, such as mind, psychiatry, madness, neurosis and schizophrenia, are not listed in the Index*

anthropophobia, 64
antidepressants, 19ff., 178
Antipodeans, 172, 212n74
antipsychotics, 19ff., 32n21, 45,
    132, 178
antiRealism, 113, 114, 173-75,
    183, 213n79
    philosophical, 173-75, 213n79
    village, 173, 213n79
antiSemitism, 45
anxiety disorders, 15-16, 20, 22,
    23, 24, 25, 69, 77, 81, 93n14,
    97, 117, 120, 122, 125, 140,
    178, 187, 193, 195
anxiolytics, 20, 23-24, 178
aphasia, 73, 121, 122
arguments, 39, 41, 44, 54-55, 57,
    75, 100-102, 105, 111-12,
    114, 116, 117-19, 129, 142,
    148-49, 154, 161-65, 166,
    180, 182, 193, 199n4, 199n7,
    200n10, 202n20, 208n50,
    210n67, 211n68, 214n87
Arica, 26
Aristotle, 181
Asendin (See amoxapine)
Asperger's disorder, 70, 205n38
atheoretical approach, 66-67, 73-
    74, 78, 82, 126
attention, 4, 104, 145-48, 150, 52-
    53, 168
attention deficit/hyperactivity dis-
    order, 66, 68, 70, 132
Austin, J., 151
autism, 16, 66, 70, 74, 98, 119,
    123, 124, 128, 130-32, 152,
    186, 187, 205-6n38, 206n39,
    214n86
autonomy, 38, 44-45, 54, 87, 166
autoscopy, 98
autosites, 97
avolition, 74, 120

bad faith, 47-49
Baldessarini, R., 32n21
bats, 114, 173-74, 203n24

Beattie, M., 27
Beauchamp, S., 198
Beck, A., 85-86, 94n21
Bears, C., 197
Behaviourism, 66, 91n4, 106-7,
    133
Bender, K., 32n20, 32n22
Berenbaum, S., 204n31
Berkowitz, B., 26
Berne, E., 88, 94n24
Berrios, G., 94n21
Bini, L., 17
Binswanger, L., 88, 94n22
bizarre/nonbizarre delusions, 74
Bleuler, E., 16, 32n19, 98
blindness of will, 156-57, 210n62
body dysmorphic disorder, 78, 79,
    83, 125, 169, 186, 190
Borch-Jacobsen, M., 205n34
Bradshaw, J., 27
brain, 2, 14-15, 20, 24, 42-43, 45-
    46, 47, 55, 56-57, 73, 77, 78,
    92n10, 92n13, 97, 98, 99, 105,
    111, 112, 113, 114, 117, 122,
    123, 132, 133, 134, 157, 61-
    62, 163, 164, 165, 166, 171,
    172, 173, 186, 189, 190, 191,
    194-96, 200n12, 210n63,
    212n76, 213n76 (See also
    neurology)
brain cases, 99, 111, 119, 124,
    140, 167, 177, 179-81, 184,
    193-96
brain-fag, 64
Branden, N., 26, 27
Brentano, F., 4
Brief (reactive) psychosis, 21, 68,
    74-75, 83, 92n12, 138-39,
    178, 189
Briquet's syndrome (See somati-
    zation disorder)
Broad, C., 105, 201n14
Brothers, J., 27
Brunton, A., 212n73
bulimia, 125
bupropion, 22

faculties, 100, 105, 117, 141-42, 148-49, 156, 183, 206n45, 208n53

families, 54, 55-56, 97-98, 138, 182, 199n3

Farber, L., 204n30

Farrell, B., 203n24

Feigl, H., 203n25

female sexual arousal disorder, 65

fetishism, 65

Fingarette, H., 31n15

First, M., 90n3

first-person, 90n1, 103-4, 107, 109, 144, 201n16

Fischer, J., 211n68

Flanagan, B., 29n3, 29n6, 59n12, 207n47

fluoxetine, 22, 23

fluphenazine, 20

Fodor, J., 201n13, 201n14, 202n21, 206n45, 208n53

folie à deux (See induced psychotic disorder)

Forman, L., 90n3

Forward, S., 27

Foucault, M., 28n1, 198-n2

Foundationalism, 102

Frances, A., 90n3

freaks, 96, 102, 185

free association, 14

free will, 37-38, 40, 42, 46, 47-49, 52, 53, 58n6, 73, 88, 105, 111, 123, 124, 128, 153, 161-67, 208n50, 210n63, 211n68, 212n73

Freeman, W., 18

Fregoli syndrome, 137

French, the, 64, 90n2, 93n15, 137-38, 205n37, 206n43

Freud, A., 88, 94n23

Freud, S., 1-14, 14 -16, 17, 25, 39, 40, 42-43, 44-45, 49, 56, 58n3, 58n6, 59n10, 60n16, 64, 65, 67, 84, 85, 86, 87, 88, 89, 91n4, 93n16, 104, 106, 107, 108, 117, 127-28, 134, 135, 139, 144, 152, 166, 168, 171, 172, 177, 178, 187, 190, 191, 193, 196, 197, 201n14, 201-2n17, 205n34, 213n77, 215n89

Friedenberg, E., 61n18

Fromm, E., 87, 94n22

functional disorders, 69, 72-73, 82, 91n6, 133, 180-81, 190, 194-95

Functionalism, 59n6, 78, 106, 110, 114, 115-16, 117, 133, 165

future, 40, 58-59n6, 110-11, 149, 164-65, 198, 202n21

game theory, 39, 44

gamma aminobutyric acid, 23

Ganser's syndrome, 98

Genaine quadruplets, 197

gender identity disorders, 65, 80, 83, 125, 140

generalized anxiety disorder, 23, 117

George III, 198

gestalt psychology, 88

giants, 97, 173, 198

Gillett, G., 211n69

Goldman, H., 33n22

Goldstein, K., 86

Goodwin, D., 215n88

grand paresis, 15, 17, 99, 194

Grant, T., 28

Grebb, J., 92n11, 92-93n13, 93n14

Guze, S., 215n88

Hacking, I., 198n2, 205n35

Haldol (See haloperidol)

haloperidol, 19, 20

Hamlet, 103

Happy Puppet syndrome, 97

Harrison, P., 197

Hartmann, H., 88, 94n23

Hauser, K., 97

hebephrenia (See disorganized schizophrenia)

Hegarty, J., 32n21